Intercultural Crisis Communication

Bloomsbury Advances In Translation Series

Series Editor:

Jeremy Munday, Centre for Translation Studies, University of Leeds, UK

Bloomsbury Advances in Translation publishes cutting-edge research in the fields of translation studies. This field has grown in importance in the modern, globalized world, with international translation between languages a daily occurrence. Research into the practices, processes and theory of translation is essential and this series aims to showcase the best in international academic and professional output.

A full list of titles in the series can be found at:
www.bloomsbury.com/series/bloomsbury-advances-in-translation

Related titles in the series include:

Collaborative Translation
Edited by Anthony Cordingley & Céline Frigau Manning

Community Translation
Mustapha Taibi & Uldis Ozolins

Global Trends in Translator and Interpreter Training
Edited by Séverine Hubscher-Davidson & Michał Borodo

Institutional Translation for International Governance
Fernando Prieto Ramos

Intercultural Crisis Communication
Edited by Federico M. Federici & Christophe Declercq

Quality in Professional Translation
Joanna Drugan

The Pragmatic Translator
Massimiliano Morini

Translating Holocaust Lives
Edited by Jean Boase-Beier, Peter Davies, Andrea Hammel & Marion Winters

Translating in Town
Edited by Lieven D'hulst & Kaisa Koskinen

Translation Solutions for Many Languages
Anthony Pym

Intercultural Crisis Communication

Translation, Interpreting and Languages in Local Crises

Edited by
Federico M. Federici and Christophe Declercq

BLOOMSBURY ACADEMIC
LONDON • NEW YORK • OXFORD • NEW DELHI • SYDNEY

BLOOMSBURY ACADEMIC
Bloomsbury Publishing Plc
50 Bedford Square, London, WC1B 3DP, UK
1385 Broadway, New York, NY 10018, USA
29 Earlsfort Terrace, Dublin 2, Ireland

BLOOMSBURY, BLOOMSBURY ACADEMIC and the Diana logo are trademarks of
Bloomsbury Publishing Plc

First published in Great Britain 2020
Paperpack edition published 2021

A catalogue record for this book is available from the British Library.

A catalog record for this book is available from the Library of Congress.

ISBN:	HB:	978-1-3500-9705-6
	PB:	978-1-3502-6100-6
	ePDF:	978-1-3500-9706-3
	eBook:	978-1-3500-9707-0

Series: Bloomsbury Advances in Translation

Typeset by Integra Software Services Pvt. Ltd.

To find out more about our authors and books visit www.bloomsbury.com
and sign up for our newsletters.

Contents

List of Illustrations   vii

Notes on Contributors   viii

Words of Empathy, Access and Relief
Christophe Declercq and Federico M. Federici   1

Section 1   Integrating People in Movement in Regional Crises

1   The Counternarratives of Migrants and Cultural Mediators
    Stefania Taviano   21

2   Language Mediation in Emergency Migration Contexts:
    A Case Study of the Migrant Crisis 2015 in Croatia
    Vedrana Čemerin   39

3   The Role of the Translator and Interpreter in Terrorist
    Conflicts *Carmen Pena-Díaz*   63

4   Language, Culture and Perceived Ethnic Homeland
    Integration: Syrian Armenian Forced Migrants in Armenia
    Daria Vorobyeva   81

Section 2   Integrating Intercultural Communication
              in Crisis-Affected Health Settings

5   Medical Translation in Crisis Situations *Vicent Montalt Resurreccio*   105

6   Intercultural Mediation in Healthcare: Thematic Analysis,
    from the Interpreters' Perspective
    Izabel Emilia Telles de Vasconcelos Souza   127

7   Interpreting for Refugees: Empathy and Activism
    Marija Todorova   153

8   Voices of Refugee Doctors in the United Kingdom:
    An Exploration of Their Linguistic and Cultural Needs and
    Aspirations *Ceri Butler and Khetam Al Sharou*   173

Section 3   Integrating Cross-National Representations of Local Crises

9   On France, Terrorism and the English Press: Examining
     the Impact of Style in the News *Ashley Riggs*   193
10 Re-Narrating Crisis: A Translation Perspective
     Maria Sidiropoulou   215
11 *Emergenza Migranti:* From Metaphor to Policy
     Federico M. Federici   233

Index   260

Illustrations

Figures

3.1 Survey participants   71
11.1 Access to information in Italy   239

Tables

1.1 Mediated interactions between doctors and migrant patients
(Amato and Garwood, 2011)   26
3.1 Survey questions   70
6.1 Advantages of addressing cultural issues   136
6.2 Disadvantages of addressing cultural issues   144
9.1 Synoptic table   197
9.2 Alliteration and connotation   203
9.3 Alliteration and government/politics   205
9.4 Alliteration and religion   206
10.1 Greek conventions in natural and human-induced disaster
reporting manifested through translation   224
11.1 Adapted excerpt from the DEMIG POLICY database   248

Contributors

Khetam Al Sharou is a post-doctoral researcher at the Centre for Translation Studies of University College London. She holds an MSc in Translation and Computer Assisted Translation Tools from Heriot-Watt University and a PhD in Translation Studies from University College London, UK. Previously, she lectured in English at the Higher Institute of Translation and Interpreting, Damascus University and other universities in Syria. She has conducted research into automatic machine translation and cross-disciplinary projects focusing on the linguistic integration of adult refugees and refugee doctors in Europe and the UK. She has published chapters and articles, with a recent one in *Translation and Interpreting Studies* (2018).

Ceri Butler is a lecturer and researcher in the fields of health services research and medical education and currently lectures at Brighton and Sussex Medical School. Her main research interests lie in global health and the experiences of refugee health professionals into the UK. She has undertaken primary research in these fields since 2002, completing her PhD at University College London exploring the integration of refugee doctors into the UK National Health Service. Ceri has also worked in national policy arenas on the employment and training of refugees, including sitting on the National Board for Refugee Employment for NHS Employers.

Vedrana Čemerin received her MA at the University of Zagreb in 2011, after which she worked for several years as a professional translator and subtitler, subsequently progressing to the position of an in-house quality control supervisor in a large Croatian AVT agency. She currently holds the position of a lecturer at the University of Applied Sciences Velika Gorica, where she teaches English for specific purposes at the Department of Crisis Management and the Department of Optometry. She is also doing her PhD research at the University of Zadar, with a focus on AVT Quality Assessment and Revision Procedures.

Christophe Declercq is Lecturer in translation at KU Leuven Brussels Campus and senior lecturer in translation at CenTraS, University College London. Christophe's research happens along three lines. First, he has been working on

Belgian refugees in Britain 1914–1919 for well over a decade. On the subject, he has published several chapters and spoken widely at conferences and commemoration projects in both Britain and Belgium. He has worked with the BBC and VRT (Belgian television) on multiple occasions. A second trait concerns application and pedagogy of language and translation technology, which has led to his working with EU institutions frequently since 2009. The two traits converge in the theme of conflict and communication, both historic (two co-edited books on Languages and the First World War with Julian Walker, Palgrave) and contemporary (language and translation provision in times of crisis) @chrisdec71 @belgianrefugees.

Federico M. Federici is Associate Professor in Translation Studies at the Centre for Translation Studies, UCL. Previously, he founded and directed the EMT MA in Translation Studies at Durham University, UK (2008–2014) as well as the Centre for Intercultural Mediation. Federico's recent publications have appeared in *Translation Spaces* and *International Journal of Disaster Risk Reduction*. Federico's research focuses on news translation and the role of translators in crises. He is member of the EU-funded INTERACT Crisis Translation Network (2017–2020) led by Sharon O'Brien (Dublin City University), with whom he is developing cross-disciplinary projects in the area of Crisis Translation.

Vicent Montalt Resurrecció is Professor at the Department of translation and Communication of the Universitat Jaume I in Spain. He is the director of the MA in medical-healthcare translation and a member of the Gentt research group, where he leads the medical translation and communication section. He has published extensively in the areas of scientific-technical, medical and drama translation; pedagogy of specialized translation; mediation of specialized knowledge; improvement of clinical communication; Shakespeare and medicine; translation and Medical Humanities.

Carmen Pena-Díaz is Professor of Translation at the Department of Modern Philology at Alcalà de Henares University (Madrid, Spain). She has previously taught at Vigo University (Spain) and at Louisiana State University (USA). Her research areas are bilingualism, translation and ESP. She is member of the FILWIT research group which researches new technologies in language and translation teaching, is leader of a nationally accredited research group InterMed and coordinates the English-Spanish section of the European Public Service Intercultural Communication, Translating and Interpreting Master's Degree at Alcalà University.

Ashley Riggs graduated with a BA from Smith College (Massachusetts) and completed her PhD, which focused on translation, feminism and fairy-tale rewritings, at the University of Geneva in 2014. She is a research and teaching fellow at the Faculty of Translation and Interpreting of the University of Geneva. She is currently writing a book about the interplay between stylistic features and cultural representation in news articles about terrorism (working title: *Stylistic Deceptions in Online News*). Ashley's other main research, focused on contemporary rewritings of fairy tales and their translations, mobilizes concepts and approaches from fairy-tale studies, gender studies and translation criticism.

Maria Sidiropoulou is Professor of Translation Studies and Chair of the Department of English Language and Literature, School of Philosophy, National and Kapodistrian University of Athens. She was Head of the Interuniversity and Interfaculty Co-ordinating Committee of the Translation-Translatology MA Programme of the University of Athens, in 2009–2011, and director of the Language and Linguistics Department of the Faculty of English in 2004–2006. Her recent publications (books, co-/edited volumes, articles) deal with intercultural issues manifested through translation in the press, in advertising, in academic discourse, in EU documentation, in literature, on stage and screen.

Stefania Taviano lectures in English at the University of Messina, Italy. She is author of *Translating English as a Lingua Franca* (Mondadori Education, 2010), *Staging Dario Fo and Franca Rame. Anglo-American Approaches to Political Theatre* (Ashgate, 2005), and she has edited a special issue of *The Interpreter and Translator Trainer*. Her current research areas include language phenomena resulting from globalization, particularly multilingualism in hip-hop music and citizen journalism, the spread of English as a Lingua Franca and its impact on translation, language and translation pedagogy. She is also a professional translator and interpreter.

Izabel Emilia Telles de Vasconcelos Souza (formerly Arocha), MEd, CMI-Spanish, PhD, is a passionate advocate for the advancement of healthcare/medical interpreting worldwide. She works as a certified interpreter, translator and educator (Bridging the Gap, Boston University, Cambridge College, Osaka University). Dr Souza has several published articles on topics related to interpreting, intercultural mediation and language access. Dr Souza served as president and executive director of the International Medical Interpreters Association (IMIA) and as Secretary General for the International Federation of

Translators. Dr Souza is an ISO and ASTM Standards Expert in interpreting and translation standards. She is currently project leading the ISO 21998 Medical/Healthcare Interpreting standard.

Marija Todorova holds a PhD in Translation Studies from the Hong Kong Baptist University, and a PhD in Peace and Development Studies from University Ss. Cyril and Methodius Skopje. She has over ten years of experience working for various international organizations including UNDP, UNHCR, DfID and OSCE. Her research interests include interpreters in conflict zones, violence in children's literature and multimodal translation. She is currently a Postdoctoral Fellow at The Hong Kong Polytechnic University. Marija is an Executive Council member of IATIS and the Editor of *New Voices in Translation Studies*. Her papers have been published in edited volumes and journals, including *The Translator* and *Linguistica Antverpiensia*.

Daria Vorobyeva holds a PhD from the School of International Relations, the University of St Andrews (UK). Her thesis was entitled: 'Forced Ethnic Migrants' Integration: Syrian Armenians in Armenia and Lebanon (2011–2016)'. During the PhD and currently Daria has also been working on the Russian foreign policy towards the Middle East, especially Syria. She has been writing and presenting on both topics.

Words of Empathy, Access and Relief

Christophe Declercq and Federico M. Federici

Crises erupt every day; they can affect an individual, a family, a vulnerable social group, a region, country, nation, or can be cross-borders. With an interconnected world and globally broadcast news, they seem to occur all the time (Federici, 2016). The scale, size, duration, impact and risks for property or people are studied in disaster risk research (Alexander, 2016). The effects of individual disruptive events (the trigger for a crisis) are considered more and more as cascading (Pescaroli and Alexander, 2016). Mitigating these effects – be they cross-boundaries, local, national or particularly significant for culturally and linguistically diverse (CALD) communities – depends on efficient, effective, timely and widely broadcast communication. Communication in disasters, emergencies and in the different phases of developing crises is crucial and is normally an intercultural interaction. Yet the area remains under-explored with very few exceptions. The need for more efficient intercultural communication among international humanitarian field operators begins to be acknowledged in those reports that focus on the consequences of inefficient communication in responding to international crises.

Few people, if any, would disagree were we to state that not enough contemporary research in intercultural communication has dedicated debates or publications to intercultural interactions and multilingual communication in emergencies, disasters and, more broadly, *crises*. More importantly, from both the limited scope of research and from the events on the grounds where crises have happened – or are ongoing – a clear need is evident on how research should draw from practical experiences in the field and how the latter can draw from

---

Our title is an explicit reference to the campaign *Words of relief* run by the non-profit organization Translators without Border to raise awareness of the significance of gaps in accommodating language needs for crisis-affected populations world-wide.

the former as well (Federici, 2016). A very recent report of the International Federation of the Red Cross and Red Crescent Societies (IFRC) leaves very little doubt about the long journey ahead: 'Language barriers can leave people left out [*sic*] of the loop. Older people and persons with disabilities who are also migrants or from linguistic minorities may not speak the official national language(s)' (IFRC, 2018: 102). Although the issue of language barriers with diverse people who do not speak the official language(s) of their authorities also resonates in systems of institutional care at national level – for asylum applicants and newly arrived migrants or at regional or local level – care for other-lingual elderly,[1] – the focus of the contributions included in this volume is on translating *ad hoc* barriers of interlingual variety at times of crises into adequate intercultural communication in the field – i.e. the very location of the disaster and/or the forefront of the crisis – so as to alleviate the suffering emerging from the respective crisis situations.

Communication is a fundamental form of intercultural interaction and all the more crucial at times of disasters, emergencies and in the different phases of developing crises. Yet the area of research into applications of this ethical-theoretical stance remains under-explored. Moreover, the field is characterized by the disproportionally low research-driven support for specific issues relating to Translation and Interpreting (T&I). A few exceptions are noted – predominantly the work of InZone in disaster interpreting and extensive work on conflict-related, translation and interpreting (Baker, 2006; Dragovic-Drouet, 2007; Coyle and Meier, 2009; Inghilleri and Harding, 2010; Tipton, 2011; Footitt and Kelly, 2012; Kelly and Catherine, 2013; Moser-Mercer, Kherbiche, and Class, 2014). The need for more efficient intercultural communication among international humanitarian field operators is a shared concern that emerges from annual reports on how international non-governmental organizations (INGOs) progress with their Grand Bargain agreement of 2016 on enhancing their accountability to, localization for, and engagement with communities that are affected by crisis (Derzsi-Horváth, Steets, and Ruppert, 2017; Metcalfe-Hough, Poole, Bailey, and Belanger, 2018). The findings that the IFRC's research acknowledges focus on the consequences of inefficient communication in responding to international crises (IFRC, 2018) and to the code of conduct that they should adopt (Sphere, 2018).

Although the UN 2018 Global Compact aims to provide a comprehensive global approach to migration and how human rights of all migrants (including refugees) can be guaranteed, intercultural communication is included as a priori condition on how risks and challenges for individuals and countries of origin, transit and destination can be addressed. The Global compact suggests that addressing them must go through child-sensitive and gender-representative support, as much as through counselling on the one hand and through a language that migrants understand on the other hand (Global Compact, 2018).[2] With the focus of the Global Compact aiming at reducing communication barriers, it is – therefore – not surprising that the contributors in this volume engage with the complexity of multilingual communication in crises, especially in those contexts in which rare or minority languages represent a substantial obstacle to rescue or humanitarian operations. These languages may be 'temporarily' minority languages or those of groups marginalized, but often the language of displaced people (asylum seekers, refugees, and migrants) ends up in a complex relationship of demand and offer for understandable information with the countries of transit and arrival. Given the new scale of migratory phenomena in the 2010s, this volume has several contributions centred on the provision of intercultural mediation in these long-term social, logistic, economic and political crises.

An additional dimension of concern relates to the representation of those contexts in the media, more in particular in news bulletins. At times of crisis or disaster relief news content provides messages with a twofold purpose: they recognize and acknowledge the population that is left vulnerable after a disaster or during a crisis and they provide access to potentially crucial information. At times of relief, communication used by health professionals, logistics teams or media journalists alike should allow for ample space for conveying compassion and empathy.[3]

Illnesses and containment

Not taking into consideration the increasingly unsurmountable issues of drinkable water provisions, pollution, energy consumption, man-made (including terror attacks) as well as disasters triggered by natural hazards and armed conflicts – each of which is often exacerbated by massive population movements – there is one ultimate threshold the planet faces: estimations about the uttermost world population limit in terms of food supply settle for 10 billion people (Henry et al., 2018). With an estimated 7.7bn people on the planet today and the estimated threshold reached in 2050 (UN, 2017), it should be clear that the critical issues and frequently ensuing transnational threats mentioned earlier increasingly play a part in the everyday lives of increasingly more people. The strain on natural resources, on supplies of varying kinds (such as water, food, petrol, electricity) and on basic commodities (such as housing, education, employment, healthcare) only increases, with no clear solution at hand. Moreover, at times of increased isolationist attitudes on a global scale (Trumpist America, fortress Europe, sparring Russia, assertively developing China and increasingly disproportional energy consumption in India, etc.) countries in – for instance – sub-Saharan Africa will suffer ever more from the illnesses that plague substantial parts of the continent.

For most of 2014 and 2015, several countries in Western Africa were hit by an outbreak of the Ebola virus. The WHO traced the origins of the outbreak to a two-year-old child in Guinea in December 2013 (WHO, 2014) but the virus quickly spread across Sierra Leone and Liberia. The latter was declared Ebola-free in January 2016, the former in June 2016 (CDC, 2017). Two Ebola outbreaks occurred in the Democratic Republic of Congo (DRC), in the summer of 2017 and 2018 respectively, but were contained in a matter of weeks (Federici, Gerber, O'Brien, and Cadwell, 2019).

However, at the time of writing, a new outbreak had taken place in DRC, in Kivu more in particular, and this was still developing (Zucconi, 2019). Among the main triggers of the disease spreading are the difficulty in accessing the area for assessing the spread and the inadequate containment efforts and medical relief provisions (Yong, 2018). And the explanation of medical processes needs to be culture-specific, yet decision-makers rarely inform their interventions through suitable socio-anthropological considerations (Bastide, 2018). Given that the wider region is characterized by military conflict and that armed groups fight one another also over the mineral wealth of the region, the Ebola outbreak in Kivu bears similarities to those in Liberia and Sierra Leone. Moreover, with over 100 ethnic groups in Congo and nearly every group speaking their own language (Worldatlas, 2018), it should perhaps come as no surprise that access and relief appeared to be equally inadequate in the three countries of the 2014–2015 Ebola crisis.

In those countries over ninety languages are spoken and more than half the population is illiterate (Laschet, 2015). However, communication about the disease and its dangers also had to overcome cultural traditions, not least the custom of burying the dead beloved one in the garden, touching the diseased body in the process, often with equally lethal consequences. Meeting a disaster or crisis with adequate communication and appropriate access to resources is the orientation from relief to the affected population. There is, however, an important reciprocity: many experts claim that the outbreak of Ebola in West Africa was in part caused by a failure to understand the cultural frameworks in which relief had to be organized (Smyth, 2014).

In any disaster relief, as in the case of the 2014 Ebola outbreak, in attempting to control an epidemic, access to information is as much key as it is to provide it in a language or form that is accessible. When provided information in their own language, communities can be reassured and trust in aid workers increases (Laschet, 2015). However, communicating how to combat the Ebola virus was exacerbated by restrictions on movements and public gatherings (ALNAP, 2017). In the absence of adequate and accurate communication, mistrust can emerge not only as a hindrance that is difficult to overcome – or distrust in government and authority can be transferred onto aid workers and mediators – but also due to a lack of understanding what is actually happening and what is needed to alleviate consequences of the disaster or crisis. The consequences are reputational and operational: the organization becomes to be perceived as inept, adding to the existing distrust and maintaining the distance between those affected and those aiming to provide relief. This hurdle needs to be overcome – or even better prevented – in case of provision of help and support to be successful in containing the effects of the crisis at hand.

During the Ebola outbreak in West Africa relief mobilization and a focus on a bottom-up approach came too late and were incorporated only at a time when the epidemic had taken much more substantial proportions. Increasingly anthropologists – working alongside faith leaders – were mobilized for a better understanding and therefore addressing of locale-specific socio-cultural and political dimensions (ACAPS, 2015). These initially absent but subsequently continued actions formed the multidimensional framework in which the relief support for the Ebola crisis could be mediated and the affected population appropriately and effectively accommodated. However, lessons learned from one crisis and best practices emerging from one situation typically do not translate well into other situations, as is evident from the situation in DRC. Best practices for crisis communication are also lacking from relief actions in countries beyond those that suffered from Ebola: despite a truce, the epidemic and humanitarian disaster in Yemen, including outbreaks of different natures as well as dramatic malnutrition represented significant linguistic challenges for international relief teams, again over limited language access and difficult accessibility on the field over continued armed interventions from one side or another.

The complicated example of Ebola in several African countries also highlights two key problems that come with – typically unexpected – crises and disasters: no accumulated experience or expertise is immediately available on site, and with this unexpectedness comes unprecedentedness, also at the level of consequences for the people who are affected. However, up to which point can one really apply the label of unexpectedness? The cyclone Idai that caused such destruction in Mozambique – and to a lesser extent Zimbabwe and Malawi but it still left up to 2.6m people affected – in March 2019 most certainly was unexpected in terms of scale and power of the cyclone, but the combination of increasing extreme rainfall and storms – arguably due to climate change, evidence provided by several reports from the Intergovernmental Panel on Climate Change (IPCC) – has happened before. Mapping out areas that would be devastated by powerful storms largely depends on housing and other infrastructure being able to withstand such forces, but areas prone to flooding should be considered part of a prevention policy along the likes of those devised in the Global North (such as the Netherlands). This is much needed for the Global South as the affected area in Mozambique is not only scarred by the many casualties and the damage to the infrastructural fabric, those who are affected the most are struck twice as the much-needed harvest from their fields – their livelihood and main source of food – is destroyed as well. Maybe the geographical location and the lack of prevention measures such as dykes, channels to carry excess water away from danger areas and the like made the affected area in Mozambique prone to disasters triggered by natural hazards. Maybe as well a cultural shift was needed in the early warning system to alert the population so that its efficiency and accuracy – through appropriately addressing people – would not be taken for granted and not leave much space for people not taking the warning seriously or even refusing to leave the area.

This volume aims to address language use as the main means to cross-cultural barriers at times of crises and/or relief. The urgency for increasing uptake of scientific support of future actions is real, not least because crises can also play at micro-level when they intersect. In New Zealand, refugees from the past decade had come from war-torn places like Afghanistan, Somalia and Sudan, predominantly from countries where the majority of people follow Muslim beliefs. These refugees were part of the local community when Christchurch was hit by an earthquake in 2011 and they subsequently helped to rebuild that community and its social and infrastructural fabric, only to find that a mere lone-wolf attack against their religion took place at the core of their existence, in their places of worship in March 2019. At times of such terror attacks, political discourse often relates diversity to tolerance and inclusion. This framework of empathy and professed leadership is much needed too well beyond the western urban centres.

Mediating crises

This volume considers languages, mediation and translation as part of disaster relief (and/or prevention) as non-PR crisis communication. Organizational factors play a part in crisis response, but crisis communication in order to alleviate the consequences of a crisis is all about management, not about public relations on behalf of an organization over product malfunctions or of a celebrity over a media blunder. Although in both cases the communicator-mediator attempts to manage and control damage, in the case of the latter this is more reputation of the main actor (typically with a contractual obligation to do so) and in the case of the former the manner in which the crisis has been responded to largely affects the reputation of the organization and no contractual relation exists between the humanitarian relief organization and the main reason for the need for relief (armed conflict, disasters triggered by natural hazards, etc.; see earlier).

There is, however, an overlap in conceptual framework in dealing with crises. Britton (2017) stipulates the ideal approach to crisis communication for companies; therefore all PR-related, and yet some vital stipulations, can easily be transferred to a non-corporate environment, including crisis relief operations. Although the general approach might sound obvious on the face it, three broad features are core to successful communication. Firstly, crisis relief communication should be as much as possible in real time or with a very fast turnaround between need and output back to those who need the information. Secondly, when available information should be accessible to all who need it, it entails a clear understanding of the geographical situation as well as local cultural traditions (see earlier) and systems of feedback from the crisis-affected populations on what information they need. Among the objectives of the much contested 2018 UN Global Compact for Migration is indeed the stipulation to 'provide accurate and timely information in all stages of migration'. Thirdly, messages should be customized, made as relevant as possible for the individual receiver. In a situation of a crisis, applying these principles on the ground demands profound collaboration between all those involved.

Among the reasons of why people feel compelled to leave their country of origin are 'natural disasters, the adverse effects of climate change, and environmental degradation'. The lesser-known purpose of the Global Compact is indeed to 'minimize the adverse drivers and structural factors' that see people become displaced. The current volume does not align itself with any frame relating to that Global Compact, but it very clearly relates to the problems of multilingual contexts in times of crisis and its ensuing relief.

Structure of the volume

Subdivided into three sections, the common thread of the contributions is the notion of intercultural communication as a vehicle for *integration* as much as interaction between interlocutors. We have not had recourse to a naïve conceptualization of integration but rather to this notion as a debatable, controversial and intangible concept, which attracts social and political conflicts as much as aspirations and hopes. Some contributions are succinctly presented because their relevance is immediately obvious in the context of crisis communication in intercultural settings. However, our mapping of the tripartite structure of this volume also happens as a contrastive, critical and reflective presentation of the contributions. In the few words that follow we *offer the readers* our conceptualization of the dialogues and diatribes embedded in the chapters that follow.

Integrating people in movement in regional crises

The four chapters in this section focus on the role of language mediation in relation to migration and institutional approaches to language mediation in prolonged regional crises.

The section opens with Taviano's chapter on the self-definition of cultural mediators working into and out of English as a lingua franca for mediation. Chapter 1 in fact focuses on issues of language justice and the position of English as a lingua franca in enabling communicative acts as acts that grant equal access to services in migrants arriving in Italy. The chosen focus allows Taviano to engage with the profiles and professional operational settings of intercultural mediators in Italy, with emphasis on the role of mediators coming from a migrant background. Compelling views of identity through language mediations are presented, discussed and analysed in a contribution that goes against narratives of help and support that could oversimplify the complex communicative acts embedded in exchanges between locals, institutions, mediators and migrants in Italy.

In her Chapter 2, Čemerin engages with the specific approach to dealing with transmigrants, intended as displaced people crossing Croatia with the purpose of reaching another destination to apply for asylum and refugee, during the recent peak of migration flows in 2015. Čemerin offers a detailed overview of the procedures of crisis management adopted by the Croatian government and the NGOs. The chapter offers an account of the challenges, practical and legislative, that the response efforts had to consider when working between under-resourced languages and the language of a (relative) minority of speakers as Croatian. The social dimension of a population that has known in its recent past the need to migrate because of conflict in its territories and the multiple institutional and private initiatives to support humanitarian operators in the 2015 crisis offer many points for discussion and reflection on what it means to consider language access as a form of social activism and solidarity.

Working on interviews with Spanish institutions and language mediators, Pena-Díaz's Chapter 3 aims to analyse to what extent the role of translators and interpreters in conflict zones can be meaningful in the prevention of international terrorism. Grounding her work on narrative theory, Pena-Díaz investigates the ways in which linguistic analysts collaborate with the intelligence services (in as much as the data allow her to consider) and assesses the role of mediated communication in creating narratives of terrorism from abroad. The chapter emphasizes the need for professional language mediation (both translators and interpreters) in intercultural crisis settings such as those of conflict and terrorism.

Chapter 4 concludes this section. Here, Vorobyeva presents the multi-layered context of people displacement of the Armenian population that used to live for centuries as diasporic Armenians in Syria, who had to return as refugees in their country of origins after the conflict in Syria erupted. The historical and social connections and contrasts are investigated with a cogent critique of expectations, tensions and overlaps in cultural understanding between populations who felt to share a distant past, which is clearly represented and viewed completely differently between the diasporic Armenians and those who stayed in Armenia. Issues of migrations are considered here with an historical and long-term perspective, whilst equally considering the immediate effects of what is to all intents an issue of intercultural communication during a crisis. With the difference, the cultural differences seem to be predominantly diachronic.

Integrating intercultural communication in crisis-affected health settings

This section opens with Montalt's Chapter 5 on medical translation in emergencies. The chapter adopts the general definition of 'translation' accepted in crisis settings whereby oral, written and multimodal forms of communication perform into a complex unicum. The chapter provides an inspired theoretical framing, pivoting around the three concepts of *ethos*, *logos* and *pathos* that colour both reflections on the activities of healthcare language mediators and on what healthcare professionals seem to expect of them, when working in extreme settings compared to their regular work environment, as occurs to the volunteers of Médecins Sans Frontières who compose the participants interviewed by Montalt for the project behind this chapter.

Chapter 6 represents a special case that deserves additional attention in mapping the contents of this volume. The chapter covers the important operational area of provision of healthcare language mediation, by drawing on a unique large data collection (458 practitioners from 25 countries) providing data from diverse and even conflicting healthcare traditions. This chapter has been included provocatively. Here, Telles de Vasconcelos Souza argues that the concept of 'advocacy' is irrelevant in interpreting in healthcare settings. The chapter gives readers access to a wealth of data from interpreters working in the sector. The data are the reasons why the chapter was included, as the ontological perspectives raise multiple questions. The data collected via interviews with professional interpreters allow the readers to access first-hand accounts of the settings in which healthcare language and culture mediation happen. The discussion of the data is filled with traditional prejudices around what it means to *interpret*, which stay away from recent tensions in interpreting studies regarding advocacy. When the groups for whom interpreting is provided belong to CALD communities, their social status is that of marginal and at times vulnerable groups. Interpreters need to transfer meaning with one of the social groups more (widely) respected in the same society, that of the medical professionals – of course exceptions to this respect equally exist. The relationship is not among equals, so the ideal of a neutral interpretation with no advocacy has been questioned in the literature (for a discussion, see the recent works, and the bibliographies therein, by Ozolins, 2010; Valero Garcés, 2014; Drugan and Tipton, 2017; Taibi and Ozolins, 2016; Tipton and Furmanek, 2016). Yet when questioned in copyediting, Telles de Vasconcelos Souza took a very traditional position known as the healthcare interpreter as a *conduit of language*. In collecting data from professionals, this approach presents two crucial risks that make the inclusion of this chapter ever so important: (1) would professionals recognize themselves in the simplistic view or would this insubstantial analysis of the interpreters' constraints and responses entrench prejudices on research on interpreting as 'academic work' in the pejorative sense? In other words, would this perspective entrench the view that practitioners do not need to engage with researchers? (2) Would the important data collected by the researcher be dismissed because of the risks that the rigour in collecting the data might be as limited as the rigour in the analysis of the data? The editors – Declercq and, in particular, Federici – felt an ethical and deontological need here to include the chapter because this debate on advocacy cannot be swiped under the carpet. Furthermore, it had to be included, as it is ever more significant to recognize that a substantial disagreement has to be followed by a frank and profound discussion and a broader discussion, rather than the simple option to exclude a chapter from the current collection of essays. There are aspects of this contribution that show how interpreters are perceived as paramount to integrate intercultural communication in healthcare interpreting with emergency medicine and with victims of assaults when seen and interviewed by healthcare professionals (see discussions in Cox and Lázaro Gutiérrez, 2016; Valero Garcés and Lázaro Gutiérrez, 2016). For the above reasons, the chapter has to be read.

Chapter 7 juxtaposes Todorova's self- and ethno-anthropological approach to consider the work of frontier interpreters to the controversial position of the previous chapter. Todorova's reflections on the self-reflective and committed role of interpreters consider the contextual challenges of interpreting for refugees, in intimidating and stressful conditions. The discussion of those contextual needs compares the challenges of other forms of interpreting, such as asylum seeks with the transient situation of refugees who live both in waiting both temporally and spatially. The chapter engages with the immediacy and effect of interpreting at the *border* (political and metaphorical for the refugees) or in large refugee camps. The vulnerable person has not been safely removed from the sensitive situation and is strongly affected by it. The interpreter is here considered, through the author's own experience and reflection with practitioners in diametrically opposing terms with the previous chapter: advocacy, empathy and other interpersonal skills for interpreting come to the core and are discussed, in situations that challenge the traditional training received by professional interpreters.

Chapter 8 is a compelling perspective of medical training, as Butler and Al Sharou engage with the complexity of integrating medical doctors from a refugee background in the UK's National Health Service (NHS). With an emphasis on training and the personal welfare, as much as the societal benefits in integrating medical practitioners through intercultural preparation to different conceptualizations of patient–doctor relationship as well as different linguistic and cultural values, the chapter reports the struggles in achieving such integration. It focuses on both the institutional point of view of planning the system to vet and enable medical professionals to work for the NHS according to its practices and standards, and that of the qualified and often highly experienced doctors from a refugee background. The chapter shows the findings of a pilot project that will hopefully be rolled out to larger groups of 'refugee' doctors as it proved to be a strong vehicle for reintegration into a society with an active role of skilled individuals who paradoxically become dependent on social welfare systems when, in fact, they have a lot to offer to the countries that has granted them asylum.

Integrating cross-national representations of local crises

This section opens with Chapter 9, an analysis of the impact of style in the translation of news by Riggs. The chapter by Riggs focuses on stylistic elements in the English press – influential rhetorical devices such as alliteration and modality – using a corpus-based methodology to try and distil how France and the French are portrayed in reports on recent terrorist attacks in France. The chapter particularly focuses on the depiction of dangers when risk is perceived through highly biased lenses. The chapter draws on textual analyses of stylistic choices as markers of bias, providing a reminder of how Islamophobia can be potentially embedded in unconscious narratives that betray journalistic and editorial policies. The perspective of assessing stylistic features when re-narrating a specific crisis, here France, terrorism and how this is reflected in the English press, makes this chapter a reminder of how linguistic practices shape perception of crises. Terrorism should not only be perceived as an international crisis but also be viewed in terms of the ideologies it foments, and which may, in turn, (further) pit different sections of society against each other. While reporting on terrorism, journalists, like translators and intercultural mediators, carry a noted responsibility. Yet it transpires that journalism covering this wider field is characterized by a culture and practice of othering, reliance on, and perpetuation of, stereotypes – all within the context of a sense of siege, of a continued state of emergency.

Chapter 10 by Sidiropoulou adds a translation perspective to the national framing and narratives when disaster strikes and the journalistic reaction is to automatically equate foreign crises, and the reactions of disaster-affected populations, to the domestic reactions to similar events. The chapter documents how English-language portrayals of disasters caused by natural hazards became embedded in traditional forms of disaster reporting when transposed into Greek. The headlines analysed show how the cultural specificity of crisis reporting manifests itself very clearly through lexical and formatting choices when introducing a remote crisis to Greek-speaking audiences. The chapter engages with concepts related to crisis management strategies and focuses on traditional (printed) press data. Results confirm that genre represents a significant variable in crisis communication also within the same culture. The study suggests that crisis management research should take into consideration a translation perspective so as to do justice to significant aspects of intercultural and intracultural crisis communication.

Chapter 11 by Federici interpreters the impact of a specific metaphor, that of *emergenza migranti*, on representations of forced migrants that deeply affect social, political and, ultimately, legislative perceptions of displaced people. The chapter argues that the aggressive metaphor of 'migration emergency' in journalistic narratives in Italy altered the perception of the arrival of migrants but also influenced political debates to take root into legislative choices and finally statutory changes to migration policies. Through the frequent use of *emergenza migranti* (in all its force as a noun-clause typical of the journalistic variety of Italian) the metaphor entrenched the perception of a global phenomenon of migration into a reductive notion of emergency. Therefore, the metaphor and its uses are discussed within the context of the movement for ethical journalism and recent discussion of news reliability. The figurative language creates a confusing form of oblique censorship, which makes soundbites useful to present challenging crises, such as the four decades of economic and social migrants reaching Italian shores. It is suggested that the reduction of complexity to soundbites enables politicians to avoid complex debates by taking sloppy shortcuts.

Concluding remarks

Already in 1997, Alexander noticed that the field of *disasterologists* needed more cohesive and holistic approaches to bring together the expertise of its many researchers and crisis managers. And despite the fact that in the following twenty-one years, many disaster relief projects have generated collaborative efforts, dialogue on the ground remains paramount, not only across all participants of that plethora of ongoing relief and developmental projects but also for future collaborations. However, little consideration has been reserved to the difficulties in accommodating language needs in such collaborations. Intercultural communication in multilingual crisis situations occurs in many dimensions. Local responders may need to work arms in arms with personnel from the international humanitarian sector. In the circumstances, intercultural communication has to consider at least three dimensions: (1) community engagement that maximizes the impact of the intervention by managing the collaborations between local and international responders; (2) including in the feedback loop the crisis-affected populations, who need to have space to assert their needs and have access to the type of information they want, in a language they understand; (3) coordination among international responders and crisis managers, and these groups with experts who get involved optimize future emergency plans and assess the impact of the crisis and the measure to mitigate it. Now, none of these approaches is fully integrated and intercultural communication in crises lacks the ethos and the civic values that other forms of language mediations in ordinary circumstances have been slowly gaining.

Maybe one general pattern is that typically none of the disaster relief and crisis communication organization is properly regulated. This is a double-edged sword as regulation is a much-needed framework for better use of language resources, but it also carries the fear of becoming a hindrance in customizing existing knowledge and experience when needed on an ad hoc basis. Flexibility is crucial in emergency management as crises do not conform to expectations and plans, which, therefore, must remain flexible to be usable and useful. Although no action has been taken just yet, it might indeed be a good plan to devise an EU-level platform that provides background details to all disaster-prevention-related initiatives and aims to provide standardized procedures that are harmonized as much as possible, but still maintain a customizable design.

With an arguably near-utopian point of collaboration, cooperation and convergence on the one hand and the utopian point of an EU-wide platform on the other, the whole field remains fragmented. The disciplinary voices that engage with the role of T&I in intercultural mediation during crises remain rare and limited. Perhaps what is needed is an online count of the field's 'should factor' and that we should strive for an ever-decreasing factor of that count and have modality as a form of contingency. In the end, we should beware of becoming Victorian or Edwardian philanthropists who expressed their perceived superiority through charity and through helping lesser fortunate fellow human beings.

In providing cross-cultural quality to disaster relief–related multilingual communication and information, translation then becomes a political action in that the world of translators, interpreters and intercultural mediators put their knowledge, experience and expertise at the service of society as a whole, more in particular at those who need it because of a man-made conflict or a disasters triggered by natural hazards. Issues with communication and coordination of volunteers and organizations in disaster response are well known (Alexander, 2010) and the addition of problems caused by multilingual contexts and intercultural incomprehension is slowly being recognized as an incremental factor in miscommunication and miscoordination. As we know these are real problems, it is high time we started looking for real solutions.

Notes

1 See for instance the UPWEB project (Understanding the practice and developing the concept of welfare bricolage, 2015–2018), which aims to reconceptualize welfare in superdiverse neighbourhoods and how all residents access healthcare (see UPWEB, 2015).
2 Among the established needs the Global Compact includes facilitating means of communication through investing in information technology solutions (Global Compact, 2018).
3 Compassion and empathy also have the capacity to drive the promotion of evidence-based public discourse and through there the elimination of discrimination, precisely two of the objectives of the Global Compact (Global Compact, 2018).

References

ACAPS (2015). 'Ebola Outbreak, Liberia: Communication: Challenges and Good Practices'. Report available online: https://reliefweb.int/report/liberia/ebola-outbreak-liberia-communication-challenges-and-good-practices (accessed 7 December 2018).

Alexander, D. E. (2010). 'The Voluntary Sector in Emergency Response and Civil Protection: Review and Recommendations'. *International Journal of Emergency Management* 7(2): 151–166.

Alexander, D. E. (2016). *How to Write an Emergency Plan*. Edinburgh: Dunedin Academic Press.

ALNAP (2017). 'Learning from the Ebola Response in Cities: Communication and Engagement'. Report available online: https://reliefweb.int/sites/reliefweb.int/files/resources/alnap-urban-2017-ebola-communication-community-engagement.pdf (accessed 7 December 2018).

Baker, M. (2006). *Translation and Conflict: A Narrative Account*. London and New York: Routledge.

Bastide, L. (2018). 'Crisis Communication during the Ebola Outbreak in West Africa: The Paradoxes of Decontextualized Contextualization'. In M. Bourrier and C. Bieder (eds), *Risk Communication for the Future*, 95–108. Cham: Springer.

Britton, C. (2017). 'What Is Crisis Communication? A Guide for Beginners'. Available online: https://www.rockdovesolutions.com/blog/what-is-crisis-communication-a-guide-for-beginners (accessed 16 December 2018).

CDC (2017). '2014–2016 Ebola Outbreak in West Africa'. Available online: https://www.cdc.gov/vhf/ebola/history/2014-2016-outbreak/index.html (accessed 6 December 2018).

Cox, A., and Lázaro Gutiérrez, R. (2016). 'Interpreting in the Emergency Department: How Context Matters for Practice.' In F. M. Federici (ed.), *Mediating Emergencies and Conflicts*, 33–58. Houndmills, Basingstoke; New York, NY: Palgrave Macmillan.

Coyle, D., and Meier, P. (2009). *New Technologies in Emergencies and Conflicts: The Role of Information and Social Networks*. Washington, DC; London: UN Foundation-Vodafone Foundation Partnership. Available online: http://www.globalproblems-globalsolutions-files.org/pdf/UNF_tech/emergency_tech_report2009/Tech_EmergencyTechReport_full.pdf (accessed 30 November 2018).

Derzsi-Horváth, A., Steets, J., and Ruppert, L. (2017). *Grand Bargain Annual Independent Report 2017*. Berlin: GPPi. Available online: https://www.icvanetwork.org/system/files/versions/Inception%20Note%20Grand%20Bargain%20%28v2%29%5B1%5D%5B1%5D%5B1%5D.pdf (accessed 30 November 2018).

Dragovic-Drouet, M. (2007). 'The Practice of Translation and Interpreting during the Conflicts in the Former Yugoslavia (1991–1999)'. In S.-C. Myriam (ed.), *Translating and Interpreting Conflict*, 29–40. Amsterdam and New York, NY: Rodopi.

Drugan, J., and Tipton, R. (2017). 'Translation, Ethics and Social Responsibility'. *The Translator* 23(2): 119–125.

Federici, F. M. (2016). 'Introduction: A State of Emergency for Crisis Communication'. In F. M. Federici (ed.), *Mediating Emergencies and Conflicts. Frontline Translating and Interpreting*, 1–29. Houndmills, Basingstoke and New York, NY: Palgrave Macmillan.

Federici, F. M., Gerber, B. J., O'Brien, S., and Cadwell, P. (2019). *The International Humanitarian Sector and Language Translation in Crisis* Situations. *Assessment of Current Practices and Future Needs*. London; Dublin; Phoenix, AZ: INTERACT. Available online: https://drive.google.com/file/d/1jGEhbiAzoxuVZw25Bpj9EnjlDFcfcAT-/view.

Footitt, H., and Kelly, M. (2012). *Languages at War. Policies and Practices of Language Contacts in Conflict*. Basingstoke and New York, NY: Palgrave Macmillan.

Global Compact (2018). Global Compact for Safety, Orderly and Regular Migration. United Nations. Available online: https://refugeesmigrants.un.org/sites/default/files/180713_agreed_outcome_global_compact_for_migration.pdf (accessed 20 March 2019).

Henry, R. C., Engström, K., Olin, S., Alexander, P., Arneth, A., and Rounsevell, M. D. A. (2018). Food Supply and Bioenergy Production within the Global Cropland Planetary Boundary. *PLOS One* 13(3): e0194695. Available online: https://doi.org/10.1371/journal.pone.0194695 (accessed 29 November 2018).

IFRC (2018). *World Disasters Report 2018. Leaving No One Behind*. Geneva: IFRC. Available online: https://media.ifrc.org/ifrc/wp-content/uploads/sites/5/2018/10/B-WDR-2018-EN-LR.pdf (accessed 30 November 2018).

Inghilleri, M., and Harding, S.-A. (2010). 'Translating Violent Conflict'. *The Translator* 16(2): 165–173.

Kelly, M., and Catherine, B. (2013). *Interpreting the Peace. Peace Operations, Conflict and Language in Bosnia-Herzegovina*. Basingstoke and New York, NY: Palgrave Macmillan.

Laschet, M. (2015). 'Words of Relief – Ebola Crisis Learning Review'. TC World November 2015. Available online: http://www.tcworld.info/e-magazine/translation-and-localization/article/words-of-relief-ebola-crisis-learning-review/ (accessed 7 December 2018).

Metcalfe-Hough, V., Poole, L., Bailey, S., and Belanger, J. (2018). *Grand Bargain Annual Independent Report 2018*. London: ODI. Available online: https://www.odi.org/sites/odi.org.uk/files/resource-documents/12255.pdf (accessed 30 November 2018).

Moser-Mercer, B., Kherbiche, L., and Class, B. (2014). 'Interpreting Conflict: Training Challenges in Humanitarian Field Interpreting'. *Journal of Human Rights Practice* 6(1): 140–158.

Ozolins, U. (2010). 'Factors That Determine the Provision of Public Service Interpreting: Comparative Perspectives on Government Motivation and Language Service Implementation'. *The Journal of Specialised Translation* 14(1): 194–215.

Pescaroli, G., and Alexander, D. (2015). 'A Definition of Cascading Disasters and Cascading Effects: Going beyond the "toppling dominos" Metaphor'. *Planet@Risk* 3(1): 58–67.

Pescaroli, G., and Alexander, D. E. (2016). Critical Infrastructure, Panarchies and the Vulnerability Paths of Cascading Disasters. *Natural Hazards* 82(1): 175–192. doi: 10.1007/s11069-016-2186-3.

Project Sphere (2018). *The Sphere Project: Humanitarian Charter and Minimum Standards Disaster Response*. 4th edition. Geneva: Mc Connan.

Smyth, C. (2014). 'Bungling Experts Allowed Virus to Overwhelm Africa'. Available online: https://www.thetimes.co.uk/article/bungling-experts-allowed-virus-to-overwhelm-africa-0zs8vznqrr5 (accessed 7 December).

Taibi, M., and Ozolins, U. (2016). 'Community Translation: Definitions, Characteristics and Status Quo'. In M. Taibi and U. Ozolins (eds), *Community Translation*, 7–28. London and New York, NY: Bloomsbury Academic.

Tipton, R. (2011). 'Relationships of Learning between Military Personnel and Interpreters in Situations of Violent Conflict'. *The Interpreter and Translator Trainer* 5(1): 15–40.

Tipton, R., and Furmanek, O. (2016). *Dialogue Interpreting a Guide to Interpreting in Public Services and the Community*. London and New York, NY: Routledge.

UN 2017, United Nations Department of Economic and Social Affairs (2017). 'World Population Projected to Reach 9.8 Billion in 2050'. Available online: https://www.un.org/development/desa/en/.../world-population-prospects-2017.html (accessed 30 November 2018).

UPWEB (2015). *Understanding the Practice and Developing the Concept of Welfare Bricolage*. Available online: https://www.birmingham.ac.uk/generic/upweb/index. aspx (accessed 30 November 2018).

Valero Garcés, C. (2014). *Communicating across Cultures: A Coursebook on Interpreting and Translating in Public Services and Institutions*. Lanham, MD, and Plymouth: University Press of America.

Valero Garcés, C., and Lázaro Gutiérrez, R. (2016). 'Perceptions from the Outside in Cases of Gender Violence. "What Are You [the Interpreter] Doing Here?"' *European Journal of Applied Linguistics* 4(1): 57–72.

WHO online (2014). *Six Months after the Ebola Outbreak Was Declared: What Happens When a Deadly Virus Hits the Destitute?*. Available online: http://www.who.int/csr/ disease/ebola/ebola-6-months/guinea-chart-big.png?ua=1 (accessed 30 November 2018).

Worldatlas (2018). *What Languages Are Spoken in the Republic of the Congo?*. Available online: https://www.worldatlas.com/articles/what-languages-are-spoken-in-the-republic-of-the-congo.html (accessed 30 November 2018).

Yong, E. (2018). 'Most Maps of the New Ebola Outbreak Are Wrong'. Available online: https://www.theatlantic.com/health/archive/2018/05/most-maps-of-the-new-ebola-outbreak-are-wrong/560777/ (accessed 30 November 2018).

Zucconi, P. (2019). 'Ebola in DRC: Violence and Instability in a Hot Zone'. *Geopolitical Monitor*. Available online: https://www.geopoliticalmonitor.com/ebola-in-drc-violence-and-instability-in-a-hot-zone/ (accessed 20 March 2019).

Section One

Integrating People in Movement in Regional Crises

The Counternarratives of Migrants and Cultural Mediators

Stefania Taviano

As the language of communication on a global scale *par excellence*, the status of English is particularly complex for a number of reasons. To start with, it is no longer defined or identified as a single language, but rather as a family of languages (Crystal, 2003). Furthermore, the World Englishes paradigm emphasizes the 'polymorphous nature of the English language worldwide' (Rudby and Saraceni, 2006: 13), leading to the use of *Englishes* to identify this language family. This approach is one among many possible ones examining the role and status of English today, and this variety of analytical approaches, together with the subsequent diversity of definitions, ranging from EFL (English as a Foreign Language), to Global English and International English, equally testify to its complexity. One of the issues complicating things even further is its double nature as both a global and a local language: English exists simultaneously as a language of international communication and as multiple local varieties of English.

Following English as a lingua franca (ELF) scholars, such as Seidlhofer (2007, 2011), Jenkins (2015), I have argued that ELF is a hybrid language inevitably affected by the languages and cultures of its speakers (Taviano, 2010, 2013). It can be empowering, particularly when its speakers appropriate the language and make it their own, for instance when it has a central role in constructing their identity, as in the case of migrant writers (Polezzi, 2012a) and activist artists (Taviano, 2016). At the same time, however, the opposite is true and knowledge of English, or better a lack of it, can have a significant impact preventing people from having access to well-paid jobs as well as affecting their social status. It can also contribute to power imbalance in high-stakes encounters, such as asylum claims.

ELF permeates the destiny of migrants and asylum seekers as a language of communication when interacting with police officers, social workers and asylum commissioners. ELF is intrinsically related to the importance of translation and interpreting in intercultural crisis communication, the themes addressed in this book. The centrality of migrants' languages as well as translation and interpreting practices, particularly in contexts of inequality and injustice, however, has so far been given scarce attention, with few exceptions (see Angelelli, 2015; Guido, 2015; Inghilleri, 2017). This chapter is thus an attempt to start filling such a gap through an interdisciplinary perspective, combining ELF and Translation Studies, focusing on the relationship between language and identity, on the one hand, and current critical notions of citizenship as affected by translation and migration, on the other. It does so by taking into account the role of cultural mediators as well as asylum seekers' perspectives, such as those narrated through the *Storie migranti* project (Storie migranti, 2011).

Challenging cultural and linguistic marginalization

As Hobsbawm and Ranger (1983) argue, the marginalization and homogenizing categorization of migrants, far from being a neutral act, is the consequence of socially and politically oriented discourses. Such discourses, as commonly known, are based on notions of identity as well-defined, fixed entities. In Bucholtz and Hall's view, establishing identities involves downplaying differences while inventing similarities. The Other can thus be perceived in opposition to those 'socially constituted as the same' (2004: 371). More precisely:

> In most cases difference implies hierarchy, and the group with the greater power establishes a vertical relation in terms beneficial to itself. Such ideological ranking enables the identities of the more powerful group to become less recognizable as identities; instead, this group constitutes itself as the norm from which all others diverge. (2004: 372)

This is clearly the case for the hierarchical relationship between Europeans and migrants/asylum seekers, whereby, as Bucholtz and Hall further explain, the first group's identity is unmarked in contrast with the identities of migrant groups. Migrants are often easily recognizable and, thus, ideologically and socially marked, particularly due to their use of language(s) that differ from the norm. Precisely because identity is a social and cultural phenomenon (ibid., 377), as Bucholtz and Hall rightly emphasize, there is often an imbalance between cultural ideologies and social practices, between what we believe about people of various social backgrounds in terms of their language and behaviour, and the actual linguistic and social practices which tend to be far more complex and strategic than expected (Bucholtz and Hall, 381–382). Challenging predominant assumptions in which language is simply considered a reflection of one's identity and culture is central to rethinking the relationship between Europe and migrants as the Other. This approach crucially recognizes that language, as a key cultural resource, is also a resource for the production of identity.

It is by taking into account the social and cultural constraints through which migrants and asylum seekers engage with their surrounding contexts that we can better understand how their use of language affects their identities, which are understood as historically, politically and socially produced. In this sense, it is particularly useful to conceptualize ELF as a translational lingua franca, as I have done elsewhere (Taviano, 2018). This means approaching ELF as a language in which translation, intended in a broad sense as the coexistence of several languages, is embedded in, thus making evident the political role of translation, translators, interpreters and cultural mediators, as Polezzi emphasizes (2012b).

Cultural mediators deserve particular attention since they play a pivotal function in *welcoming* migrants to EU countries, such as Italy, whose borders are currently being reinforced through the enclosure of migrants in identification camps where they are all categorized as non-European/Other. However, in Italy such figure is far from being fully recognized in professional terms with subsequent low hourly rates and the lack of a single definition, with multiple terms adopted varying from 'cultural mediator' to 'intercultural mediator'. In 2014 the EU co-funded with the Italian Ministry of the Interior a project aimed to better identify the skills and competencies required to become an intercultural mediator (see Melandri et al., 2014). The latter's low professional profile is in contrast with the complexity of a role which goes well beyond that of facilitating communication between migrants and civil servants, as Amato and Garwood (2011) and Katan (2015), among others, argue. The debate on the relationship between the role of translators and interpreters and that of cultural mediators, which is also framed as a debate about language skills, on the one hand, and metalinguistic competences, such as the ability to listen and understand people's needs and to resolve conflicts, on the other, continues to take place among academics and interpreters and mediators themselves.

The lack of a commonly recognized definition (see Rudvin and Spinzi, 2014) and professional recognition on a national level in Italy is indicative of the contradictions inherent in the profession of the cultural mediator and how this figure is perceived. The role of community interpreters, as they are defined in English, and cultural mediators, as well as the differences between the two (see

Martin and Phelan, 2010), has been and continues to be studied from a variety of critical approaches, as Vargas-Urpi shows (2011). These include anthropological perspectives, such as Bahadir's (2004) view of the ideal interpreter-ethnographer as a professional who can understand both cultures and undertake different roles, depending on the context. There are also sociological approaches, such as Inghilleri's (2003), which draw on both sociological and Translation Studies theories to argue for mediation as 'a socially situated activity', and applied linguistics approaches which emphasize how interaction between participants affects the message being conveyed – as in the case of the difference in use and tone of the imperative between English, on one hand, and Romance languages on the other (Mason and Steward, 2001). Finally, there are psychological approaches (see Valero Garcés, 2005) that focus on the cultural mediator's skills in facing particularly stressful contexts, such as court appearances and hospitals.

Needless to say, interdisciplinary approaches that take into account the connection between language and the context in which the former is produced, as well as the hierarchical relations existing among participants, are particularly useful. This is largely because all the approaches mentioned above can be combined to contribute to a better understanding of cultural mediation as a socially produced profession (Inghilleri, 2003). As such, it needs to be contextualized to shed light on the impact that the social, political and cultural backgrounds of the actors involved, both individually and while communicating with others, can have.

According to Taronna (2015), for instance, experiences and processes of cultural mediation can contribute to transforming our views of language, negotiation, neutrality and resistance. Taronna argues that cultural mediators function as 'activists in the creation of cross border networks of solidarity' within a 'community of practice' based on common values and narrations contributing to a translational and translocal sense of citizenship (2015: 173). Interestingly enough, before Taronna's study, ELF scholars, such as Seidlhofer (2007), had adopted Wenger's notion (1998) of community of practice in their conceptualization of ELF as a fluid language of international communication, rather than as a precise and codified variety of English. Such views of ELF as a dynamic language, constantly shaped by its speakers, parallel Taronna's argument on translation practices and cultural mediation as acts of resistance in the Mediterranean.

At the centre of translation and cultural mediation practices are migrants and cultural mediators who determine the dynamics of such interactions and, at the same time, are affected by the norms and expectations about who they are and what they are supposed to do. Inghilleri's study on the interpreters' 'uncertainty zones' (2005: 70) examines precisely such contradictions; other scholars have similarly focused on the problematic status of a professional figure who can be conceived on the one hand as a social worker, who is required to intervene, and on the other as a neutral and objective interpreter (see Merlini, 2009; Katan, 2015). Such pressure and expectations placed on cultural mediators make them vulnerable and render their work particularly demanding, as Minervino and Martin (2007) have shown. However, it is through precise translation and mediation practices as acts of negotiation and narration of the self that both migrants and cultural mediators can play an active role in putting forward cross-border notions of citizenship.

Translation as the interconnecting link

The interconnections between migration and translation were addressed at the 2018 symposium *Mutations in Citizenship. Activist and Translational Perspectives on Migration and Mobility in the Age of Globalisation*, held at the University of Manchester, which took its title from Aihwa Ong's argument about 'mutations in citizenship' (2006: 499). While migration is intrinsic to human history and, thus, historically and geographically vital for the 'evolution of the social and physical world', as Inghilleri (2017) claims, traditional notions of citizenship, closely related to nation states and dating back to the seventeenth and eighteenth centuries, are, and continue to be, challenged by ever-growing migratory flows in the current dynamic and borderless world. Staggering figures, such as those of stateless people, estimated to be at least 10 million by the UNHCR, as Inghilleri points out (2017), confirm that such notions are no longer valid. Like Ong, translation scholars taking part in the symposium have for a long time now been arguing for a renegotiation and rethinking of the concept of citizenship. This might involve strategies adopted by migrant artists, as explored in Inghilleri's presentation at the symposium, or new understandings of the nexus between translation and migration, which, given the centrality of both practices and phenomena, have been addressed by several scholars in a variety of fields in the last few years. Polezzi (2012b), for instance, argues that migration seen from a translation perspective reminds us that it is people who travel, as well as texts. This assumption, which is at the basis of new ways of conceptualizing citizenship, is also central to my argument on the role of cultural mediators and migrants, first and foremost as human beings.

The second section of this chapter focuses precisely on those cases and sites in which renegotiation of identities, and thus of citizenship, has occurred. Needless to say, other cases studies, such as those collected by eight Italian universities through the AIM project (Analysis of Interaction and Mediation), testify to different mediation practices. The consortium has collected hundreds of mediated encounters, some of which have been examined by Amato and Garwood (2011). The excerpts in Table 1.1 are taken from interactions between Italian-speaking doctors, migrant women from Nigeria and Ghana, and mediators in a family planning clinic:[1]

In these dialogues the migrant woman is either partially or totally excluded. In the first case when the mediator takes the initiative to ask her what contraceptives she is taking, thus inverting doctor and mediator's roles, and then when the doctor addresses the mediator directly, she is side-lined. While, in the second exchange, the mediator transforms the interaction even further by totally excluding the migrant's voice. In Amato and Garwood's view, cases such as these are quite telling of mediated interactions whose dynamics are inevitably controlled by doctors and mediators with a frequent risk of minimizing or silencing the migrant's voice due, among other things, to time constraints and lack of qualified staff. However, they conclude hoping that further studies and the dissemination of their results might lead to an improvement in cultural mediators' skills and the adoption of best practices. Similarly, Angelelli (2015)

Table 1.1 Mediated interactions between doctors and migrant patients (Amato and Garwood, 2011)

	Back translation
General doctor: Usa il condom lei di solito? Mediator: Do you use condom normally? Patient: No. Mediator: You don't use condom? So what do you use to avoid pregnancy? General doctor: [Sta prendendo Arianna.] General doctor: Are you taking pills? Patient: Yes.	General doctor: Do you usually use condoms? General doctor: [She is taking the pill, Arianna.]
Doctor: OK (…) Va bene. Questa gravidanza com'è andata? Mediator: Eh io lo so dottoressa perchè lo vedo [al consultorio] [è andata così così perchè la gravidanza è andata bene, cioè a un certo punto, dottoressa ha fatto l'ecografia e ha visto che il bambino non è cresciuto bene e poi.].	Doctor: Ok. Fine. How is the pregnancy going? Mediator: I know because I see her [at the clinic]. [It is not going that well, at some point, doctor, she had a scan and she saw that the child was not growing properly and then.]

emphasizes the importance of quality interpreting given that access to justice by linguistic minorities can be hindered by those same figures who are supposed to ensure it. This was the case, among others, of a Spanish-speaking driver who was sent to jail, and only subsequently set free, because his answers were misinterpreted by the ad hoc telephone interpreter during an interview by a US Border Patrol. More generally, research shows that the use of non-professional, ad hoc interpreters can cause miscommunication leading to medical errors, for instance in Emergency Departments (see Cox and Lázaro Gutiérrez, 2016), and that, in the absence of formal legislation and policy guidance, public service interpreting offered to EU citizens might not be appropriate, thus resulting in unequal access to cross-border healthcare (Angelelli, 2015b).

Resistant translation practices

The cultural mediators whose interviews I report here, and who prefer to remain anonymous,[2] testify instead to mediation practices and processes that seek to create spaces of negotiation and resistance, as mentioned above. Far from offering such cases as exemplary, I have chosen to present the experiences of both a Nigerian (CM1) and an Italian mediator (CM2), as both profiles represent a snapshot of the mediators who can be employed in Italy. The small sample offers an insight into the opposite perspectives: one of the mediators shares the migrants' cultural background and the other comes from the receiving culture. Furthermore, they both work with particularly vulnerable migrants, i.e. Nigerian women victims of trafficking. These women, whose asylum claims have been approved and completed, are housed in Protection System for Asylum Seekers and Refugees (SPRAR) centres.

Other analyses, such as Vigo's (2015), focus on the efficiency of Italian and non-Italian mediators in understanding whether and why non-Italian mediators tend to be preferred by migrants and recruiters, and apply ethnographic methods aiming, among other things, to have a quantitative, as well as a qualitative, relevance. In contrast, I hope to demonstrate that my case studies are significant as instances of radical social and political change, occurring in the here and now of individual experiences and/or within small communities, rather than being representative of widespread practices. It is from such sites of translation that new forms of mediation can start to emerge before becoming collective, if this will be the case. In this sense it is particularly interesting to note that these mediators, despite their different social and cultural backgrounds, and their personal experiences, share common views on the role of cultural mediation and transcultural interactions as possible forms of activism.

The Nigerian cultural mediator CM1 speaks Igbo, Nigerian English and the so-called Pidgin English. Igbo is one among several native languages, such as Hausa, Yoruba and Kanuri, spoken in Nigeria where multilingualism tends to be the norm, rather than the exception. As she has told me, besides a native language, educated people speak Nigerian English, whereas Pidgin English, also known as broken English, is commonly spoken as a lingua franca in Nigeria, particularly by uneducated people, and its pronunciation is clearly influenced by local languages. Pidgin English is also understood and/or spoken in neighbouring African countries; however, it can create comprehension problems in an international context, as often occurs in Italy. In fact, she raises an interesting issue: the language of mediation cannot be taken for granted in the sense that mediators who speak the migrant's language or mediators in general are not always and necessarily available. While the Italian Decree Law 286/98 grants all migrants the right to have access to written and oral communication directed to them in a language they understand, for instance when applying for asylum status or whenever they are interacting with civil servants and public institutions in general, social workers often have to compensate with their knowledge of ELF. This means, as CM1 emphasizes, that Italian social workers' limited knowledge of English can have a negative effect when they happen to interact with migrants without the help of a mediator. In cases such as these, 'the pivotal role of translation in acknowledging and attempting to safeguard the right of all persons to express and defend themselves', in Inghilleri's words (2017: 74), is denied. Consequently, migrants are then believed not to follow the rules of the receiving society or not to listen, whereas in actual fact Italian professional figures with whom they interact might cause misunderstandings, and thus affect their subsequent relationships.

Legislation on migration and its implementation through regional policies and provisions – which are far from being uniform in Italy – do not seem to take into account the extent to which language and cultural differences permeate migrants' lives, for instance in relation to their documents, given the frequency with which they become invalid because of wrong spellings or differences in transliterations. Uneducated migrants might not know how to spell their names and this can cause discrepancies between how they pronounce them and how they are transcribed in their passports and residency permits – for them English, although an official language in principle referring to their country of origin, may be the second or third language. Transliteration of their names from the original language, let alone their English transliteration, varies, in fact, according to the migrant's country of origin, and thus depends on the colonizing country, as well as according to the mediator's background. For instance, the Arabic for 'thank you' can be spelled either 'shukran' or 'chukran', according to the English or French transliteration. Furthermore, most African countries do not tend to document their citizens' date of birth; thus Italian doctors indicate the first of January of a given year, which does not necessarily correspond with the date indicated in migrants' documents. Transliteration differences and indication of dates, which might be considered as basic issues and/or deviations in relation to an ideal of standard norms and languages, acquire a completely different significance when we consider ELF as a translational language. ELF is in fact a functional tool of communication that changes according to the agents involved and the surrounding cultural and social context, as Seidlhofer (2011), among others, argues.

What is particularly significant is that, when meeting a Nigerian migrant for the first time, CM1 asks which English he/she would like to speak. For her, it is a question of respect and it is a way to put these people at ease. If she interacts with an uneducated elderly person, she adopts Pidgin English to avoid embarrassing her addressee. This is a first of series of examples on which I am going to focus testifying to the active role that cultural mediators have in their interactions with migrants and between migrants and institutions. Mediating, like translating, always implies precise choices, and as such has a political significance, as Polezzi rightly emphasizes (2012b). Both mediators' choices in fact provide a clear indication of their ethical approaches to practices of mediation.

CM2 is Italian; she has learned to understand Pidgin English after a long-term experience of mediating. Over the years, she experienced several instances in which migrants managed to communicate using accommodation techniques, such as slowing down, repetition, paraphrasing and explanations. Thus, Nigerian women speak to CM2 in Pidgin English or Nigerian English, depending on their cultural background, and she speaks the British English she has learned through her studies combined with an American accent. Like CM1, CM2 pays particular attention to her tone of voice and the words she uses to make sure she avoids offensive terms. In addition, when working in a team with social workers and lawyers, she translates in the third person adding her views as a mediator to the others' opinions, which she translates for the migrants. When translating critical comments about a migrant she also uses the third person to create a distance between her and the professional figure she is translating for, in order to maintain the trust that migrant women have in her. They constantly contact her and ask her to mediate, to help them better communicate with civil servants.

She also questions the fact that mediators can be criticized for letting a migrant take too long when answering a question. This attitude indicates a lack of recognition of their skills and demanding role as mediators, corresponding to the relatively uncertain social position of translators and interpreters, as Inghilleri (2005), among others, emphasizes. The latter claims, in fact, that there is a 'discursive gap' resulting from 'democratic iterations', aimed at encouraging mutual understanding, and 'authorized discourses', which tend to maintain power relations (Inghilleri, 2005: 72). The contrast between CM1 and CM2's democratic iteration to allow migrant women to talk longer than requested, when they realize that a specific question requires a long answer, and the authorized discourse of social workers, is evident. As Inghilleri argues, the choice and/or predominance of one kind of iteration over another depends on the public service providers, but also on the interpreters themselves, and mediators, who are inevitably affected by their political, social and cultural backgrounds. Interpreters, like translators, as emphasized by Boeri and Maier (2010) and Baker (2006, 2013), cannot be neutral in contexts of social and political injustice and thus acquire an active political role, which goes well beyond ensuring linguistic fidelity.

Mediation as activism

Professional and personal activities characterize CM1 and CM2 as activist mediators, which I explore in this section with reference to their initiatives and their discourse about them. Both CM1 and CM2 try to create active spaces of resistance in a number of ways, for instance by encouraging intercultural and transcultural understanding while collaborating with social workers to make them reflect on the importance of accepting diversity beyond one's own prejudices. In CM2's view, this is vital to prevent migrants from creating barriers towards the receiving culture and reinforcing those same prejudices they fight against. When, for instance, a social worker was annoyed by the fact that a migrant woman was not looking at him while he was talking to her, she mediated explaining how avoiding a direct gaze was a sign of respect towards him, rather than the opposite.

CM2 pursues an active role as a mediator also through teaching a course on cultural mediation. She is currently training, of her own initiative, a selected number of Nigerian women in the SPRAR centre where she works. Since several of them have expressed an interest in this profession and have related language skills, she is giving seminars on key notions and principles of cultural mediation and its main techniques, based on both training and her personal experiences. This initiative is particularly relevant given that formal education and non-academic professional training are not uniform on a national level and can vary across regions. In Sicily, for instance, training is mainly limited to BA and MA courses, while extensive professional training is lacking compared to other regions, such as Emilia Romagna and Veneto (see Angelelli, 2015).

CM2's seminars, combining key themes, such as mutual understanding, empathy, conflict solving, identity and human rights, on a theoretical level, with practical instances of how these issues are and can be addressed through cultural mediation, are thus an attempt to fill such a gap, even though on a limited scale. She started with small-group seminars, then moving onto individual tuition, as she has found out that this type of tutoring is more effective as she can tailor her training sessions to match and build on the individual migrant/learner's skills. The very personal initiative of CM2 in holding these ad hoc seminars/training for migrant women is a significant example of activism on several levels. First of all, she encourages them to become agents of their own identities by meeting their interests and demands as migrants and asylum seekers who try and begin a new life in the host country. However, she is also training them to become mediators hoping that such a role will give them the opportunity of overcoming the stigma and prejudices they are subject to as prostitutes, as well as contributing to future employment. As Cronin (2006) argues, migrants in this case use translation as a way to negotiate spaces of resistance or survival, and thus they may become translators who make use of 'the opportunity to shift from objects of translation to active subjects, to agents in the process' (Polezzi, 2012b: 348).

The fact that this takes place through a training course on mediation practices is significant, as it helps migrant women acquire those specific skills, and above all makes them aware of what translation and mediation involve, so that they can become future agents of resistance. As CM2 argues, being activist mediators requires a personal journey on the part of the migrant allowing him/her to overcome his/her traumatic experiences, and thus to be able to effectively mediate for others. Furthermore, let us bear in mind that, as Inghilleri (2005) argues, following on Bourdieu, the weak social position of public service interpreting allows members of this profession an opportunity to define their role according to 'who they are', rather than according to 'who they must be' (Bourdieu, 2000: 158–159). This is what CM1 and CM2 do: they define their role as mediators on the basis of their own personal views and experiences of what this role involves, rather than according to predominant practices or predefined rules. In this sense their initiatives, drawing on the informal acquisition of competences and skills, show how long-life learning can be even more significant than official formal training, as also indicated by Melandri et al. (2014).

Cultural mediation thus conceived becomes a mutual enriching experience, albeit with its difficulties and problems, whereby both their and migrant women's identities are shaped and transformed during these encounters made possible by and through translation and mediation practices and by becoming aware of the agency they can be afforded. As previously argued, such cases are not necessarily indicative of common trends, in the same way as the number of migrant writers who manage to find their voices as self-translators can remain isolated and restricted to small groups (Polezzi, 2012b). However, it is precisely through such singular, albeit significant, acts of resistance that spaces of negotiation can be created and alternative mediation strategies start being adopted to challenge those imposed by legal and political institutions determining migration laws and political asylum procedures.

Cultural mediators, such as CM1 and CM2, can play an activist role also when preparing asylum seekers for their interviews with the committee evaluating individual applications for asylum. They take part in mock interviews, together with psychologists, if required, and lawyers or guardians, in the case of minors, to make sure that migrants are well equipped for such interviews and do not make those mistakes that might prevent them from obtaining their rights as asylum seekers. In this sense, interviews with three asylum seekers in the Mineo Reception Centre for Asylum Seekers (CARA), near Catania in Sicily, testify to the dehumanizing nature of such procedures. One of these migrants, in fact, unmistakably confirms how one mistake can make a significant difference in their lives:

> If you are going to make one mistake in your commission, you are done, they give you negative. We are not normal people, living normal life, we make mistakes, we have families, problems, we are not as lucid as you are. People make mistakes for example with dates: on your report you said that something happened on the 19th and during the commission you say it happened on the 21st: it's a straight denial. But even their own spelling mistakes give you denials, their spelling mistakes with your names. And if you should correct them for their own spelling mistakes, then it's negative: straightforward.

Two key elements emerge clearly from this narrative: bureaucratic issues and emotional impact. The bureaucratic complications derive from a lack of uniformity in the spelling of migrants' names in their documents and records with a subsequent delay or denial of asylum claims and/or residency permits, as previously argued. The emotional impact, above all, attests to the migrants' vulnerable psychological state in these complex – and to them often unclear – legal proceedings.

This is why preparing them for such interviews, particularly on a psychological level, is vital, as witnessed by the following migrant's narration:

> Let me tell you my story. I went in front of the commission last month and as I was starting to embroid [*sic*] my story they tell me: this is enough, sign your paper! [...] I spent 5 hours but they translated only 45 minutes. Because most of the time they are distracted, they disturb you. Understand? You enter the commission and they tell you, wait now I am going to smoke, then they come back after a long time and you want to start telling your story and they interrupt you again [...]. And after two hours they ask you the same stupid question again and you are frustrated.

This person's experience further testifies to one among many examples of the Italian system's fallacies, which are far from being limited to Italy, as Barsky's study on Canadian Convention refugee hearings shows (1996):

> They asked me, they told me they are supposed to be 3 people but there are not 3 people here now and so they ask me: do you accept to do it now, are you ready to do it now? What do I say? Of course I accept. One commissioner and one translator. Also the translator is from Belize and can't translate into English very well, they just patch. I speak French but I don't understand Italian and I come from an English country, I don't understand what they are saying. And I don't want to understand because I want to leave Italy.

This migrant's rights are repeatedly denied since he is interviewed by a commission formed by two, rather than three, people, including a non-professional interpreter who appears to prevent, rather than facilitate, communication. The basic requirements for an interview are further denied when he is convened for a second time to be asked the same questions all over again:

> They call me for commission on day/month and the commission is one old man. The man's psychological faculties are very fatigued, he's very old. [...] Then they call me back a week later to ask me the same questions I had already answered. And I ask why am I getting the same questions. And they said that the way the old man interviewed me he did not do it well. [...] You people talk about democracy, democracy but when you people are talking about it and what you are doing is two different things, two different things. (Storie migranti, 2011)

These asylum seekers' experience, together with the experiences of CM1 and CM2, among many others, clearly shows the pressing need to rethink and renegotiate citizenship in Italy, as well as in other European and non-European countries. Such renegotiation has to be radical, so that migrants' lives are not reduced and categorized through hierarchical relations and systems that fail to recognize the fluid nature of cultures, diasporic identities and languages. Spelling differences and psychological traumas should be taken into account in migration legislation and asylum procedures so that, rather being an obstacle and one of the contributing factors leading to a barrier, i.e. a denial of asylum and residency claims, they are recognized as inherent aspects of the dynamics of interactions between migrants and the receiving society.

Concluding remarks

Cultural mediation and translation practices can thus represent a point of departure, a site of negotiation where we can conceive citizenship through the lens of translation. We can start doing so by recognizing migrants' dramatic experiences as human beings, as particularly vulnerable human beings who, as Barsky puts it (1996), have left their home because they were persecuted or for other financial or political reasons, hoping to have better opportunities in the host country to then find a hostile system which makes their lives impossible. The way these experiences affect not only their memories, thus the possibility of recalling their traumatizing journeys, but also their ability to put them into words, cannot go unnoticed. Ultimately, 'translation as an act of witnessing' (Polezzi, 2012b: 354) and its agents allow for the humanity intrinsic in the experience of migration to become central, rather than marginalized, 'if the heart not be so callous' – adapting the title of a recent article condemning Israeli's shooting of Palestinians, *If the heart be not callous: on the unlawful shooting of unarmed demonstrators in Gaza* (B'Tselem, 2018). Adopting a translation perspective when addressing migration means understanding that these people's languages and identities, far from coinciding with their country of origin, are strongly affected by that same journey, which started in another place but is still ongoing in the host country. As a result, these languages and identities continue to change through inherent translation practices and processes which make interactions between varied languages and cultures fluid. As Inghilleri rightly argues (2017), the limited availability and poor quality of translation resources for labour migrants show that quality translation provision is still not considered as a relevant aspect of human and labour rights. Research with an agenda of social change – as in the case of Boeri's current, yet unpublished, project on video- and interpreter-mediated asylum hearings in France – is thus vital in identifying solutions to intercultural communication crisis and failures. If, also thanks to such research, migration policies start to embrace the complexity and hybridity of migrants' languages, particularly ELF, thus the centrality of translation and interpreting, those intercultural encounters encouraging radical social and political change will be facilitated, rather than hindered.

Notes

1   The lines in square brackets are those when the mediator is communicating directly to the doctor and vice versa, followed by the translation.
2   To be precise, only one of the two mediators wishes to remain anonymous, but for the sake of consistency I have decided to extend anonymity to the other too and I have obtained written formal consent to refer to their interviews.

References

Amato, A., and Garwood, C. (2011). 'Cultural Mediators in Italy: A New Breed of Linguists'. *InTRAlinea*, 13. Available online: http://www.intralinea.org/archive/article/Cultural_mediators_in_Italy_a_new_breed_of_linguists (accessed 12 July 2018).

Angelelli, C. V. (2015a). 'Justice for All? Issues Faced by Linguistic Minorities and Border Patrol Agents during Interpreted Arraignment Interviews'. *MonTI: Monografías de traducción e interpretación* (7): 181–205.

Angelelli, C. V. (2015b). *Study on Public Service Translation in Cross-Border Healthcare: Final Report for the European Commission Directorate-General for Translation.* Available online: https://publications.europa.eu/en/publication-detail/-/publication/6382fb66-8387-11e5-b8b7-01aa75ed71a1/language-en (accessed 1 September 2018).

Bahadir, S. (2004). 'Moving in between the Interpreter as Ethnographer and the Interpreting-Researcher as Anthropologist'. *Meta* 49(4): 805–821.

Baker, M. (2006). *Translation and Conflict. A Narrative Account.* London and New York: Routledge.

Baker, M. (2013). 'Translation as an Alternative Space for Political Action'. *Social Movement Studies: Journal of Social, Cultural and Political Protest* 12(1): 23–47.

Barsky, R. (1996). 'The Interpreter as Intercultural Agent in Convention Refugee Hearings'. *The Translator* 2(1): 45–63.

B'Tselem (2018). *If the Heart Be Not Callous: On the Unlawful Shooting of Unarmed Demonstrators in Gaza.* Available online: https://www.btselem.org/publications/summaries/19201804_if_the_heart_be_not_callous (accessed 14 April 2018).

Boeri, J., and Maier, C. (ed.) (2010). *Compromiso Social y Traducción/Interpretación. Translation/Interpretation and Social Activism.* Granada: ECOS.

Bourdieu, P. (2000). *Pascalian Meditations*, trans. Richard Nice. London: Polity Press.

Bucholtz, M., and Hall, K. (2004). 'Language and Identity'. In A. Duranti (ed.),
    A Companion to Linguistic Anthropology, 268–294. Oxford: Basil Blackwell.
Cox, A., and Lázaro Gutiérrez, R. (2016). 'Interpreting in the Emergency Department:
    How Context Matters for Practice'. In F. M. Federici (ed.), *Mediating Emergencies and
    Conflicts*, 33–58. London and New York, NY: Palgrave Macmillan.
Cronin, M. (2006). *Translation and Globalization*. London and New York, NY: Routledge.
Crystal, D. (2003). *English as a Global Language*. Cambridge: Cambridge University Press.
Guido, M. G. (ed.) (2015). 'Mediazione linguistica interculturale in materia d'immigrazione
    e asilo'. *Lingue e Linguaggi*, Numero Speciale, 16.
Hobsbawm, E., and Ranger, T. (eds) (1983). *The Invention of Tradition*. Cambridge:
    Cambridge University Press.
Inghilleri, M. (2003). 'Habitus, Field and Discourse: Interpreting as a Socially Situated
    Activity'. *Target* 15(2): 243–268.
Inghilleri, M. (2005). 'Mediating Zones of Uncertainty: Interpreter Agency, the
    Interpreting Habitus and Political Asylum Adjudication'. *The Translator* 11(1): 69–85.
Inghilleri, M. (2017). *Translation and Migration*. London and New York, NY: Routledge.
Jenkins, J. (2015). 'Repositioning English and Multilingualism in English as a Lingua
    Franca'. *Englishes in Practice* 2(3): 49–85.
Katan, D. (2015). 'La mediazione linguistica interculturale'. *Lingue e Linguaggi* 16: 365–391.
Martín Mayte, C., and Phelan, M. (2010). 'Interpreters and Cultural Mediators –
    Different but Complementary Roles'. *Translocations: Migration and Social Change* 6(1).
    Available online: http://doras.dcu.ie/16481/1/Martin_and_Phelan_Translocations.pdf
    (accessed 10 June 2018).
Mason, I., and Steward, M. (2001). 'Interactional Pragmatics, Face and the Dialogue
    Interpreter'. In I. Mason (ed.), *Triadic Exchanges. Studies in Dialogue Interpreting*,
    51–70. Manchester: St. Jerome.
Melandri, E., et al. (2014). *La qualifica del mediatore interculturale. Contributi per il
    suo inserimento nel futuro sistema nazione di certificazione delle competenze*. Rome:
    ISFOL.
Merlini, R. (2009). 'Seeking Asylum and Seeking Identity in a Mediated Encounter. The
    Projection of Selves through Discursive Practices'. *Interpreting* 11(1): 57–93.
Minervino, S., and Martin, M. (2007). 'Cultural Competence and Cultural Mediation:
    Diversity Strategies and Practices in Health Care'. *Translocations* 2(1): 190–198.
Ong, A. (2006). *Neoliberalism as Exception. Mutations in Citizenship*. Durham, NC and
    London: Duke University Press.
Polezzi, L. (2012a). 'Polylingual Writing and the Politics of Language in Today's Italy'. In
    G. Parati (ed.), *New Perspectives in Italian Cultural Studies*, vol. 1, 87–111. Madison,
    NJ: Fairleigh Dickinson.
Polezzi, L. (2012b). 'Translation and Migration'. *Translation Studies* 5(3): 345–356.
Rudby, R., and Saraceni, M. (2006). *English in the World. Global Rules, Global Roles*.
    London: Continuum Publishing Group.
Rudvin M., and Spinzi, C. (2014). 'Negotiating the Terminological Borders of
    'Language Mediation' in English and Italian. A Discussion on the Repercussions

of Terminology on the Practice, Self-Perception and Role of Language Mediators in Italy'. *Lingue Culture Mediazioni – Languages Cultures Mediation* 1(1–2): 57–79. Available online: http://www.ledonline.it/index.php/LCM-Journal/article/view/748/646 (accessed 1 April 2018).

Seidlhofer, B. (2007). 'English as a Lingua Franca and Communities of Practice'. In S. Volk-Birke and J. Lippert (eds), *Halle 2006 Proceedings*, 307–318. Trier: Wissenschaftlicher Verlag.

Seidlhofer, B. (2011). *Understanding ELF*. Oxford: Oxford University Press.

Storie Migranti (2011). Intervista con tre richiedenti asilo del CARA di Mineo (Mineo, statale Catania-Gela, dicembre 2011). Available online: https://www.storiemigranti.org/spip.php?article1020 (accessed 10 September 2017).

Taronna, A. (2015). 'La mediazione linguistica come pratica di negoziazione, resistenza, attivismo e ospitalità sulle sponde del Mediterraneo'. *Lingue e Linguaggi* 16: 159–175.

Taviano, S. (2010). *Translating English as a Lingua Franca*. Milan and Florence: Mondadori Education/Le Monnier.

Taviano, S. (2013). 'English as a Lingua Franca and Translation: Implications for Translator and Interpreter Education'. *The Interpreter and Translator Trainer* (ITT), Special Issue 7(2): 155–167.

Taviano, S. (2016). 'Translating Resistance in Art Activism: Hip Hop and 100 Thousand Poets for Change'. *Translation Studies* 9(3): 282–297.

Taviano, S. (2018). 'ELF as a Translational Lingua Franca: Reciprocal Influences between ELF and Translation'. *The Translator* 24(3): 249–262.

UNHCR (2017). *I Belong Report*. Available online: https://www.unhcr.org/ibelong/wp-content/uploads/UNHCR_EN2_2017IBELONG_Report_ePub.pdf (accessed 15 May 2018).

Valero Garcés, C. (2006). 'Community Interpreting and linguistics: A Fruitful Alliance? A Survey of Linguistics-Based Research in CI'. *Linguistica Antverpiensia* 5: 83–101.

Vargas-Urpi, M. (2011). 'The Interdisciplinary Approach in Community Interpreting Research'. *New Voices in Translation Studies* 7: 47–65.

Vigo, F. (2015). 'Mediazione e competenza interculturale. Quando l'emergenza si tramuta in risorsa'. *Lingue e Linguaggi* 16: 179–214.

Wenger, E. (1998). *Communities of Practice*. Cambridge: Cambridge University Press.

2

Language Mediation in Emergency Migration Contexts: A Case Study of the Migrant Crisis 2015 in Croatia

Vedrana Čemerin

Migration flows of refugees and migrants through routes from Asia and Africa into Europe are an ongoing and complex crisis. In the Mediterranean, the crisis is playing out against the backdrop of the conflicts and transition processes arisen from Arab Spring, most notably the Syrian Civil War, as well as conflicts and economic uncertainties in several Asian and African states (Townsend, 2015; Dragović et al., 2016). While the Mediterranean Sea remains the main theatre of migratory flows towards Europe, during the summer and autumn of 2015 the land route over the Balkan Peninsula gained prominence. The UNHCR Emergency Handbook specifies a terminological difference between *refugees*, defined as people forced to flee to save their lives or personal freedom, and *migrants*, defined as people who move due to a variety of other reasons, be it to escape a disaster triggered by natural hazards, to join their family abroad or to seek livelihood. Yet, due to the temporary nature of journeys and transitory character of the crisis this terminological difference did not play a significant part in the public perception of events and the crisis response.

Contemporary sources, such as newspaper articles, social media content and governmental decrees and documents, used both terms interchangeably. As a European Union member state in the middle of the Balkans migration route, Croatia occupies a geostrategic position. Croatian rescue and protection services were heavily involved in relief efforts as hundreds of thousands of refugees and migrants passed through the Croatian territory following the overland route to the West, typically towards EU member states who – unlike Croatia – are also members of the Schengen Area. The transitory nature of their stay in Croatia makes these refugees and migrants 'transmigrants' (Glick

Schiller et al., 1995). However, the discussion of the concept transmigrants is beyond the scope of this chapter.

This chapter in fact focuses on a case study of interlingual translation and interpreting processes during the peak period of the crisis in 2015, considered as forms of language mediation according to the definition of the Common European Framework of Reference for Languages (Council of Europe, 2001: 4). Research into the communication and translation processes experienced by language mediators involved in the European refugee crisis has so far been mostly focused on the transcultural contact realized in the Mediterranean region (Giordano, 2008, 2014; Taronna, 2016; Ghandour-Demiri, 2017a). This study therefore aspires to fill the extant gap in literature regarding the role of language mediation and crisis communication in refugee aid operations on the Eastern European land routes. It purports to do so by examining both the state-run crisis response led by specific bodies in Croatia and independent community-driven initiatives organized by volunteers from various non-governmental organizations. Their activities were conducted in parallel and complementary to each other, frequently intertwining throughout the duration of the crisis, so both of those angles need to be examined.

Migration flow as a crisis and intercultural communication

The 16th of September 2015 can be considered the starting point of the refugee crisis in Croatia, since this was the date when the Republic of Hungary closed its border with the Republic of Serbia, thus diverting the flow of refugees from Serbia to Croatia (see Zrinjski, 2016). Not all migrants registered in Serbia officially entered Croatia: some remained in Serbian camps, some managed to cross to Hungary – the border was officially closed, but unofficial crossings continued – some continued to Bosnia, some entered Croatia unofficially and were thus not registered and some returned to Bulgaria to either meet up with family members or possibly seek another route.

It may be noted that while the Balkans have for centuries been a contact zone between different cultures, religions and languages, they are not a traditional contact zone for this scale of migration patterns: despite the extremely large influx of people in the mid-2010s, for a large majority of refugees and migrants Croatia was not what may be termed a 'hot spot' or a destination country, but rather a transit country and a temporary stop on their way to the West. This is reflected in the numbers: according to official data by the General Police

Directorate, Department of Border Management, a total of 658,068 migrants entered Croatia between 16 September 2015 and 4 March 2016. Of that number, 558,724 migrants were registered at entry in the last four months of 2015. Only 39 refugees/migrants requested asylum in Croatia, while the rest moved on to Western Europe (Zrinjski, 2016). Citing the official documents by the Department of Border Management, Dragović et al. (2016: 38–39) provide specific numbers for the period between 16 September 2015 and 10 December 2015: of the 420,753 registered migrants up to 10 December 2015, 231,032 were male, 70,173 were female and 119,548 were children. With regard to stated nationality, 211,404 migrants were Syrians, 125,452 were Afghans, 53,754 were Iraqi, 13,597 Iranian, 6,659 Pakistani, whereas all the other stated citizenships amount to 9,887.

The brunt of the influx, often labelled a 'crisis', lasted for seven months in total until March 2016 when the joint EU-Turkey Statement was signed. The agreement stipulated that the EU would provide three billion euros' worth of financial support for refugee camps in Turkey, while Turkey agreed to accept the return of all new irregular migrants and asylum seekers who try to cross to the Greek islands (*EU-Turkey Statement: one year on*, 2017: 2–3). In the first four months of 2018 the Croatian Ministry of Interior has recorded 1,761 attempts to cross the Croatian borders illegally, a 72 per cent increase to 2017. Likewise, the composition of the migrant population has changed, with Syrians recently constituting a relatively small percentage, and the majority consisting of Afghans, Pakistanis, Kosovars, Algerians, Turks, Libyans and Moroccans. (Haidar Diab, 2018; *Index.hr*, 2018a).

Public perception of the events and the response by the competent authorities had been somewhat influenced by relatively recent memories of the Homeland War which lasted from 1991 to 1995, and during which Croatia had faced a refugee crisis of its own, accepting and accommodating more than 700,000 refugees from the occupied Croatian territories and Bosnia and Herzegovina (Toth, 2001: 57–60 and 143–147; Esterajher, 2015:15). While the refugee crisis of the 1990s had likewise been a complex issue, it had also been spread out over several years and involved the Croats and the Bosnian Muslims, culturally similar peoples who spoke mutually intelligible languages and had been living in the same country – former Yugoslavia – for several decades. Interlingual interpretation had had a vigorous lifespan during the conflicts of the 1990s, but its use was primarily related to the presence of international peacekeeping forces (Apter, 2001; Kelly and Baker, 2013).

This chapter focuses exclusively on those migrants who legally entered Croatia and were officially registered in refugee camps during the response operations of 2015, as they required the engagement of all competent services at once. The refugee crisis of 2015 represented a peculiar event, whereby the relevant services had been forced to act quickly and in a short time frame (Dragović et al., 2016: 31).

Methodology and data collection

Methodologically, this chapter relies on qualitative data in the form of discourse analysis of contemporary newspaper articles and written documents of relevant actors, such as the ministries and NGOs involved in crisis response. These are integrated with qualitative interviews conducted with the language mediators involved in the relief efforts, in line with the ethnographic methods and case studies to conduct research in Translation Studies (Hubscher-Davidson, 2011: 2–3; Susam-Saraeva, 2014). When it comes to qualitative interviews as a method used in social sciences, Edwards and Holland emphasize their usefulness in exploring the working processes of institutions and personal experiences, reflections and imaginings of research participants, as well as in uncovering the meanings that individuals and groups affix to experiences, social processes, practices and events (2013: 90–91). They likewise point out the fact that data obtained through a qualitative interview by its very nature cannot be generalizable in the way quantitative data is. This prompts the need to make the research process as transparent as possible (Edwards and Holland, 2013: 92).

However, since the refugee crisis entailed a specific set of conditions whereby most of the actual events and the language mediators' work took place in person and through oral interpretation, the author considers the use of qualitative interview as a research method warranted. The semi-structured interviews were conducted with six translators: four from the Croatian Red Cross as the main body which coordinated the mediators in the field, one with a translator from the Jesuit Refugee Service and one with a volunteer who participated in the development of the Refugee Phrasebook as a printable language aid to incoming refugees. Three respondents were interviewed in person, while the remaining three were interviewed using email. The questions used were open-ended and the respondents were encouraged to focus on anything they deemed relevant to the topic.

Crisis response: Basic overview

Specific crises call for bespoke responses, and this crisis had been primarily humanitarian, involving many people in need of medical and other types of physical and psychological assistance. Considering it as a humanitarian crisis meant providing relief, temporary accommodations, basic food items and water, warm clothing and footwear, hygiene and sanitation, personal safety and security, psychological support, reuniting separated families and other similar activities, and, finally, further transport towards their intended destinations.

The Croatian government adopted its official policy, known as *open borders policy* (Zrinjski, 2016; Vitas, 2017: 22), as of 16 September 2015. The policy was applied in the following manner: refugees and migrants were allowed entry, transported to transit camps and makeshift refugee centres; sick and infirm were treated for their respective medical conditions and then finally transported by specially organized trains and buses to borders with Slovenia and Hungary. Within the framework of the open borders policy, a Coordination Centre for Activities led by the Interior Minister was established by a governmental decree on the 17 September 2015, enabling rapid decision-making in the field. The Ministry of the Interior and the following actors were involved in managing the crisis:

- various other ministries such as the Ministry of Health,
- governmental bodies such as the National Protection and Rescue Directorate, which is the main body responsible for civil protection and defence,
- the Directorate for Commodity Reserves whose duties involve keeping the reserves of food, tents, medical supplies and other goods that may be deemed necessary to sustain the functioning of the state in the event of a possible crisis until the re-establishment of normal conditions and
- the police and the army.

Approximately twenty-five local and regional non-governmental organizations (NGOs) from the broad political and civil spectrum participated in the relief operations. These ranged from large NGOs with established facilities such as the Croatian Red Cross as the UN coordinator, or the local branch of the Jesuit Refugee Service, to independent NGOs organized by volunteers such as the local initiative called Are You Syrious and the international volunteer initiative assembled in an open collaborative project to provide important vocabulary to refugees, called the Refugee Phrasebook.

The Are You Syrious community was formed in the summer of 2015 precisely to support the refugees arriving in Croatia by the Balkans route. Like other initiatives of this type, including the analogous Refugee Phrasebook project, its members used social media to organize themselves and communicate. Hundreds of volunteers from all those organizations worked long hours and provided their skills and knowledge to sustain the relief efforts. However, as mentioned in the introduction, due to the very number of organizations and people involved in the crisis response, the lines regarding the issues of responsibility and authority were occasionally blurred, since various organizations were performing tasks that sometimes overlapped. For instance, volunteers of one NGO would plan their daily activities to include the sorting of donated winter clothes, only to discover that another NGO had already taken up that task for the day. Similar miscommunications occasionally caused tensions but most inter-organizational complications were dealt with as and when they occurred, and they did not interfere with the overall course of the operations.

Inter-organizational tensions and coordination issues in disaster response are commonly associated with the difficulty of managing spontaneous volunteers and responders (see Alexander, 2010). Whittaker et al. (2015: 359–361) discuss this phenomenon, claiming that those volunteers who are formally unaffiliated with the official agencies but participate in the management of crisis events tend to be viewed as a nuisance or liability, their efforts frequently undervalued and seen as falling outside the purview of the official emergency and disaster management system and even potentially impeding effective crisis response. This tendency is mitigated by obtaining legitimacy through the system, usually by becoming an accredited or formally affiliated volunteer.

However much the goodwill and hard work of spontaneous volunteers are invaluable, difficulties may arise from the lack of experience, practical, psychosocial and intercultural training among the volunteers operating in the aftermath of a disaster. Fernandez et al. (2006: 61) identify two types of risk connected to the presence of spontaneous volunteers in crisis situations: the first is the potential failure of emergency managers to effectively utilize the volunteers they have got, leading to potential inability to save some victims of the disaster, inability of victims to benefit from the volunteers' activities and subsequent poor perception of the overall disaster response by competent authorities. For instance, one of the respondents in this study claimed that one of the volunteers almost caused a stampede in the reception centre in Bregana when she started doling out pre-prepared meals ahead of schedule. However, this situation was quickly spotted and stopped before it could develop into an actual problem. The second type of risk involves the potential for untrained and uncoordinated volunteers to harm disaster victims, emergency responders and their own selves. Any disaster response ought to be cohesive in terms of human resources available to provide relief on the scene.

Managing a multilingual crisis

Most refugees in Croatia spoke rare or emerging languages (Lai and Mulayim, 2010: 49), such as Levantine Arabic, Farsi, Dari, Urdu, Pashto, Amharic, Tigrinya or dialects of Kurdish (Kurmanji and Sorani). Therefore, the relief coordinators dealt with the need to find large numbers of interpreters able to face up this linguistic diversity. This need was urgent, as extant legislation regarding the process of asylum and international protection complies with relevant European Union directives and requires the presence of case-appropriate translators or interpreters for processing refugees' applications.

On 12 June 2015, the Croatian Parliament adopted the Act on International and Temporary Protection, replacing the earlier Asylum Act (2008–2015); Article 14 of this new Act defines the right of asylum seekers and applicants for international protection to have recourse to a translator/interpreter for a language in which they are able to communicate and which they may be justifiably presumed to understand. The translator/interpreter is further specified to ought to be of the same sex as the applicant, if possible, to ensure the full account of the applicant's reasons for seeking asylum, and the applicant is obliged to cooperate with the interpreter unless they deem such cooperation might have a negative effect on the full account of the reasons for their application. In such cases, the applicants need to provide reasons for their refusal to cooperate with the interpreter, as well as providing certified translations of the documents on which they are basing their asylum application.

Article 13 of the same Act defines the duties and obligations of translators and interpreters employed to assist in the asylum proceedings, specifying that the translator/interpreter shall be employed if it has been assessed that he/she has good knowledge of Croatian and the language for which they are being engaged, in both writing and speech, and if it has been established that there are no circumstances which would be a hindrance to employment in civil service according to extant regulations, as well as that no security hindrances exist subsequent to basic security checks. However, these provisions refer to the conditions pertaining to standard asylum procedures in the official – and frequently long-lasting – legal proceedings, rather than a large-scale emergency necessitating immediate action through a broad spectrum of relief activities. The difference between crisis communication and traditional translation exists because with the former 'content is generally concise, and time is a highly critical factor' (O'Brien, 2016: 96). Furthermore, in order to properly assess the interpreters' professional credentials and abilities, one first needs a sufficient pool of available interpreters for relevant language combinations, as well as the established and verified assessment procedures. When it comes to rarely utilized language combinations, these may generally be quite difficult to come by, much less to do so quickly and efficiently.

As demonstrated by the Crisis Management Team of the Ministry of Health's checklist of 15 September 2015 (Ministarstvo zdravlja, 2015), language barriers were identified as the greatest issue in providing emergency medical services, as it had been determined that some migrants might need medical assistance but spoke no European languages. After stating the anticipated language difficulties, the checklist provided a list of potential solutions, stating that 'only some of those solutions may be in use at an individual centre, but it would be best if at least two of them were utilised' (Ministarstvo zdravlja, 2015):

1. Determining the availability of interpreters for Arabic and Farsi (difficult due to organizational and financial reasons).
2. Usage of machine translators such as Google Translate (vocal for Arabic, vocal and textual for Farsi).
3. Usage of standardized communications resources, such as dictionaries and glossaries.
4. Using trilingual (Croatian/Arabic/Farsi) or quadrilingual (Croatian/English/Arabic/Farsi) text cards with frequently asked questions and answers.

Practical constraints

Considering the extant drawbacks and hazards inherent to the improper use of machine translation (MT), their utility in crises and emergencies remains somewhat limited for now, especially when it comes to non-Indo-European languages and languages whose reference data sets and online corpora are relatively small. Translators Without Borders rely on machine translation on their Kató platform (see Translators Without Borders, 2018), which developed and effectively used offline MT engines for Sorani and Kurmanji, specifically focusing on content for refugees (Translators Without Borders, 2016). These engines are rule-based, rather than statistical or neural. Even though the MT output is somewhat rudimentary, it can be used on low-spec smartphones without an internet connection by providing support with relatively basic and limited lexical needs. However, if used with due diligence, i.e. with proper revision instead of taking MT at face value and with full human translation instead of inappropriate MT output, machine translation tools may be an asset in the crisis language mediation process.

According to the respondents of this study, Google Translate and similar tools were used very rarely and only to resolve issues related to dialectal language varieties. Differences in pronunciation of Arabic occasionally caused issues when the refugees received two different pieces of information from two different mediators due to specific slang or sociolect used, so sometimes the mediators would look up particular words using Google Search or Google Translate. The overall situation required mainly oral interpretation – in the form of community interpreting – with regard to medical assistance or the provision of basic items such as food – and the language mediators present on-site were native speakers of relevant languages. If language mediators were unable to provide their services (for instance, if they were engaged in other camps or on other urgent tasks in the same camp), then other volunteers would use Google Translate or even Google Images, by asking the refugees to search for an image of what they needed (e.g. a bottle of water or a pair of shoes) in their own language and then show the result to the volunteers.

The lack of trained interpreters was perceived as a significant problem by all relief organizations, both Croatian and international. Mediators were present in all reception camps both at the borders and within the country proper, and their work was coordinated by the Croatian Red Cross. The mediators were mostly non-professional linguists fluent in languages needed, who performed both written translation and oral interpreting on an ad hoc basis, as the need for their services arose according to the flow of events. The notion of using ad hoc translational solutions in emergency mediation is almost a staple of crisis translation, since emergency and crisis situations in multilingual settings frequently demand finding many skilled translators at short notice (Federici, 2016: 3), who are then recruited 'last minute' (Taronna, 2016: 290). The 2015 refugee crisis in Croatia followed this very pattern, as the number of interpreters available for specific language combinations was quite low since their learning and use are not economically viable in the Croatian language market, and for some there are no established translational relations at all, such as Urdu or Amharic. Furthermore, while Arabic is taught as an optional course at the Zagreb University Faculty of Humanities and Social Sciences' Department of Turkish Studies, it involves standard literary Arabic, rather than spoken dialects. Currently, there is no Croatian-Arabic dictionary or vice versa. Therefore, finding professional translators or court interpreters for those language pairs proved to be a daunting task. The Croatian Association of Court Interpreters offered to provide its expertise, but as it turned out that they did not have interpreters for the languages needed, their members ultimately provided general volunteer services. Eventually, the language mediators were mainly recruited from a pool of native speakers with ties to Iraq, Iran or Syria who already lived in Croatia. They voluntarily offered their services and their profiles fitted in one of the four categories described below.

1. People who came to Croatia to study and who already spoke Croatian fluently. During the 1980s, as the former Yugoslavia had been one of the founding members of the Non-Aligned Movement,[1] there were fewer restrictions for students from the non-aligned countries or the Middle East to register as university students. Students taking up these opportunities continued to live in Croatia after graduation by gaining employment and acquiring citizenship (see Pašiček, 1977/2015). Bilingual speakers of Croatian and Arabic or Farsi belonged to this group (Patković, 2015).
2. People who had sought asylum in Croatia and were granted international protection, and who spoke English or Croatian in addition to their mother tongue – including speakers of Arabic, Farsi and some Kurdish dialects.
3. People who have been granted temporary residence in Croatia (e.g. through being reunited with their families who have been granted asylum).
4. The Jesuit Refugee Service mainly deployed Farsi-speaking language mediators from Iran and Arabic-speaking language mediators from Eritrea, Libya, Sudan and Somalia to encompass diverse Arabic dialectal varieties. They were all either past or present asylum seekers, whose knowledge of Croatian or even English was quite limited.

None of the mediators used by various organizations in the camps had a university language degree or experience as a professional translator. Some had previously worked for the police and served as ad hoc court interpreters. They received basic training with regard to Red Cross operational practices, but they had no specific training in intercultural mediation. While the Croatian Red Cross' printed manual on refugee protection in English and Croatian (Lalić and Kraljević, 2014: 101) underscores the importance of language and cultural mediators – especially their selection, training and competences – it also recommends avoiding interpreters who are prone to excess criticism and the use of negative or demeaning phraseology in their manner of speaking in order to facilitate a welcoming environment for refugees. Furthermore, it provides guidelines on potential communication obstacles and difficulties (lack of linguistic knowledge or misusing particular words, falling prey to negative stereotypes and prejudice, with an additional emphasis on avoiding such pitfalls). However, in actual crisis fieldwork the engagement of interpreters is mostly dependent on their availability, and less upon their individual personal qualities, especially in circumstances as extreme as the 2015 crisis.

In ideal conditions, any personnel engaged in the performance of a particular activity would be thoroughly screened, vetted and trained following a proper recruitment process. This is sometimes difficult to achieve even in regular market conditions, when the workforce pool is limited, such as may be the case with minor language combinations where translational relations are almost non-existent, or they may have to resort to using pivot or relay languages in order to complete their clients' orders. In the 2015 crisis settings in Croatia, these issues become magnified due to a high-stress environment requiring the rapid completion of tasks in the constantly evolving conditions, which are discussed in the next section.

Crisis response: The working process

Temporary reception centres were established at border crossings, where the incoming refugees were admitted into the country (such as Tovarnik and Bapska on the border with Serbia) and subsequently transferred to further temporary transit centres and reception camps within the Croatian territory (such as Lovas, Beli Manastir, Opatovac and Slavonski Brod, Ježevo and the centres in the capital city of Zagreb, at the Porin Hotel and in the Zagreb Fair facilities) and those where the refugees were transferred out of the country to Slovenia (such as Bregana and Trnovec). As stated above, mediators were present in all reception camps both at the borders and within the country proper, and their work was coordinated by the Croatian Red Cross. Those mediators who had already been working for the Red Cross before the crisis belonged to the Red Cross' Asylum and Migration Department and Search Service whose duties and tasks frequently corresponded to each other and overlapped during the crisis. They translated all logistical items for all organizations which needed them. They likewise interpreted in emergency dispensaries and hospitals, as well as during the activities of psychosocial support. Depending on the specific task they needed to perform, the mediators were accompanied by the psychosocial support coordinator or someone from the Search Service who acted as their supervisor. They worked in twelve-hour rotation shifts, with one mediator spending one week per camp and then being replaced by another according to the rotation schedule, which are standard Red Cross shifts for their personnel but are very physically and mentally demanding. They translated all written materials utilized in the relief process, such as informative leaflets, posters or signs posted in camps, into relevant languages. In addition, large written signs were posted at camp entrances, containing information on the location of the incoming refugees' arrival, what kind of help they could obtain there and the general procedure on what will happen in the following few hours.

However, the mediators and the relief personnel soon realized that the dissemination of spoken information was much more pertinent than written information on posters and information boards. Signs with ten to fifteen lines of text containing information have proven themselves to be cumbersome, with a refugee population consisting largely of pre-school or school-age children and many illiterate adults (similar conditions are described in Ghandour-Demiri, 2017b). The varying degrees of literacy and education among the refugee population, for Ghandour-Demiri (2017a: 7–8), subsequently affect the comprehension of information generating the need for further mediation.

Given the similar nature of the language mediation needed by humanitarian aid workers in Greek camps (Ghandour-Demiri, 2017a: 31–32), it is not surprising that the respondents to this case who had been involved in relief operations in 2015 reported similar issues. These included shortage of interpreters for particular languages which caused the organizations to borrow language mediators from one another, lack of interpreters for Kurdish dialects (the Croatian Ministry of the Interior had two mediators for Kurdish who worked for all organizations but one respondent who mentioned this did not know which Kurdish dialect they spoke). Also, insufficient knowledge regarding specific cultural and linguistic nuances was an issue, as was dissemination of written materials in English, Arabic or Farsi, whereas a portion of the refugee population spoke none of those languages. Nevertheless, the similar results between the study by Translators Without Borders and this case study in Croatia emphasize the importance of catering for the linguistic needs of the affected population in order to achieve successful communication in the field.

As claimed by one of the Red Cross mediators interviewed for the purposes of this study, some refugees did not want to read communication in the form of written materials but through personal touch and having the relevant data conveyed by spoken word. This kind of approach would at the same time provide them with reassurance and emotional support. This ultimately led to the relief personnel in camps such as Opatovac utilizing oral interpreting through megaphones and loudspeakers, as written information from the posters and signs was then recorded and continuously played on loudspeakers in order to make necessary information accessible to everyone. The mediators would join refugees upon arrival in the railway station and loudly repeat the information and relevant announcements. All pertinent information, such as where to obtain winter clothes or food and other types of information, had also been distributed through printed leaflets simultaneously with the loudspeaker recordings, but the primary mode of language mediation used throughout the duration of the crisis had been face-to-face interpreting.

Likewise, language mediators also served as intercultural mediators for other volunteers on-site, explaining them the specificities of body language and non-verbal gestures, cultural aspects related to individual ethnic groups and the reasons behind certain instances of refugees' behaviour, which were ingrained in their cultural background. As one of the Red Cross coordinators claimed: 'Since our mediators came from relevant cultures and ethnicities, we considered them experts for those cultures and deferred to their opinion on all matters related to specificities of culture.' The coordinator from the Jesuit Refugee Service supported this opinion, claiming that their volunteers were taught by their mediators all relevant cultural specificities (tradition, customs, expected behavioural patterns), which greatly facilitated and improved their own performance. In addition to their language mediation duties, the mediators themselves sometimes searched for the refugees' family members, without the psychosocial support coordinators, as their familiarity with language and culture enabled them to eliminate pronunciation difficulties with individual names.

Language mediation in practice: Strategies, potential issues and pitfalls

When asked whether they encountered any language and comprehension difficulties, and the perceived importance of their tasks, all respondents agreed that the most important aspects of their work in the camps had been the transfer of meaning and provision of accurate and timely information to those in need, in addition to being as professional as possible in those circumstances and treating the refugees with kindness. Despite the fact that none of them were employed as full-time interpreters, and had no professional linguistic qualifications, they strongly emphasized the importance of a professional approach to the performance of their duties.

When asked about their motivation why they volunteered, they invariably claimed the desire to help those in need, their own past experience as refugees or as participants in the asylum process, and the desire to be useful as they possessed specific language skills that were in great demand. In particular, they pointed out the human factor in relief and empathy. This is in line with the findings of other studies on volunteer translation in disaster triggered by natural hazards, which found the emotional response to the unfolding crisis and the sense of civic or moral duty to be very strong motivating factors when it comes to offering one's volunteer services to relief organizations (Barraket et al., 2013: 27). The same study puts an emphasis on experiential factors (being a survivor of a past disaster or personally affected by the unfolding crisis, past experience with volunteering, exposure to people who were directly affected by the current crisis, having relevant professional skills and/or professional exposure to disasters, and the desire to give something other than money or other types of aid). Personal identification with the victims is likewise noted as a powerful emotional motivator to volunteer (Fernandez et al., 2006: 58).

The mediators emphasized how the core issue they faced was one of scale, having to deal with such a large number of people who needed the mediators' assistance in the camps, which amounted to several thousand per day. These demands entailed quite strenuous physical exertion on the part of the mediators. Regarding specific problems, the mediators mentioned the differences in the dialects of Farsi or Arabic. The mediators resolved this issue by adapting their accents to be closer to standard literary Arabic or Farsi, or by using mediators who spoke closer dialectal varieties to the ones spoken by individual refugees, if it had been possible. Some mediators, coming from a refugee background themselves, had very little or no knowledge of Croatian and somewhat limited knowledge of English, so they relied on other mediators to communicate with the volunteers. One respondent mentioned communication issues with Somali migrants who had hardly a working knowledge of Arabic but were then directed to those mediators who came from Somali background. Another mentioned an issue occurring in medical dispensaries when male mediators did not want to ask or translate vocabulary items related to female genitalia, or vice versa. Already accounted for in Article 14 of the Act on International and Temporary Protection, this requirement was met by assigning same gender mediators whenever possible.

Most of the complications were resolved by utilizing several approaches:

1. By using language accommodation strategies: simplification, code-switching, code-mixing, frequent repetitions of what has been said. Sentences used needed to be short and clear, vocabulary choices were quite basic.
2. Any dialectal or slang doubts or difficulties were occasionally resolved through teamwork and the use of several languages until a satisfactory solution has been achieved (e.g. Croatian-English-Farsi, or Kurdish-Farsi/

Arabic-English). As the mediators themselves noticed, when relay translations are used and if a conversation has two or three speakers, there are always certain errors and deficiencies present, so it was important to use short sentences, frequently repeat important pieces of information and not to complicate the discussion with irrelevant or superfluous speech.

3. Dictionaries or Google Translate and similar supporting tools were used rarely as there had been no extremely complex vocabulary for native speakers and only to resolve dialectal issues, but Google Images were used as a non-verbal communicative resource and since the items needed by the refugees were quite basic, such as food or clothing items, for some mediators they proved to be the best communicative variety with the least margin of comprehension errors.

4. By using either English or French as a relay/pivot language to help explain difficult points. While English was the main language used, besides Arabic and Farsi, as some of the migrants originated from French-speaking countries or knew a little German, those languages were sometimes used to enhance communication or clarify certain points. However, their use was quite limited since the communication mostly relied on English, Arabic and Farsi. One of the respondents mentioned that she had a lot of problems understanding migrants from the Maghreb, since she herself was Iraqi and the Arabic dialects spoken in the Maghreb contain many calques from French, so she tried to steer the flow of the conversation towards standard Arabic.

All respondents agreed that no difficulty they encountered during their work had been so complex that it could not be resolved in a timely and successful manner. In addition, the people who needed their assistance were people on the move, so most of them were just passing through and needed their issues – which revolved around basic human needs and finding their lost family members – to be resolved quickly and up to the point. This meant that language mediation mostly involved relatively simple and repetitive types of information, as opposed to complex and highly specific language such as legalese which may be present in formal asylum proceedings. Mediators belonging to the Jesuit Refugee Service claimed that, after their shifts in the camps, they used their free time at home to go through vocabulary issues which they had experienced first-hand to be problematic and often also learned vocabulary items which were crucial but relatively rarely used. As individual mediators worked closely with specific volunteers from a specific organization, they spent a lot of time together and learned each other's idiolects which greatly enhanced mutual communication, so if a volunteer from another organization needed the services of that specific mediator but would not understand them completely, volunteers from their parent organization would help them to communicate effectively. This greatly facilitated the working process.

Refugee Phrasebook: Volunteer translation in a digital space

In addition to the professional first responders and spontaneous volunteers present in the camps and reception centres, the relief efforts also involved online volunteers who participated in the projects aimed at providing refugees with helpful information throughout the duration of their passage over the Balkans route. Some volunteers participated both online and in situ, not limiting their activities to language services but also sorting clothes or handing out meals to incoming refugees.

The most distinctive online initiative discussed here was the Refugee Phrasebook (for the latest version, see Refugee Phrasebook 2018), created as an open collaborative translation project spanning several countries and utilizing the Creative Commons licence to develop a large glossary and phrasebook in several languages, both those spoken by the refugee population (Arabic or Farsi) and the languages of the countries located along the transit route (Greek, Hungarian, Bosnian, Croatian, Serbian, Macedonian, Albanian, etc.), as well as German and English as the primary and possibly pivot languages of the master file. A Berlin-based group initiated the Refugee Phrasebook in August 2016; when it became clear that the refugee flow will arrive to Croatia, Croatian volunteers joined the extant project. The project itself functioned as an open Google Docs spreadsheet which the translators could edit and add their own phrases. The contents included several important terminological fields, varying from simple phrases in given languages, such as greetings, to more complex juridical and medical terminology. One column included phrases for helpers, meaning volunteers and other personnel in contact with refugees. Minefields represented an important sub-domain as, following the 1990s war, Croatian and Bosnian territories – through which the refugees passed – are still covered with minefields. The Phrasebook team included the images of Croatian language minefield warning signs together with their translations into relevant languages.

Volunteer translators for the project were recruited mainly through Facebook and using the word-to-mouth method: volunteers would ask their friends and acquaintances to recommend someone for a particular language (e.g. Macedonian or Albanian) and then those contacts would bring their own contacts into the project team. People who invested a little more time and effort into their work would later serve as a sort of 'project managers', organizing and managing work for their respective languages. Medical and legal subsections were respectively translated by medical or legal professionals who were native speakers of relevant languages, or certified court interpreters, and whose work was then proofread by language specialists. The main languages of the Phrasebook were German and English, and there were translators whose main task was to confirm that those two versions were in compliance and without errors and mistranslations. Translators for relevant languages (including Croatian) proofread and verified each other's translations, comparing them to each other and to the German and English 'originals'. Volunteers who translated from both German and English could spot inconsistencies and inform the 'project managers'. All communication regarding the project was conducted by email or through Facebook.

When it comes to Croatian, as it shares a lot of similarities with Bosnian and Serbian, there was an acute need to harmonize the versions in those languages. The solution was to use one column for all three languages, with the words that occur in all of them written only once, but different vocabulary written in all three languages. Translators who were tasked with working on a specific language would receive a link with an editable table solely for that language. If they spotted an issue elsewhere, they could add a note next to it, but they could not edit other languages. Translations for languages spoken by the refugee groups were proofread by native speakers, who were likewise recruited via social media or through existing personal networks. Those translations were, subsequent to proofreading, posted on the dedicated Facebook group and left open for people to comment on potential errors and changes to the text. Translators recruited for those languages were always asked whether they had any previous experience with translating or a university degree. Translations in languages such as Arabic or Farsi were checked and verified by five or more people, in order to eliminate all potential errors or inconsistencies. Since the Phrasebook was envisioned to cover the entire Balkans route, and the volunteers from relevant countries were in constant contact with each other, phrases, terms and sentences were added to the spreadsheet in accordance with extant needs and the information obtained from the fieldwork.

The refugees, as the final users of the project, received the Phrasebook in progressive steps since it was created and completed following the changes in the direction and movement of the refugee wave across the Balkans route. The first part to be completed was the Greek version, since it was the first stop on the route and the one which commanded the most urgency, so the volunteers worked day and night to finish this version. A similar thing occurred with Hungarian and Croatian. For the Croatian version, translators worked several weeks in advance of the increase of refugee numbers as it had been known that Hungary would close its border with Croatia, so they worked sixteen hours per day to have the finished version ready for that exact moment. When the refugee flow reached Croatia, the Phrasebook was ready to be downloaded and volunteers started sharing links for download. When the first refugees crossed the border, the border police officers printed out the Phrasebook in order to facilitate communication.

As there was a master version in German and English, it was relatively easy to complete the larger part of the work in a relatively short time frame, so as the need arose for each individual language, the volunteers would simply seek translators and proof-readers for those languages. For instance, after the Hungarian border had been closed, there was no need for the Croatian version to contain Hungarian phrases, but certain other languages were added to this version according to the path the refugee route moved. This meant that at any given time, several versions of the Phrasebook existed.

This proved to be somewhat of an issue when the Croatian branch of the Bisnode Ltd company donated funds to print out 100,000 copies of the Phrasebook, which they printed in a shortened version to increase the number of copies. This caused some discussions among the volunteers, but, ultimately, they agreed on incorporating certain elements of the digital version, while leaving out others. This was the largest printed edition of the Phrasebook. It was given out to refugees in the reception centre in Bapska and throughout the route, as well as shipped to Serbia, Bulgaria, Macedonia, Austria and Germany.

However, despite the enormous and quite professional amount of work that went into the development of the Phrasebook, there were certain issues related to its utilitarian function, and those issues were similar to the ones encountered by language mediators in the reception centres with regard to written signs: its very size proved to be too cumbersome for people on the move to utilize properly, so it was soon discovered that – while its use had been somewhat limited for its intended purpose on the route itself – it proved to be of great assistance and benefit to those refugees who reached Austria and Germany and had time to settle down and start learning the relevant language. To them it served as a learning aid. The printed-out versions were thus dispensed among the refugees in the camps in Germany, and a certain number of copies were even sent to England by truck, so as to be of use to those refugees who had arrived in asylum centres in the UK.

While most digital volunteering does not reach the level of professionalism and organization shown by the project team gathered around the Phrasebook, crowdsourced online translation in crises is a vibrant field (Munro, 2010; Sutherlin, 2013) that can be expected to grow only as more initiatives arise following various disasters and adverse events. This again prompts the issues regarding the quality of volunteer output and the overall management of volunteer work. Research into translation quality assessment of translations produced by volunteers for non-profit organizations is relatively scant. However, Gigliotti's study (2017: 52–55) found that the quality of her corpus of such translations varied greatly, with a few examples of good work but overall quite poor. Moreover, she determined that in some instances not only were the translators used non-professional and volunteer, but some of them were non-native speakers of either the source or target language (Gigliotti, 2017: 59). While she cautions that her study has been conducted on a small sample of texts, those issues tie into the broader perspective of utilizing volunteer translators in crises, as well as the issues related to volunteer translator training and quality control over the translations produced by them.

Conclusions

Due to the ongoing and complicated geopolitical situation in the countries of refugees' origin, Syria and Iraq in particular, the refugee crisis is still a live and serious issue across Europe. Even though the Balkans route was formally closed in 2016, the spring and summer of 2018 have seen a resurgence in the number of those attempting to use new routes across the Balkans, following an already existing smuggling corridor for drugs and illegal weapons (*The Voice of Croatia*, 2018, *Index.hr*, 2018a, Haidar Diab, 2018). Due to the fact that such routes are illegal and maintained by human traffickers, the incoming migrants are exposed to high-risk conditions, which may lead to serious injuries or even death (*Index. hr*, 2018b) and are liable to legal prosecution and return to their point of origin in Greece or Turkey if discovered by the authorities if they are without valid documents. This means that, despite the scale of the issue being much smaller than in 2015, certain elements of the crisis persist and need to be accounted for. The issue of language mediation is among them.

In December 2016, the Croatian Ministry of Interior published a tender (see Ministarstvo unutarnjih poslova, 2016) that sought candidates for translation work in the process of obtaining international protection for these languages:

Pashto, Urdu, Punjabi, Hindi, Bengali, Sanskrit, Tamil, Burmese, Tigrinya, Tigre, Farsi, Kurdish (Bādīnān, Sorani and Kurmanji dialects), as well as Macedonian, Roma and Albanian. It may be noticed that among the languages sought were not Arabic or Farsi, meaning that at least those language needs were covered by that point. However, since the Croatian language market is by itself relatively small and that translational relations with those languages (except Macedonian and Albanian) are at best of an occasional and transitory character, it may be surmised that certain problems regarding language mediation in those combinations will persist. Lai and Mulayim (2010: 57) note similar difficulties with providing education in interpreting for rare and emerging languages (in their case Khmer, Amharic and Dari) in the Australian context, likewise mentioning economic viability as the main obstacle for maintaining such interpreting courses. Nonetheless, if we give a closer look to the issues examined in this study, we may observe that the issue of economic viability, while presenting some obstacles, did not inhibit the crisis response in extreme conditions. It should also be noted that information presented to the victims of a disaster needs to be accessible, readable, comprehensible, useful and trustworthy (Ghandour-Demiri, 2017a: 9). Depending on the immediate challenges and a specific set of circumstances for each crisis, the notion of providing information which fulfils all those criteria may be compromised by the lack of able and available language mediators or by using unsuitable mediation practices.

Most international and local organizations engaged in humanitarian and relief work use their own guidelines and frameworks to deal with language mediation needs, while spontaneous volunteers are left to devise their own working patterns and learn by practice. While this notion does not preconceive a necessarily flawed or lacking crisis response, it may be of use to develop a certain set of tentative language mediation guidelines based on the review of extant literature and best practices noted by the members of relevant relief organizations, which would then be taught to crisis language mediators or at least made openly available online in order to provide a firm and useful foundation for future crisis language mediation. At the very least, these tentative guidelines ought to take into consideration not only major language pairs, but also mediation in the situations when two rarely interacting pairs are used, or mediation in cases when no interlingual communication can be established at all, thus addressing the use of relay interpreting, non-verbal communication or the use of machine translation tools for non-linguists, in order to reduce – if not necessarily minimize – comprehension errors, mistranslations and their sometimes quite grave consequences for both the relief personnel and the recipients of their services.

Note

1 Founded in 1956, the Non-Aligned Movement provided a third path for states that were not formally aligned with or against the NATO or the Warsaw Pact blocs during the Cold War, and it involved many Asian and African countries. Formalized by the Declaration of Brijuni on 19 July 1956, its signatories included Yugoslavia's president, Josip Broz Tito, India's prime minister Jawaharlal Nehru, and Egypt's president, Gamal Abdel Nasser.

References

Alexander, D. E. (2010). 'The Voluntary Sector in Emergency Response and Civil Protection: Review and Recommendations'. *International Journal of Emergency Management* 7(2): 151–166.

Apter, E. (2001). 'Balkan Babel: Translation Zones, Military Zones'. *Public Culture* 13(1): 65–80.

Barraket, J., Keast, R. L., Newton, C., Walters, K., and James, E. (2013). 'Spontaneous Volunteering during Natural Disasters', Working paper no. ACPNS 61. Queensland University of Technology, Brisbane. Available online: http://eprints.qut.edu.au/61606/1/Spontaneous_Volunteering_Final_Report_July_31_(2).pdf (accessed 30 November 2018).

Council of Europe (2001). *Common European Framework of Reference for Languages: Learning, Teaching, Assessment (CEFR)*. Cambridge: CUP. Available online: http://www.coe.int/lang-CEFR (accessed 30 November 2018).

Dragović, F., Tadić, J., and Tadić, T. (2016). 'Migracijska i izbjeglička kriza, sigurnosni rizici za EU (Migrant and Refugee Crisis – Security risks for EU)'. *Policija i sigurnost* 1(16): 14–41.

Edwards, R., and Holland, J. (2013). *What Is Qualitative Interviewing?*. London: Bloomsbury.

Esterajher, J. (2015). 'Iskustva zbrinjavanja prognanika i izbjeglica i suvremena izbjegličko-migrantska kriza u Hrvatskoj (Experiences of accepting refugees and displaced persons and the contemporary refugee and migrant crisis in Croatia)'. *Političke analize* 6(23): 15–22.

EU-Turkey Statement, One Year On (2017). Available online: https://ec.europa.eu/home-affairs/sites/homeaffairs/files/what-we-do/policies/european-agenda-migration/background-information/eu_turkey_statement_17032017_en.pdf (accessed 30 November 2018).

Federici, F. M. (ed.) (2016). *Mediating Emergencies and Conflicts – Frontline Translating and Interpreting*. Basingstoke and New York, NY: Palgrave Macmillan.

Fernandez, L. S., Barbera, J. A., and Van Dorp, J. R. (2006). 'Spontaneous Volunteer Response to Disasters: The Benefits and Consequences of Good Intentions'. *Journal of Emergency Management* 4(5): 57–68.

Ghandour-Demiri, N. (2017a). *Language & Comprehension Barriers in Greece's Migration Crisis. A Study on the Multitude of Languages and Comprehension of Material Provided to Refugees and Migrants in Greece.* Translators without Borders. Available online: https://translatorswithoutborders.org/wp-content/uploads/2017/07/Language-Comprehension-barriers.pdf (accessed 30 November 2018).

Ghandour-Demiri, N. (2017b). *Bridging the Gap. A Study on the Impact of Language Barriers on Refugee and Migrant Children in Greece.* Translators without Borders. Available online: https://translatorswithoutborders.org/wp-content/uploads/2017/07/Bridging-the-Gap.pdf (accessed 30 November 2018).

Gigliotti, G. (2017). 'The Quality of Mercy: A Corpus-Based Analysis of the Quality of Volunteer Translations for Non-Profit Organizations (NPOs)'. *New Voices in Translation Studies* 17: 52–81.

Giordano, C. (2008). 'Practices of Translation and the Making of Migrant Subjectivities in Contemporary Italy'. *American Ethnologist* 35: 588–606.

Giordano, C. (2014). *Migrants in Translation: Caring and the Logics of Difference in Contemporary Italy.* Berkeley, CA: University of California Press.

Glick Schiller, N., Basch, L., and Szanton Blanc, C. (1995). 'From Immigrant to Transmigrant: Theorizing Transnational Migration'. *Anthropological Quarterly* 68(1): 48–63.

Haidar Diab, H. (2018). 'Migranti na novoj balkanskoj ruti kojom se godinama krijumčare oružje i droga'. *Večernji list*, 28 May. Available online: https://www.vecernji.hr/premium/migranti-na-novoj-balkanskoj-ruti-kojom-se-godinama-krijumcare-oruzje-i-droga-1248485 (accessed 30 November 2018).

Hubscher-Davidson, S. (2011). 'A Discussion of Ethnographic Research Methods and Their Relevance for Translation Process Research'. *Across Languages and Cultures* 12(1): 1–18.

Index.hr (2018a). 'Migranti se kreću novom balkanskom rutom preko BiH, vlasti strahuju da će ih od proljeća biti sve više'. 28 March. Available online: http://www.index.hr/mobile/clanak.aspx?category=vijesti&id=1035042 (accessed 30 November 2018).

Index.hr (2018b). 'Migranti pokušali preko Kupe prijeći iz Hrvatske u Sloveniju, jedan se utopio' 10 April. Available online: http://www.index.hr/black/clanak/migranti-pokusali-preko-kupe-prijeci-iz-hrvatske-u-sloveniju-jedan-se-utopio/1037791.aspx (accessed 30 November 2018).

Kelly, M., and Baker, C. (2013). *Interpreting the Peace. Peace Operations, Conflict and Language in Bosnia-Herzegovina.* Basingstoke and New York: Palgrave Macmillan.

Lai, M., and Mulayim, S. (2010). 'Training Refugees to Become Interpreters for Refugees'. *The International Journal of Translation and Interpreting Research* 2(1): 48–60. Available online: http://www.trans-int.org/index.php/transint/article/view/29/68 (accessed 30 November 2018).

Lalić Novak, G., and Kraljević, R. (2014). *Priručnik za edukatore – Zaštita izbjeglica i ranjivih skupina migranata (Handbook for Educators – Protection of Refugees and Vulnerable Migrant Groups).* Zagreb: Hrvatski Crveni Križ (Croatian Red Cross).

Ministarstvo unutarnjih poslova (Ministry of Interior) (2016). 'Javni poziv za prijavu kandidata za poslove prevođenja u postupku odobrenja međunarodne i privremene zaštite'. *Official Gazette* 112/2016. Available online: http://narodne-novine.nn.hr/clanci/oglasi/o8200814.html (accessed 30 November 2018).

Ministarstvo Zdravlja (Ministry of Health), krizni stožer (2015). 'Mjere za zaštitu od zaraznih bolesti i sadržaj pregleda osoba tražitelja azila i azilanata, stranaca pod privremenom zaštitom i stranaca pod supsidijarnom zaštitom', 15 September. Available online: http://kohom.hr/mm/wp-content/uploads/Postupnik_migranti_-KS-MIZ.pdf (accessed 30 November 2018).

Munro, R. (2010). 'Crowdsourced Translation for Emergency Response in Haiti: The Global Collaboration of Local Knowledge'. Paper presented at the Association of Machine Translation for the Americas Conference AMTA, 2010. Available online: http://amta2010.amtaweb.org/AMTA/papers/7-01-01-Munro.pdf (accessed 30 November 2018).

O'Brien, S. (2016). Training Translators for Crisis Communication: Translators without Borders as an Example. In F. M. Federici (ed.), *Mediating Emergencies and Conflicts.* Basingstoke and New York, NY: Palgrave Macmillan. 85–115.

Pašiček, M. (1977/2015). 'Hrvatska – obrazovna meka za studente iz nesvrstanih zemalja' (2015). *Moje vrijeme* 6 April. Originally published in *Arena* 1977. Available online: https://www.mojevrijeme.hr/magazin/2015/04/hrvatska-obrazovna-meka-za-ucenike-iz-nesvrstanih-zemalja/ (Accessed 30 November 2018).

Patković, N. (2015). 'Sirijski doktor koji u Hrvatskoj živi 30 godina: "Smirio sam sunarodnjake rekavši im da su došli u lijepu zemlju divnih ljudi"'. *Jutarnji list,* 16 September. Available online: https://www.jutarnji.hr/vijesti/hrvatska/sirijski-doktor-koji-u-hrvatskoj-zivi-30-godina-smirio-sam-sunarodnjake-rekavsi-im-da-su-dosli-u-lijepu-zemlju-divnih-ljudi/301174/ (accessed 30 November 2018).

Refugee Phrasebook (2018). Available online: https://www.refugeephrasebook.de/ (accessed 30 November 2018).

Susam-Sarajeva, Ş. (2014). 'The Case Study Research Method in Translation Studies'. *The Interpreter and Translator Trainer* 3(1): 37–56.

Sutherlin, G. (2013). 'A Voice in the Crowd: Broader Implications for Crowdsourcing Translation during Crisis'. *Journal of Information Science* 39(3): 1–13.

Taronna, A. (2016). 'Translation, Hospitality and Conflict: Language Mediators as an Activist Community of Practice across the Mediterranean'. *Linguistica Antverpiensia, New Series: Themes in Translation Studies* 15: 282–302.

The Voice of Croatia (2018). 'Experts Fear New Balkan Migrant Route'. Croatian Radiotelevision, 28 March. Available online: http://glashrvatske.hrt.hr/en/news/politics/experts-fear-new-balkan-migrant-route/ (accessed 28 June 2018).

Toth, I. (2001). *Civilna zaštita u Domovinskom ratu.* (*Civil Protection in the Homeland War*). Zagreb: Defimi.

Townsend, R. M. (2015). *The European Migrant Crisis*. Lulu.com.

Translators without Borders (2016). 'Translators without Borders Develops the World's First Crisis-Specific Machine Translation System for Kurdish languages'. 11 December. Available online: https://translatorswithoutborders.org/translators-without-borders-develops-worlds-first-crisis-specific-machine-translation-system-kurdish-languages/ (accessed 30 November 2018).

Translators without Borders (2018). 'Use of Machine Translation in Humanitarian Crisis Situations'. 24 July. Available online: https://www.translatemedia.com/machine-translation-email/use-of-machine-translation-in-humanitarian-crisis-situations/ (accessed 30 November 2018).

Vitas, P. (2017). 'Sustav civilne zaštite i zbrinjavanje migranata'. *Zaštita* 10: 22.

Whittaker, J., McLennan, B., and Handmer, J. (2015). 'A Review of Informal Volunteerism in Emergencies and Disasters: Definition, Opportunities and Challenges'. *International Journal of Disaster Risk Reduction* 13(2015): 358–368.

Zrinjski, I. (2016). 'Kako se odvijala migrantska kriza: na početku su izbjeglice bile prihvaćene otvorenih ruku, a sada se zatvara ruta kojom je prošlo 800.000 ljudi'. *Jutarnji list*, 9 March. Available online: https://www.jutarnji.hr/vijesti/hrvatska/kako-se-odvijala-migrantska-kriza-na-pocetku-su-izbjeglice-bile-prihvacene-otvorenih-ruku-a-sada-se-zatvara-ruta-kojom-je-proslo-800.000-ljudi/29593/ (accessed 30 November 2018).

3

The Role of the Translator and Interpreter in Terrorist Conflicts

Carmen Pena-Díaz

The aim of this chapter is to analyse the extent to which aspects of the role of translators and interpreters in conflict zones can be meaningful in the prevention of international terrorism.

Terrorist attacks such as those in the United States (New York, 11 September 2001, subsequently abbreviated as 11S), Spain (Madrid, 11 March 2004, 11M) and the United Kingdom (London, 7 July 2005, 7J) were the turning points for the commencement of common strategies to combat Islamist terrorism. Since then, further attacks have caused more personal sorrows and international indignation. In this context, it is essential to provide linguistic analysts who can collaborate with the intelligence services, and to provide mediating experts who can communicate with immigrant civilian populations. Navarro (2004) considers that information and knowledge management are key to succeed in such situations. However, public administrations do not always consider translators and interpreters as professional and visible mediators.

In this chapter, the role of the translator and interpreter working in conflict situations (in terrorism contexts) will be analysed as a project of added political value and from a Narrative Theory perspective (Baker, 2006, 2010) which views human behaviour as determined by the histories and the events that have taken place, i.e. the predominant narrative in the environment that surrounds them. Using this approach, the chapter tries to emphasize the need for professional translators and interpreters to work in conflict areas and to provide support in the fight against terrorism together with intelligence services and public administration. In parallel lines with Bielsa (2009), one of the main objectives of this chapter is therefore to vindicate the role of translation as a necessary project for society.

Premise

Terrorist attacks such as the 11S in New York, the 11M in Madrid and the 7J in London created a widespread perception of a jihadist threat and constituted the turning point for the commencement of common strategies to fight against Islamist terrorism. Until the attacks in New York, terrorism in Europe had been largely confined to the state level (ETA in Spain, RAF in Germany, IRA in Northern Ireland etc.), but combatting terrorist threats has increasingly grown into a global concern. Thus, terrorism had to be dealt with at an international level and subsequently also from an intercultural and interlinguistic perspective.

Translators and interpreters have shown to be of a paramount importance for preventing international terrorism and terrorist acts with national origin and within national boundaries. More specifically I will bring the example of Spanish combat strategies against international terrorism and how it has promoted linguistic initiatives to train new translating-interpreting professionals. The examples also raise awareness of the need to master conflict languages, i.e. those languages relevant to a certain crisis settings. Among the common strategies was the use of translators and interpreters, who were put into practice and tested through the long and painful experience of Spanish society dealing with home terrorism during the infamous years of activity of the terrorist organization ETA. During that time, translation from Basque into Spanish and vice versa was a matter of life and death. Therefore, translators and interpreters were vital for questions of national defence, security and civilian protection and for the creation of a more competent society, better equipped to deal with threats of such magnitude. Our society, today, is facing a new scenario where international terrorism requires a complex response to the challenges it posits. This chapter will analyse this by using findings that were drawn from a survey carried out among representative members of relevant Spanish governmental and administrative bodies in relation to the application of foreign languages and defence such as CNI (National Intelligence Agency), CNP (National Police Force), Guardia Civil (National Judiciary Police Force) and CSID (Military Intelligence).

Information and knowledge management will be the real key to succeed in international terrorism (Lahneman, 2004). It is essential to train linguistic analysts who can collaborate with the intelligence services, but also experts who can communicate with the immigrant civilian population. The latter sometimes cannot see their basic needs met due to a lack of communication. Communication is essential in crisis situations and it must be dealt with effectively. Information management and knowledge as the object of communication are key to be able to organize and be effective not only for intelligence services but in crisis contexts as well (Navarro, 2004).

Communication in crisis situations

A crisis situation is typically defined as a serious disruption of how communities and societies function. Crisis situations usually involve widespread human, material, economic or environmental losses and impacts. Equally typically the ability of the affected community or society is not able to suffice (UNISDR, 2009: 9). Moreover, we can include to the label of crisis situation disasters due to natural hazards, violent outbreaks, epidemic or pandemic outbreaks, or any unexpected situation in which emergency services need to take part, such as the one which concerns this chapter, terrorist attacks which can be considered according to Alexander (2016) as teleological disasters.

In crisis and disaster contexts, it is essential for people to communicate, as it is the only way that they can understand an emergency situation. It is also important for them to empower themselves as to what they can do for themselves and for their families and peers. Personal communication in times of crises also allows people to be in contact with administrations and different organizations. If people cannot communicate properly, they will be left to their own devices, possibly adding to a sense of anxiety or even a public fear. It is essential for the affected population to understand emergency communications. These can include alerts and warnings, as well as directives about evacuation scenarios and different actions and information about response, assistance and other matters that impact response and recovery. Effective communication during a crisis is thus strategically important (Fischer, 2008; Seeger, 2006; World Health Organization, 2012) and insufficient linguistic and cultural competences limit access to and comprehension of important crisis-related information (Nsiah-Kumi, 2008). When messages are delivered effectively during crises, they can help ensure cooperation, public safety and a collaborative response. However, when there is a lack of communication, many breakdowns can occur. In multicultural settings, communication is very frequently difficult, but in emergency situations, usually amidst chaos, clear, accurate and accessible lines of communication become even more complex. In crisis situations, measures to help communication flow better become essential. In that context, the role of the translator or interpreter can become life-saving.

Although there is growing concern about communication in crisis situations, literature on this issue is growing at a slower pace with regard to language mediation and it far from being abundant or comprehensive (for translation-specific literature, see discussion in Federici, 2016). Existing research normally refers to specific geographical situations that have taken place, such as the earthquakes in Turkey (Bulut and Kurultay, 2001; Doğan and Kahraman, 2011; Kurultay and Bulut, 2012); the conflict in Somalia, its effect on the people and in refugee camps in Kenya (Moser-Mercer and Bali, 2007; Moser-Mercer et al., 2014); conflicts in Syria or Iraq and in refugee camps in Jordan (Kherbiche, 2009; Businaro, 2012); conflicts involving Finnish military interpreters (Snellman, 2014); the combined earthquake, tsunami and nuclear disaster in Japan (Tsuruta, 2011; Mizuno, 2012; Naito, 2013; Cadwell, 2014, 2015). All of this research studies the influence of linguistic and cultural barriers within the specific context. Often these contexts are characterized by the 'absence of specialised training in the interpreting work done in these high-risk settings' (Cadwell, 2015: 9–10); it is in the subject literature where we find proof of the lack of professionalization and lack of awareness of the need for interpreters. Both lacunas typically spawn the emergence of the non-trained language mediators. Research has been done on these improvised, *ad hoc* interpreters and the professional status of translators (McDonough Dolmaya, 2012; Pérez-González and Susam-Sarajeva, 2012).

There are studies dedicated to the ways in which key stakeholders, such as health personnel, can improve their interactions with translators and interpreters during crises (Freeth, 1993; Bolton and Weiss, 2001; Businaro, 2012; Powell and Pagliara-Miller, 2012), as this is fundamental in order for the communication channel between language professionals and the general public. As O'Brien and Cadwell (2017) show in their work on health-related communication during the Ebola crisis for a government-driven project in Kenya, written modes of communication for health-related crisis information are not always the most suitable for some countries and cultures. Their project showed that in that context (2017: 41) 'public gatherings, church, and radio were listed as preferred modes of communication for health-related information'. Each specific context is bound to have particular needs; however, common ground must be established in order to create management procedures that could be applied to most scenarios, including to terror attack crises.

Another essential element in crisis and emergency situations where translation is needed is the use of ICT (Lin et al., 2009; Ikeda et al., 2010). Including ICT platforms and capacities to crisis communication facilitates collaborative translation in disasters (Kageura et al., 2011). Computer-assisted translation and post-editing of machine translation could be of great help (for recent discussions of these technologies, see O'Brien et al., 2014). Aside from using crowdsourcing in emergency situations when no professional help is available, it is highly important to train translators to work in crisis settings (McKee, 2014; O'Brien, 2016). Training is the most important element that different authors establish as a key feature for translators and interpreters in any crisis context (Kelly and Baker, 2012; Lázaro et al., 2015).

Narrative Theory and the translator as a media worker

Narrative Theory applied to Translation Studies, in particular with regard to crises, was first introduced by Baker in her book *Translation and Conflict: A Narrative Account* in 2006. Baker (2009 and 2010) subsequently built on that pioneering work. Since then, many other authors (in chronological order, Apter, 2005, 2009; Inghilleri, 2008; Baker, 2009, 2010; Bielsa, 2009; Inghilleri and Harding, 2010; Beltrán, 2013) have researched translation topics from the perspective of the Narrative Theory exposed by Baker.

Framing the role of the translator and interpreter working in conflict situations (in terrorism contexts) while using Narrative Theory, we can view human behaviour as determined by the histories and the events that have taken place. In other words, there is a predominant narrative in the environment that surrounds humans; individual and, by extension, local narratives are part of larger narratives. This configuration of human relations and events is populated by humans in need of clear communication exchanges and takes place in a setting of a variety of media as well. As we have explained before, it is of paramount importance to emphasize the need for professional translators and interpreters to work in conflict areas and work together with intelligence services and public administrations in the fight against terrorism. According to this research perspective, different narrative accounts that relate to terror-related conflicts are temporarily embedded; they unfold in time and space and always have a perceived beginning and a projected end.

Not only due to the usual professional skills needed, but also because interpreters in crisis zones need to be 'more sensitive to the background situation, emotions, and need to be able to sense perceptions and feelings' (Todorova, 2016: 227), their narratives can help us understand the scope of the scenarios from all perspectives. This ties in with one of the main historical concerns for translators, with Nida (1964) as the starting point, which has been the issue of equivalence: the translator retells the story from her/his own perspective and thus positions her/himself to elaborate a narrative.

This mediating role of a translator turns the issue of equivalence into a much wider and flexible concept, as the translator is faced with profound conflicts and issues due to the real and physical conflict. Translators who work on-site at the time of a crisis or conflict typically perform alongside of and in support of official channels and authorities such as military officers and government officials, but very often they also provide information for media outlets. A translator/interpreter working in a crisis context has an influence he/she can exert by creating, for example, new public narratives in a mediated world in which there is a clear predominance of Anglo-speaking and Western culture, as opposed to Eastern cultures, turning translation into a complex and highly responsible public media task, thus broadening mentalities in Western cultures by describing and becoming the eyes of those who live in safer places and raising awareness about those conflicts.

Despite their alliance through contractual stipulations when it comes to the role of the translator in armed conflicts, there is still a lack of trust from governmental agencies towards translators, and, by extension, to cultural mediators and interpreters. Despite recognition of the value of interpreters to their operations, military and political institutions do not grant them equal status within their ranks (Inghilleri, 2010: 179) as they are not military personnel trained by them and applying their same codes. Rafael (2007) states that the interpreter is 'unsettled and unsettling inasmuch as [his or her] presence generates both relief and suspicion among soldiers'. In conflict zones, interpreters work for different people – e.g. the locals, the military, administration personnel – and this may generate suspiciousness.

In conflicts and war situations, or in terror attack contexts, translators are used by governments as instruments to deal with the enemy (in some cases the countries of origin of the translators from which they are exiled), a role and position from which they are later thrown out and left without protection, without granting them, for example, visas or asylum, as the only way to guarantee their safety. There are initiatives to offer help and train interpreters (AIIC, InZone, IRAP) but in most cases, interpreters and translators are left unprotected when their commission ends and their services are no longer required. There are hundreds of striking situations of interpreters in different areas, such as Afghan interpreters who had to apply for refugee asylum in the UK.

Following on from Bielsa (2009) who emphasizes the need for professional translators and interpreters to work in conflict areas and to provide support in the fight against terrorism together with intelligence services and public administration, we would like to vindicate the role of translation as a political project. Although all translators are limited by their own culture and by the narrative that has surrounded them, translation is a means to renew and increase cultural horizons, conceived to combine different disciplines and treat a social phenomenon, to facilitate dialogue within society, who must move away from their individual points of view with the aim of opening up to a new interdisciplinary context, especially in the globalized world we live in and with an international threat aimed at everyone: the current conceptualization that there is an international jihadist threat for which international initiatives and strategies are being implemented. The aim of the chapter is to study the response capacities of the Spanish government in the military and intelligence fields in order to highlight the current linguistic initiatives and the consideration that the country gives to the role of the translator to fight against this current threat.

Methodology

In order to study how Spain integrates linguistic policies and, in consequence, translators and interpreters, in their strategies to combat international terrorism, a survey was carried out to representative members of relevant governmental administrations, such as CNI (National Intelligence Agency), CNP (National Police Force), Guardia Civil (National Judiciary Police Force) and CSID (Military Intelligence), relating to the application of foreign languages and defence. A total of 74 responses were received.

On the one hand, the survey was directed towards members of the Spanish state security and the Armed Forces, and to administrative institutions (universities, hospitals, NGOs, and so on) and interpreters on the other. The survey was distributed by email in order to reach as many participants as possible and it was composed of 16 questions that explored two variables. The first variable aimed to

- determine to what extent the workers consider it necessary to be trained in conflict languages (those languages that may be used in the contexts under

Table 3.1 Survey questions.

Who carries out translating and interpreting in your organization?
What resources have been created to help communication in conflict zones?
Are there courses offered for conflict languages?
Are opportunities provided to those individuals with ethnic origins other than Spanish to preserve and accentuate their inherited language skills and use them for the benefit of the country?
How is the work of the translator/interpreter carried out in your work?
How do you feel about the creation of a national Spanish linguistic authority?
In the war against international terrorism, is it considered important for public administrations to invest in linguistic initiatives to train professionals in conflict languages?

analysis, such as those used in conflict zones where the Spanish army could be present at the time, such as Afghanistan and Syria).

The second variable explored in the survey aimed to

- assess the level of cooperation between the State Security Forces and the Intelligence Services to create an Intelligence Community.

In order to design the questionnaire, the survey design drew upon the work of Valero-Garcés, Schnell, Rodríguez and Cuñado (2015). Given the representation of the United States as a pioneer country in matters of linguistic policy and national defence, the survey based our research study on the objectives established at the National Conference of Languages held in Maryland in 2004 and in the language policy plan developed by the US Sub-Department of Justice.

The first set of questions in the questionnaire intended to gather essential personal information about the participants (gender, professional status and organization). The second set of questions focuses on the linguistic initiatives carried out by the Spanish administration and are listed in Table 3.1.

Analysis

As can be seen in Figure 3.1, from the amalgamated responses of the first questions – general information about gender, professional status and the like – it transpired that 39 per cent belonged to the Police and the Armed Forces, 12 per

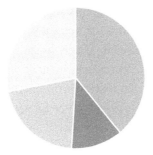

▨ Police & Armed Forces ▨ Academics

▨ Interpreters and translators Health personnel & NGOs

Figure 3.1 Survey participants.

cent were personnel from academic institutions related to foreign languages, 21 per cent were interpreters and translators of the administration hired as staff and freelance, and 28 per cent were representatives of the health field and public services (NGO).

As the second set of questions concerned the linguistic initiatives carried out by the Spanish administration, they aimed to elicit more target answers than the information that could be found in official documents. Although Spain has modified its legislation on translation and interpretation in legal proceedings, marked by the mandatory compliance with Directive 2010/64/EU and the requirement that the assigned translator must be included in the lists of the competent administration, the translation services of the State Security Forces and the Courts are regulated by three private companies: *Atlas Servicios Empresariales, Ofilingua* and *Seprotec.*

In theory, professionals from the State Security and the Armed Forces are encouraged to learn languages that can be strategic in conflict zones and approximately 50 per cent of the police and Armed Forces agree that from their institutions, conferences are created to promote the study of languages and raise awareness about the importance of multilingualism. However, it was unanimously confirmed that the languages taught are usually English or French, or another language of the UN countries (English, French, German, Russian, Arabic and Chinese) but none other.

Asked about scholarships to study languages of strategic conflict areas, as offered by the government of the United States, the author is not aware whether or not the Spanish administration grants support to learning the language(s) of troubled geographical regions or countries. In fact, although military exchanges are carried out, these are usually organized in Allied countries and clear information on Spain-driven management of such courses was not found. Members from the Police stated that there are incentives for students to enrol in training courses in face-to-face and online foreign languages; the police also detailed that classical Arabic is the only critical language that can be strategic in the face of the jihadist threat – for a contrasting position to this, see Chapter 2 in this volume.

As for the answers obtained from the academic institutions, there are three important initiatives: dictionaries have been created in different languages with very elementary vocabulary to communicate with foreign families. Moreover, the Cervantes Institute – a government institution responsible for promoting the study and the teaching of Spanish – has more than seventy offices around the world, although some of them are located in areas with high levels of terrorist attacks and threats (Beirut, Tel Aviv, Cairo, Istanbul, Damascus). On the one hand, then, there are initiatives to teach Spanish abroad, but, on the other hand, in the same locations there are no opportunities for Spanish nationals to learn critical languages.

However, embassies from countries such as Turkey, Kuwait and Israel annually issue specific scholarships for Spaniards interested in studying Arabic or specializing in the Middle East conflict to study in their countries. Asking specifically about the critical languages and whether they had attended a training course or not, all the representative respondents from all public institutions agreed that there are no training courses in conflicting languages such as Pashtun, Farsi, Dari or any dialectal variety of Arabic from the Middle East area, but only in the other six UN languages. Participants stated that Spanish public institutions should organize more courses on conflict languages, so that those languages can be learned that can be of strategic value for national defence. Organizing these courses would help motivate workers to communicate with people who speak the respective language and could learn cultural aspects from them as well at the same time.

The next set of questions related to issues of inherited languages other than Spanish: whether or not opportunities are provided to those individuals with ethnic origins other than Spanish to preserve and accentuate their inherited language skills and use them for the benefit of the country. Aiming to establish whether or not Spanish administrative institutions have qualified linguists with cultural, historical or political linguistic knowledge of the strategic regions, practically all the respondents from the police affirmed that they themselves sometimes had to turn to people of foreign ethnic group to help them in translation or interpretation processes and that they did so whilst assuming that their institution was not capable enough in finding professionals in critical languages (including dialectal varieties of Arabic, Urdu, Farsi, Romanian, etc.). It must be noted that one of the policemen conveyed that the participation of 'external' professionals potentially poses a risk in the flow of information, a risk he considered dangerous. One of the interpreters confirmed that from her institution (the NGO *Salud entre Culturas*, which collaborates with the Department of Infectious Diseases of the Ramón y Cajal Hospital in Madrid), people with a foreign ethnic background are also used to assist in translation processes or interpretation. Previously, those 'interpreters' were trained and instructed in translation and interpretation by the NGO itself. For example, the NGO hired people of African origin who are native speakers in such language as Wolof, Bámbara and Arabic, then trained them as health interpreters. They considered that in order for the health professionals to communicate with the immigrant community, it was very profitable to train interpreters from strategic countries who understood Spanish.

However, when the participants on the survey were asked about whether or not in the war against international terrorism it is considered important for public administrations to invest in linguistic initiatives to train professionals in critical languages, all participants agreed that it is one of the best methods to create a safer society. Spanish administrations should follow similar strategies such as the United States with English for Heritage Language Speakers, and the Spanish administration should train immigrants from strategic regions to swell their ranks with a more civil society, prepared and specialized in critical languages, increasing, consequently, the Spanish capacity for defence and national security, thus instructing native professionals of Arabic and other critical languages in a higher level of Spanish, to later facilitate work in their administration.

Respondents from inside the military apparatus claimed that their institutions provided a sufficient number of professional linguists and translators, in particular of the six UN languages, so that they did not have to resort to people of different ethnic origin for translation purposes. Like that, they could continue to rely on the military personnel who have been on a mission in the specific areas, or, failing that, to employ several translators, who were drawn from the military corps. In the words of one of the military respondents, 'sometimes to understand the discourse in Dari of an Afghan, it is usual to resort to a Dari interpreter who speaks Arabic, and then from Arabic the message is translated into English or French, and from there into Spanish'. This activity is usually carried out by soldiers with a working knowledge of specific foreign languages, rather than by professional interpreters, unlike the CNP (National Police Force). This approach contrasts sharply with the Spanish central administration which does make use of professional interpreters.

Regarding the way of hiring by the police, we consider that the crucial cause for the evolution of the hiring of freelance translators to translators of the administration is based on the modification of our legislation (Organic Law 5/2015), influenced by the Directive 2010/64/EU which is committed to the role of the translator certified by the administration to perform profession in judicial and investigative processes. Thus, in investigations concerning terrorism, the police require from translators and interpreters the knowledge of the dialect, knowledge of the law, the ability to transmit messages with fidelity and correctness, professional ethics and secrecy. In addition, a thorough knowledge of international politics and situations of terrorist conflict is considered important.

For the purpose of the chapter, the survey also enquired about sentiments in relation to creating a national Spanish linguistic authority to develop and implement language strategies for non-native Spanish speakers working abroad, coordinate legislation on security and defence, and conduct campaigns to raise public and private awareness of the importance of possessing linguistic and cultural knowledge in any field of work; it is curious to note that the group of interpreters and officials of academic institutions unanimously supported this idea, as opposed to the members of the police, who did not consider it necessary.

An interesting project, led by the Ministry of Foreign Affairs and Cooperation, has been created, Casa Árabe, which is a pioneer in linguistic initiatives in the field of critical languages, providing dialectal varieties of Egyptian and Levantine Arabic (from the areas of Syria, Lebanon, Palestine and Jordan). Casa Árabe is an initiative to establish a direct approach to the Arab and Islamic world, fostering economic ties, spreading cultural knowledge. The project is committed to intercultural dialogue, to show the clear commitment of the Spanish administration to promote understanding and understanding between cultures, on the one hand, and, interculturality, on the other. The latter is understood as the active interaction between different cultures. Therefore, the author considers that Spain, aware of its strategic needs, is taking steps in the right direction when trying to encourage the study of foreign languages, although it is still in the process of development if we compare it with the United States or the United Kingdom, which publicly demand in their institutional pages the need for translators of Arabic, Farsi, Hindi, Pashtun, Dari, Russian, Urdu and West African languages.

Conclusions

The main conclusion we can draw from the survey is that there is a clear awareness of the need for language learning both in *lingua francas* such as English or French, and especially in languages which may be critical in terrorism conflicts. Several branches of Spanish administrations have initiated linguistic projects to train professionals in foreign languages, but only in the main communication languages (Arabic, Chinese, English, French, German and Russian) which are not necessarily the most necessary ones for combatting terrorism and terrorism threats. Arabic represents the only language native to conflict areas. There is thus no training in other languages which would probably be more useful than Standard Arabic such as different Arabic dialects and other languages (Pashtun, Farsi, etc.). Interpreters with knowledge in these languages would be highly useful, but they would undoubtedly be difficult to find in Spain. Therefore, local interpreters should be used.

In the military field there are exchange scholarships for those military interested in carrying out international missions. In the police force, incentives are in place for training courses in both face-to-face and online foreign languages. However, the fact that none of the respondents attended training courses suggests that the professional incentives (whether economic incentives or better working conditions) are not sufficient to have people actually take on a language training course.

In order to fight international terrorism, it is a strategic priority to include people of different ethnic origins and encourage the training of professionals of the administration and citizens of the civil society in linguistic and cultural matters over conflictive geographical areas, in order to have the capacity to delegitimize extremist narratives. There also ought to be greater inclusion of members of vulnerable groups in their host or original societies, so as to avoid extremist radicalization and stimulate the development of linguistic initiatives in strategic languages that can provide appropriate and specialist support to professionals of the administration and members of civil society in carrying out their official duties, with a view to creating a society that is better equipped to deal with crisis communication.

Having broader access to interviews with interpreters who have operated in conflict scenarios would be highly useful to raise awareness about the type of situations and contexts in which they work. These first-hand accounts could create the narratives of translators and interpreters to be shared more broadly, for instance making interpreters and translators more central in media reports. Spanish and other citizens of countries at risk of terrorist attacks would become more cognizant of the risks in the conflict zones and the hazards that emerge from there. Not only should the general public be more aware of the operational settings for conflict interpreters, but also the interpreters' narrative could also be used to train military and other forces intending to work in those areas. The working languages and materials needed could also be identified. Terrorism discourse could be analysed from a social and linguistic perspective in order to understand it better and be more prepared to combat it.

The lack of linguistic skills by the different professionals based in conflict areas not only undermines intercultural communication inside and outside our borders but limits the physical mobility of a large part of our population, reduces the commercial competitiveness of our country and hinders the effectiveness of public diplomacy. Therefore, drawing from the objectives established in the National Conference Language in 2004 (Department of Defense, 2004), which was organized to design a national language policy plan after the 11S attacks, the study considers it essential to address the following areas of work in crisis situations, including terrorist attacks:

- Identifying ways of preparing qualified individuals in as many languages as possible, including critical languages that can be of crucial help in maintaining national economic security and well-being.
- Providing opportunities to individuals of different ethnic origins to preserve and accentuate their inherited linguistic knowledge and use it for the benefit of the country.
- Increasing the number of linguistic professionals specialized in cultural, historical, political and economic knowledge of strategic nations and regions.

The training of professionals in critical languages can be a safe strategy to train professionals of the administration with more appropriate skills to face the current international terrorist threat better, not only because of the importance of understanding the terrorist discourse, in particular when in relation to anti-terror policies and initiatives.

Relations between East and West are more tense than ever, and although many Arab countries are now allied with Europe and the United States in the fight against terrorism marked by ISIS, the polarization of ideologies and cultures remains abysmal; if we add the language barrier, communication will be very minimal, too minimal for creating the opportunities in which cross-language barriers can be overcome. Translation and language learning for conflict and critical languages add value to the microcosm that is terror threat prevention. Bearing in mind the limitations of the above study, we consider the need for more extensive research in the field of investment in linguistic initiatives within the administration and the role of the translator and interpreter in situations of terrorist conflict essential. In short, it is crucial to give priority to the creation of a more intercultural society in which translators and linguistic experts help to renew and increase cultural horizons, based on a dialogue that allows us to approach conflict zones communication from an interdisciplinary perspective.

References

Alexander, L. (2016). 'The Means Principle'. In K. K. Ferzan and S. J. Morse (eds), *Legal, Moral, and Metaphysical Truths: The Philosophy of Michael S. Moore*, 251–264. Oxford: Oxford University Press.

Apter, E. (2005). 'Translation after 9/11'. *Transit* 2(1). Available at: https://escholarship. org/uc/item/3fg8h2g8 (accessed 18 November 2018).

Apter, E. (2009). 'What Is Yours, Ours and Mine', *Angelaki: Journal of the Theoretical Humanities* 14(1): 87–100.

Baker, M. (2006). *Translation and Conflict*. London and New York: Routledge.

Baker, M. (2009). 'Resisting State Terror: Theorizing Communities of Activist Translators and Interpreters'. In E. Bielsa and C. Hughes (eds), *Globalization Political Violence and Translation*, 222–240. Basingstoke and New York: Palgrave Macmillan.

Baker, M. (2010). 'Interpreters and Translators in the War Zone. Narrated and Narrators'. *The Translator* 16(2): 197–222.

Beltrán, G. (2013). *El papel y la ética de los intérpretes en situaciones de conflicto*. Master's dissertation. Máster en Traducción Profesional e Institucional. Universidad de Valladolid.

Bielsa, E. (2009). 'Globalization Political Violence and Translation. An Introduction'. In E. Bielsa and C. Hughes (eds), *Globalization Politic Violence and Translation*, 1–21. Basingstoke and New York: Palgrave Macmillan.

Bolton, P. A., and Weiss, W. M. (2001). 'Communicating across Cultures: Improving Translation to Improve Complex Emergency Program Effectiveness'. *Prehospital and Disaster Medicine* 16(4): 252–256.

Bulut, A., and Kurultay, T. (2001). 'Interpreters-in-Aid at Disasters: Community Interpreting in the Process of Disaster Management'. *The Translator* 7(2): 249–263.

Businaro, R. (2012). 'Relief Operations across Language Barriers: The Interpreter Factor'. Unpublished Master's dissertation. University College Dublin.

Cadwell, P. (2014). 'Translation and Interpreting Needs in the Great East Japan Earthquake of 2011'. In W. Baur, B. Eichner, S. Kalina, N. Kessler, F. Mayer, and J. Orsted (eds), *Man versus Machine: Proceedings of the XXth FIT World Congress* (vol. II), 752–760. Berlin: BDÜ.

Cadwell, P. (2015). 'A Place for Translation Technologies in Disaster Settings: The Case of the 2011 Great East Japan Earthquake'. In M. O'Hagan and Q. Zhang (eds), *Conflict and Communication: A Changing Asia in a Globalising World*, 248–282. Bremen: EHV Academic Press.

Doğan, A., and Kahraman, R. (2011). 'Emergency and Disaster Interpreting in Turkey: Ten Years of a Unique Endeavour'. *Hacettepe University Journal of Faculty of Letters* 28(2): 61–76.

Federici, F. (ed.) (2016). *Mediating Emergencies and Conflicts: Frontline Translation and Interpreting*. Basingstoke and New York, NY: Palgrave Macmillan.

Fischer, H. (2008). *Response to Disaster*. 3rd edition. Lanham, MD: University Press of America.

Freeth, S. J. (1993). 'On the Problems of Translation in the Investigation of the Lake Nyos Disaster'. *Journal of Volcanology and Geothermal Research* 54(3–4): 353–356.

Ikeda, Y., Yoshioka, Y., and Kitamura, Y. (2010). 'Intercultural Collaboration Support System Using Disaster Safety Map and Machine Translation'. In T. Ishida (ed.), *Lecture Notes in Computer Science*, 100–112. Berlin and New York, NY: Springer-Verlag.

Inghilleri, M. (2008). 'The Ethical Task of the Translator in the Geo-Political Arena: From Iraq to Guantánamo Bay'. *Translation Studies* 1(2): 212–223.

Inghilleri, M. (2010). 'You Don't Make War without Knowing Why: The Decision to Interpret in Iraq'. In M. Inghilleri and S.-A. Harding (eds), *Translation and Violent Conflict*, Special Issue of *The Translator* 16(2): 175–196.

Inghilleri, M., and Harding, S. (eds) (2010). *Translation and Violent Conflict*. Special Issue of *The Translator* 16(2).

Kageura, K., Abekawa, T., Utiyama, M., Sagara, M., and Sumita, E. (2011). 'Has Translation Gone Online and Collaborative? An Experience from Minna no Hon'yaku'. In M. O'Hagan (ed.), *Translation as a Social Activity: [Community Translation 2.0]*, 47–73. Brussels: University Press Antwerp.

Kelly, M., and Baker, C. (2012). *Interpreting the Peace: Peace Operations, Conflict and Language in Bosnia-Herzegovina*. Basingstoke and New York, NY: Palgrave Macmillan.

Kherbiche, L. (2009). 'Interprètes de l'Ombre et du Silence: Entre Cris et Chuchotements (Réflexion sur l'Interprétation dans un Contexte Humanitaire auprès du CICR)'. Master's dissertation. Université de Genève.

Kurultay, T., and Bulut, A. (2012). 'Re-Evaluating Community Interpreting: Emergency and Disaster Interpreting'. *I. U. Journal of Translation Studies* 3(6): 75–102.

Lahneman, William, J. (2004). 'Knowledge Sharing in the Intelligence Community after 9/11'. *International Journal of Intelligence and Counter Intelligence* 17(4): 614–633.

Lázaro, R., Sánchez-Ramos, M., and Vigier, F. (2015). *Interpreting at War: Fighting Language Manipulation*. Madrid: Ed. Comares.

Lin, K. Y., Chou, K. W., Lin, H. T., Hsieh, S. H., and Tserng, H. P. (2009). 'Exploring the Effectiveness of Chinese-to-English Machine Translation for CLIR Applications in Earthquake Engineering'. *Journal of Computing in Civil Engineering* 23(3): 140–147.

McDonough Dolmaya, J. (2012). 'Analyzing the Crowdsourcing Model and Its Impact on Public Perceptions of Translation'. *The Translator* 18(2): 167–191.

McKee, R. (2014). 'Breaking News: Sign Language Interpreters on Television during Natural Disasters'. *Interpreting* 16(1): 107–130.

Mizuno, M. (2012). 'Community Interpreting in Japan: Present State and Challenges'. In N. Sato-Rossberg and J. Wakabayashi (eds), *Translation and Translation Studies in the Japanese Context*, 202–221. London: Continuum.

Moser-Mercer, B., and Bali, G. (2007). 'Interpreting in Zones of Crisis and War: Improving Multilingual Communication through Collaborative Virtual Learning'. In *The Fourth Annual Conference of Learning International Networks Consortium* (LINC, 2007) 28–30 October 2007, Amman, Jordan.

Moser-Mercer, B., Kherbiche, L., and Class, B. (2014). 'Interpreting Conflict: Training Challenges in Humanitarian Field Interpreting'. *Journal of Human Rights Practice* 6(1): 140–158.

Naito, M. (2013). 'Sōdantsūyaku ni okeru komyunititsūyaku no senmonsei'. *Shirīzu tagengo tabunkakyōdōjissennkenkyū* 16: 31–56.

Navarro Bonilla, D. (2004). 'Introducción'. In D. Navarro Bonilla (ed.), *Estudios sobre Inteligencia: fundamentos para la seguridad internacional*. Cuadernos de Estrategia 127, Instituto Español de Estudios Estratégicos (IEEE).

Nida, E. A. (1964). *Towards a Science of Translating*. Leiden: E. J. Brill.

Nsiah-Kumi, P. A. (2008). 'Communicating Effectively with Vulnerable Populations during Water Contamination Events'. *J Water Health* 6(1): 63–75.

O'Brien, S. (2016). 'Training Translators for Crisis Communication: The Translators without Borders Example'. In F. M. Federici (ed.), *Mediating Emergencies*, 85–111. Basingstoke and New York: Palgrave Macmillan.

O'Brien, S., and Cadwell, P. (2017). 'Translation Facilitates Comprehension of Health-Related Crisis Information: Kenya as an example'. *JoSTrans* 28: 2–22.

O'Brien, S., Winther Balling, L., Carl, M., Simard, M., and Specia, L. (eds) (2014). *Post-Editing of Machine Translation Processes and Applications*. Newcastle upon Tyne: Cambridge Scholars Publishing.

Pérez-González, L., and Susam-Sarajeva, S. (2012). 'Non-Professionals Translating and Interpreting: Participatory and Engaged Perspectives'. *The Translator* 18(2): 149–165.

Powell, C., and Pagliara-Miller, C. (2012). 'The Use of Volunteer Interpreters during the 2010 Haiti Earthquake: Lessons Learned from the USNS COMFORT Operation Unified Response Haiti'. *American Journal of Disaster Medicine* 7(1): 37–47.

Rafael, V. (2007). 'Translation in Wartime'. *Public Culture* 19(2): 239–246.

Seeger, M. W. (2006). 'Best Practices in Crisis Communication: An Expert Panel Process'. *Journal of Applied Communication Research* 34(3): 232–244.

Snellman, P. (2014). 'The Agency of Military Interpreters in Finnish Crisis Management Operations'. Unpublished Master's dissertation. University of Tampere.

Todorova, M. (2016). 'Interpreting Conflict Mediation in Kosovo and Macedonia'. *Linguistica Antverpiensia, New Series – Themes in Translation Studies* 15. Available at: https://lans-tts.uantwerpen.be/index.php/LANS-TTS/article/view/392/372 (accessed 28 November 2018).

Tsuruta, C. (2011). 'Broadcast Interpreters in Japan: Bringing News to and from the World'. *The Interpreters' Newsletter* 16: 157–173.

UNISDR (2009). *Terminology on Disaster Risk Reduction*. Geneva: United Nations.

Valero-Garcés C., Schnell, B., Rodríguez, N., and Cuñado, F. (2015). 'Estudio preliminar sobre el ejercicio de la interpretación y traducción judicial en España'. *Sendebar* 26: 137–166.

World Health Organization (2012). *Emergency Risk Management for Health Overview*. Geneva: WHO.

4

Language, Culture and Perceived Ethnic Homeland Integration: Syrian Armenian Forced Migrants in Armenia

Daria Vorobyeva

By March 2018 over 5.6 million people had fled Syria, among them Syrian Armenians, escaping insecurity and violence (UNHCR, 2018). While states such as Lebanon, Turkey or Jordan have received the largest waves of refugees, others, including Armenia, accepted smaller numbers. Although the forced nature of Armenian immigration precludes the possibility of identifying the migratory process as 'repatriation', policies implemented by the Armenian state can be referred to as such. Since 2011, but especially since 2012, Armenia has introduced various policies such as simplified visa procedures and access to citizenship for Syrian Armenians; full access to health, educational and other public institutions, as well as to the employment market. This became an important reason encouraging between 20 and 25 per cent (around 20,000) of the total Syrian Armenian population, to flee to Armenia. Still, while welcoming state polices have benefitted the newcomers in many ways, integration into Armenia has been complicated by several socio-cultural and economic factors. Thus, this chapter analyses the role of language and culture in the process of integration of Syrian Armenians in the Republic of Armenia, based on empirical data collected during fieldwork in Armenia in 2015 and interviews conducted in 2015 and 2016 with representatives of relevant state and non-state institutions, and Syrian Armenians themselves. The analysis is done in the framework of forced migration and perceived ethnic homeland integration. Due to the sensitive nature of some interviews and the potentially vulnerable position of Syrian Armenians, all interviews have been anonymized.

It has been widely acknowledged that command of the host country language is the *sine qua non* of social and to a large extent economic integration (Home

Office, 2004; Spenser, 2006; Hess, 2010; UNHCR, 2013), while importance of cultural compatibility can be found in academic literature (e.g. Olsson and King, 2008; Maruyama and Stronza, 2010) and seen in recent issues of European integration of immigrants from different ethno-cultural backgrounds. In regard to language, firstly, it facilitates easier access to employment and educational and other public institutions, and allows establishment of social connections with members of host societies. Secondly, language influences, and is highly interrelated with, identity and culture (Vinokur, 2006; Goebel, 2010; Bonvillain, 2011) – key components affecting the integrational process. In relation to Syrian Armenians, language carries additional significance. In the context of diaspora in general and in the Armenian diaspora in particular, especially in the Middle East (where Armenians generally have kept stronger ethnic identity and traditions than in the West), it serves as a highly important component of ethnic and national identity (Panossian, 2006).

In this case study, both newcomers and host country citizens speak Armenian, though Western (Syrian Armenians) and Eastern (Armenians in the Republic) versions of it. Thus, it should be noted that even when people speak the same language, some accents and dialects of it can be perceived differently. This in turn can lead to unconscious bias towards representatives of different accents, including among representatives of the same ethnic group from different geographical locations. Furthermore, for Syrian Armenians, Arabic became the second language, while for Armenians in the Republic, Russian – which is not a member of the same language group as Armenian or Arabic – had been the second language since Russian Imperial and Soviet times and remains important to the present day. Therefore, the newcomers have had to adapt to another version of one language, as well as, at least to some extent, to a completely different second language. Additionally, many decades of living under different cultural and linguistic dominance significantly affected the culture, values and identity of the two groups with the same ethnic origin, leading to evident socio-cultural differences between the two and affecting the process of integration in the perceived ethnic homeland since 2011. This can be linked to the notion of specific difficulties of perceived homeland integration, which are discussed in the chapter. For Syrian Armenians the already difficult element of integration into the perceived homeland has been further complicated by aspects of forced dimension of immigration, such as high levels of stress and trauma related to experiences in the country from which they emigrated. Thus, further stress has been experienced, leading to additional integrational difficulties and potential resistance.

To address these complex aspects of the integration of the Syrian Armenians in Armenia, the chapter first discusses the role of language and cultural differences in the process of integration. It then proceeds to specific effects of forced migration and perceived ethnic homeland integration on immigrants. Then, after a short introduction to the linguistic and core cultural features of the Armenian society in the Republic of Armenia, empirical analysis is provided in two ways: language and integration on the one hand and the cultural and psychological factors of integration on the other.

Language, culture and identity

The main function of language is to enable social interaction and understanding (Vinokur, 2006: 13). While this sounds uncomplicated, understanding language is a multilayered process, involving not only understanding of pronounced words, but also categorization of these through various socio-cultural filters. The way a person speaks constructs their interlocutor's assumptions and conclusions about the speaker's nationality, race, ethnicity, social class and education and usually subconsciously makes the listener like or dislike, trust or mistrust their counterpart. It is also recognized that different accents are perceived positively, i.e. warm, friendly, intelligent or negatively, i.e. unfriendly or unintelligent (Sophocleous, 2006: 71).

Therefore, language is identified as a symbol of social and collective identity (Vinokur, 2006: 11) and 'a socially significant form of reflecting reality and a means of acquiring new knowledge about the existing reality' (Gentner and Goldin-Meadow, 2003: 12; Goebel, 2010: 13; Bonvillain, 2011: 32; Voevoda et al., 2017: 122), which is automatically recognized and interpreted by both people involved in communication. If we see language as a 'given social tradition', then it could be said that individuals can express their individual thoughts and characteristics through speech and understanding, but only within the frame of the given tradition (Vinokur, 2006: 17). That is why when people talk, they employ meanings not in an exactly the same way. Even where people use one language, but come from different socio-cultural or geographical backgrounds, depending on the scale of these differences, minor or larger differences in perception can emerge, thus leading to possible misunderstandings and even potential lack of empathy.

Furthermore, communication includes appropriate intonations, repetitiveness, style, gestures, body moves and facial expressions, recognition of personal space, behavioural adaptations, and so on. People from different cultures or various socio-economic groups can employ different or the same gestures or phrasings, but these can have altered meanings, while norms of using these may also differ (Vinokur, 2006; Bonvillain, 2011: 32, 102; Chubareva, 2017). Grammar and vocabulary also directly influence a person's perception of the world (see Whorf, 1956). For example, gendered aspects of languages influence a person's understanding of reality, its concepts and associations. In the case study, while Russian and Arabic languages have genders, this is not the case in the Armenian language, where to identify gender-binaries (girl-boy), feminizing vocabulary (woman driver) or feminizing postfix (prince-princess), gendered vocabulary is used (Sindelar, 2013; Santrosyan, 2017). Therefore, the Syrian Armenian forced migrants and citizens of Armenia in this study – people from different cultural, social and partially linguistic groups (Russian and Arabic) and backgrounds – are likely to have different norms and perceptions of reality, which can be a potential hindrance to adaptation and subsequent successful integration. The argument made thus far will be demonstrated firstly by considering linguistic and socio-cultural differences between Armenian and Syrian Armenian communities and then by analysing the implications of these in the integration process that takes place in daily life in Armenia.

Forced migration and perceived ethnic homeland immigration effects

Forced migration is defined as a relatively permanent physical movement from one geographical site to another in circumstances, such as conflict, violence, ethnic cleansing, lack of security or disasters triggered by natural hazards, when a person is forced to leave their place of settlement (Mangalam, 1968: 8; Hansen and Oliver-Smith, 1982: 2; Zetter, 2014: 21). In such cases, immigrants rarely have enough time to gather full knowledge of the structures of the host society, to establish necessary networks prior to arrival and to psychologically accept the idea of mid- or long-term emigration. Trauma related to negative experiences in the country of settlement, separation from friends and relatives, leaving belongings and work behind, and facing uncertainty of the future further complicates and usually slows down their integration in a host country (Van Hear, 1998: 152). Moreover, the newcomers have already awoken 'collective fears', which emerge among ethnic groups when a state is no longer capable of protecting them and an ethnic conflict starts. This leads to increased in-group favouritism (Syrian Armenians) and out-group exaggerated negative perception or mistrust (host country citizens) during the integration process (Lake and Rothchild, 1996: 41).

The host society's perception of migrants differs depending on such factors as the number of newcomers (the larger the number, the more negative the attitude tends to be, as these are more likely to be seen as job-takers and a potential security threat), socio-economic status (low-skilled workers are usually seen more as 'migrant' than highly skilled or elites) and ethno-racial (minorities from a different race would often be seen as more migrant than the ones from the same or close race or ethnicity) (Castles and Miller, 2003: 5; Guild, 2005: 101–112). Referring to the role of language and associated factors, a non-welcoming perception is often based on differences from local language norms, behaviours, clothes, facial expressions, as well as ideological and other socio-political differences (Olsson, 2008: 259; Maruyama and Stronza, 2010: 35).

Integration of migrants in a perceived ethnic homeland is also associated with several difficulties. Syrian Armenians mostly arrived in Syrian from the territories of the Ottoman Empire during the First World War as a result of anti-Armenian terror conducted by the Turkish authorities. The territory of the modern Armenia, however, belonged first to the Russian Empire and then to the Soviet Union. Thus, Armenia can be perceived by Syrian Armenians only as an ethnic homeland – a land where representatives of the same ethnicity live, but not from where their ancestors came. Although the 'myth of return', including to a perceived homeland, is a common and usually strong theoretical trope in diaspora studies, including the Armenian, in practice very few diaspora members 'repatriate' (Safran, 1991: 256; Olsson, 2008: 255). As recent research demonstrates, even ethnic tourism, recently gaining popularity, is associated with self-identity struggles (Maruyama and Stronza, 2010: 31–32). Due to significant socio-cultural differences, such visits often lead to reconsideration of what is perceived as a real and ancestral homeland and sometimes even to identity crises when a person no longer knows where they belong and so begin to feel they are in 'double exile' (Sen, 2011: 242). Exceptions to this trend have been ethnic visits based on philanthropic adventure ideas (Darieva, 2013: 33–34), but the current Syrian Armenian migration to Armenia does not fall into this category.

Reasons for permanent migration – economic, spiritual, as a result of persecution, etc. – affect integration, but generally such 're'-integration rarely goes smoothly or easily. Despite ethnic sentiment, years of life (for the first generation) or being born and having grown up in a different state (second and further generations; perceived ethnic homeland cases) highly affect the culture and values of diaspora members. To a large extent such movement can be called return to 'a foreign country' (Ben-Rafael, 2010: 12). A combination of an unrealistic perception of the country prior to arrival and the realization of clear socio-cultural differences between themselves and host society members on arrival (see Safran, 1991;

Olsson, 2008; Hess, 2010) often leads to feelings of frustration, disappointment and disillusionment, causing weakened attachment to the ancestral or perceived ethnic homeland (Tsuda, 2009: 9). It was also noted that even if tourist visits took place previously, and close relations were kept with some community members, when a permanent movement takes place, at least some level of difficulties and misunderstandings with the known people in the country are likely to emerge (Van Hear, 1998: 248–249). As a result of the aforementioned factors, it is often claimed that 'repatriation' is likely to lead to the emergence of new minority groups, rather than reconciliation of these (Tsuda, 2009: 11). Considering these factors, it becomes clear that forced migrants in a perceived ethnic homeland are likely to go through a more challenging and likely longer process of integration than voluntary migrants.

Russian language and its cultural influence

To demonstrate the depth of the Russian language's influence on Armenian culture and world perception, several historical facts have to be highlighted. From the first half of the nineteenth century until the 1917 Revolution and then from 1922 until 1991, the territories of modern Armenia were under the Russian rule – first as part of the Russian Empire and later as part of the USSR. In Imperial Russia, from 1835, the titular language in Armenia was used to teach children passing through the first and second grades at schools and Russian was a separate subject, while from the third year subjects were taught in Russian, and Armenian was taught separately. From 1906, Russian was defined as the language of the state apparatus and all its institutions. As such, Russian was used in the educational system, army, navy and all other state institutions, therefore 'Russifying' population of the Empire (Yamskov, 1994: 2; Voevoda et al., 2017: 125–127). Titular languages could be and were used mostly in informal and sometimes formal communication, but Russian was required for receiving good education and working for/with the state institutions or in/with other parts of the Empire.

After the 1917 revolution and a short independence (1918–1922), Armenia became part of the USSR. The Soviet policy-makers used the Russian language to spread socialist ideology and Soviet values, including through educational institutions (see Brandist, 2011: 1–16). The function of language as a means of unity, overarching culture and values was well understood in the USSR and so implemented, whereas 'ethnoterritorial national-cultural autonomy' became a guiding principle for both Lenin and Stalin (Smith, 2011: 109–110). Stalin insisted on the central role of Russian in various spheres, including modernizing the economy, while in 1938 it became a compulsory school subject across the USSR and in the late 1950s local languages were no longer a compulsory school subject (Smith, 2011: 107; Duncan and Mavisakalyan, 2015: 628). As a result of the Soviet language policies, command of Russian was seen as necessary for attractive employment opportunities and as a language of communication among the Soviet republics. Consequently, by 1989 about half of Armenians in the Republic fluently spoke Russian (Dietrich, 2005: 2).

Since the dissolution of the Soviet Union, the former USSR member states, including Armenia, have changed state language policies. According to the 1993 Armenian language law, Armenian became the only official language of the Republic (National Assembly of the Republic of Armenia, 1993). Despite this, Russian is still a mandatory language in Armenian primary schools, and there is discussion whether 'Russian [should] be taught to an advanced level at a greater number of schools' as Russian 'is the most widely used language' in the country (AFP b, 2017). Additionally, at present Russian TV and radio channels are widely used in the Republic and it is even claimed that the majority of information about world events is learned from Russian news, thus maintaining the population's command of it, influencing culture and affecting the perception of international and regional events (Marinosyan and Kurovskaya, 2015: 90–91; Vardanyan, n.d), thus reconfirming that the Russian socio-cultural influences on Armenia remains high. According to the 2001 census, 85 per cent of Armenian citizens spoke Russian (Marinosyan and Kurovskaya, 2015: 90).

At present, Russian is seen as an important language, which those employed in various professions are likely to speak, as it is the *de facto* language of communication among the post-Soviet states; it facilitates trade – it is used as the communication language within the Eurasian Economic Union (Dietrich, 2005: 14, 19–20); Russian is an attractive place for labour migration (Minasyan, 2013: 1); it is essential for state security, as Armenia and Russia have close security and defence cooperation, in which the working language is Russian, while Armenian officers are often trained in Russia (AFP b, 2017). More generally, recent research confirms that command of Russian improves labour market opportunities (for both genders), which was emphasized by Armenia's education minister, who noted that command of Russian is a matter of modern market competitiveness (Duncan, 2015: 626, 629, 639). Therefore, Russian language and culture have had a significant influence on Armenian daily life and mentality. While some impact of the modern Russian culture is visible, influence of the Soviet and early post-Soviet culture and values still has a significant impact on the Armenian culture. Therefore, some of these are discussed below.

Language in the process of social and economic integration

In regard to the Armenian language and Western-Eastern differences of it, the research, based on numerous interviews with both Syrian Armenians and Armenians from the Republic, NGO reports and personal observations, showed that generally social interaction and understanding, especially in informal communications, represented a minor issue. Although slight misunderstandings occasionally took place (mostly due to grammatical and occasional slight word meaning differences), generally it was possible for both sides to comprehensively understand each other. It was also claimed, that as long as inter-community verbal communication was present on a regular basis, overcoming these did not represent a significant challenge.

At the same time, this was a general trend and the process occurred differently depending on personality, age and educational group. Previous research suggests that youth tends to adhere to a new (semi-new in this study) language faster, largely as a result of more socially inclusive behavioural patterns, including education and socio-cultural activities. Linguistic adaptation of middle-age people depends on personal characteristics and whether they regularly interact with representatives of the host community in daily job-related activities, as well as during their free time. The elderly generally adapt slower, partly as they are usually more isolated from inter-community communications.[1] Even though exact figures were not available, based on interviews and personal observations, this tendency seems to represent the position of Syrian Armenians in Armenia. The following part of the chapter will analyse these conclusions more in detail.

School children and education

In 2012, a school called Cilicia was opened in Yerevan for Syrian Armenian children, where a Syrian Arabic curriculum was used and which employed Syrian Armenian teachers. This initiative aimed to ensure that children did not fall behind at school while (as it was widely believed the Syrian uprising would have been resolved shortly) being in Armenia for a short period, and because differences in Western-Eastern Armenian languages could potentially lead to educational problems if children studied in local schools ('Hürriyet Daily News, 2012'). However, later it became clear that the Syrian crisis was likely to continue and so the school was closed, whereas children from Syria were welcomed to join local educational institutions, as this would ensure their better socio-cultural integration (Malek, 2012; Harutyuyan, 2014). According to a personal interview with an NGO representative, at first language barrier problems were raised and so several steps were taken to overcome these. Actions included the UNHCR initiating free Eastern Armenian and Russian courses for school children, as well as arranging additional teaching assistance to Syrian Armenian students. According to interviews with Syrian Armenian parents and representatives of the relevant NGOs in Armenia, most of the primary school children had already adapted to Eastern Armenian to a large extent by mid-2015. One NGO representative said there were still some cases of language adaptation problems (predominantly among teenagers, rather than primary school children), but those were already minor in 2015. The main exception from this was terminology of science subjects at school. To address the problem, 'the education department of Yerevan municipality, with support from the private sector, had organised free training to address this' (Lena Halajian, director of the Centre for Syrian Armenian issues, in Harutyunyan, 2014). It is likely that additional language courses and assistance fostered an important positive dynamic, as in the case of Iraqi forced migration to Armenia a decade before, children experienced noticeable school integration difficulties largely due to the language barrier (Save the Children, 2011: ii). At the same time, many parents still hoped to return to Syria and wanted their children to maintain command of Arabic, and so, several initiatives to support these preferences were implemented. For example, an Aleppo NGO provided free Arabic courses twice a week, which aimed at 'straightening and development of linguistic knowledge and communication skills' (Aleppo NGO), ensuring smoother re-integration in Syria if circumstances would allow for a return.

Youth and university education

Regarding university students, it is important to note that the Armenian state recognized Syrian diplomas, and Eastern Armenian, Russian and English courses were provided to the Syrian Armenian students and a large number of Syrian Armenian university students were provided with scholarships ('More scholarships ...', 2017; 'AEF announces ...'). These steps were made in order to create viable chances for the newcomers to get involved in higher education in Armenia and so to integrate linguistically and culturally (Ministry of Diaspora representative, Yerevan, 2015; Personal interviews head of a university department, Yerevan, 2016). Interviews suggested the minor nature of issues related to the Eastern Armenian language adaptation. For example, during an interview with a Syrian Armenian student (Yerevan, 2015), it was suggested that linguistic difficulties (including unintentional adding of Russian words into conversations) occurred at the start, but by mid-2015 this became a more minor issue for many. It was claimed that as long as inter-group communication took place regularly, Eastern-Western Armenian adaptation was relatively smooth and by then they had even learned some of the most commonly used Russian words. Despite this, differences in language and curriculum in Syria and Armenia led to some students needing to repeat a year at university in order to fit into the new system (Personal interview, NGO director, Yerevan, 2015).

Adult Syrian Armenian population

Data extracted from interviews also suggested that the adaptation of mid-age Syrian Armenians largely depended on their need (or absence of it) to communicate with the local population, especially for business purposes (Personal interview, Syrian Armenian male, 20s, 2015). In regard to business, the Eastern-Western Armenian issue has been more salient, especially if the employment required written language (Lieberman, 2017). For example, one Syrian Armenian woman claimed it was hard enough to become accustomed to Eastern Armenian, but writing correctly in it was a significant difficulty (Personal interview, Syrian Armenian female, 30s, 2015). When written language was not or minimally required, a majority of male and a large number of female respondents claimed that linguistic integration into the Armenian business required effort, but was achievable.

However, it was highlighted repeatedly that a significant number of elderly people were still experiencing problems, mostly due to the low levels of communication with local people and to the preference to communicate with Syrian Armenians. This was at least partly based on a strong will among many group representatives to return to Syria. For instance, during one interview with an elderly Syrian Armenian woman, she rather emotionally stated: 'I only want peace in Syria and that I can return there!' (Personal interview, Syrian Armenian woman, 80s, 2015).

Finally, no interviews mentioned significant misunderstandings as a result of misuses of intonations, body language or facial expressions. Both in interviews and in the published literature (Campos, 2016: 36) the Syrian accent was usually perceived positively (usually defined as fine, pleasant or funny, but not unpleasant). In terms of pronunciation some minor differences were noticeable. For example, a name would be pronounced *Tiran* in Eastern Armenian and

Diran in Western Armenian, *Tigran* – *Dikran*, *Janik* – *Chanik* respectively. Some words would be used by both, but would have slightly different meanings. For example, *Paekel* in Eastern Armenian means to lie and in Western Armenian – to sleep, *Akhoyan* – rival and champion respectively. These, however, were seen as minor differences, which did not have significant influence on the understanding of each other.

Use of Russian in daily life in Armenia caused some level of frustration for many Syrian Armenians. First, as the language has been widely used in the country for decades, Armenians tend to mix Russian words into conversations in Armenian without noticing it, making Syrian Armenians feel uncomfortable, as this makes it no longer possible to understand the entire conversation or even take part in it (Personal interviews, Armenian female from the Republic in her 40s, Syrian Armenian male in his 20s, Yerevan, 2015). As discussed earlier, lack of command of the language is problematic when it comes to work in services in Yerevan, where the majority of Syrian Armenians resided AFRa (2017), due to a large number of Russian-speaking tourists and business visitors. This is especially significant, as a large number of Syrian Armenians have been finding employment in food services (opening their own restaurants and cafes or sometimes working for others).

In terms of the use of Russian outside of the work environment, it was claimed that children in primary schools usually picked up the language relatively quickly (Personal interview, Syrian Armenian father, Yerevan, 2015). For other age groups, the language remained a noticeable obstacle, which can at least partly be overcome in time. Syrian Armenians would learn the main Russian words borrowed by Armenians and frequently used in conversations, while Armenians, hearing the Syrian Armenian accent, could get used to keeping the conversation in Armenian, minimizing the use of Russian. Additionally, a lack of command of Russian limited media access of Syrian Armenians – as discussed earlier, the Russian media is widely consumed in Armenia. These factors have a cultural component as well, as Armenians in the Republic often refer to Soviet film sciences, and sayings from these in general conversations and when joking, thus leaving Syrian Armenians out of this part of cultural integration. Generally, a director of an NGO working on business integration of diaspora Armenians in the country stated during an interview (Yerevan, 2015) that: 'Their [Syrian Armenians] lack of knowledge of Russian is probably the only serious problem' in terms of linguistic integration.

As mentioned earlier, to overcome this problem, courses of Russian were opened. However at least until 2015, these were not popular among the newcomers, due to the inherent difficulties in learning to write it, as it belongs to a different language group from Armenian or Arabic (the first two are sub-groups of the Indo-European family – separate and Slavic branches respectively, while Arabic is a member of Semitic family). At the same time, problems related to the necessity of speaking Russian could be partly overcome by learning a limited number of widely used phrases and leaving service of Russian speakers to local Armenian workers, while with younger generations English could be employed.

Cultural and psychological factors affecting integration of Syrian Armenians

In the case of Syrian Armenian forced migration, stress and ethnic homeland integrational difficulties were combined, thus leading to potential integrational obstacles, even for such highly adaptive groups as Armenian diaspora members. On the one hand, even though socio-cultural differences between Syrian Armenians were substantial, appreciation of a country where Armenians were the majority, the Armenian language (even if a different version of it) was spoken, the same religion was practised and which had historical importance and important historical sites was likely to lay positive foundations in terms of the attitude towards it and its population. Additionally, the differences would still be referred to as leading to 'moderate cultural conflict' rather than 'serious conflict', leading to 'culture shock' and 'mental disease' (Berry, 1997: 13), thus at least ensuring viable chances of integration. On the other hand, 'the presumed existence of historic, cultural and/or religious heritage shared with the host society leads to the expectation of fast and painless social integration' while in reality the 'socio-cultural makeup [of the newcomers] is much closer to their countries of origin than to that of the newly acquired national homeland' (Remennick, 2003: 25).

When discussing positive factors with Syrian Armenians, the answers could be summarized in terms of sightseeing in Armenia being spiritually and ethnically awakening and uplifting, but to enjoy this beauty in full financial stability had to be ensured first. Difficulties related to the socio-cultural differences were addressed in a number of interviews. For example, one NGO representative (Personal interview, Yerevan, 2015) stated: 'Syrian-Armenians have a different mentality ... Plus they viewed Armenia "through rose-tinted glasses", because most of them did not even visit Armenia [before], because 100 years from generation to generation they grew up thinking that Armenia as a heaven ... and suddenly it was such a disappointment.' Thus, it can be seen that the historical place of Armenia provided a valuable foundation for socio-cultural integration, but differences in modern-day cultures and values in combination with socio-economic uncertainty of the future lessened the effects of these.

An overall positive attitude of the Armenian citizens towards their Syrian counterparts, however, likely had a positive effect on overcoming these. Such an attitude could be explained by several factors. Firstly, the Syrian Armenian diaspora was: 'one of the oldest [Armenia diaspora] in the world and [it was] the centre of the cultural life in the diaspora ... it was always considered to be a centre of unity and preservation of the Armenian identity and that is why Armenians in Armenia have always had a friendly attitude towards Syrian-Armenians' (Personal interview, former ambassador of the Republic of Armenia, Yerevan, 2016). Secondly, prior to the war in Syria Armenian families used to come to the country for holidays and created a positive image of themselves (Personal interviews, Syrian Armenian woman; NGO representative, Yerevan, 2015). Thirdly, circumstances of migration, violence and insecurity in Syria also often ensured a positive attitude towards Syrian Armenians. Fourthly, it was stated a number of times that Syrian Armenians brought cultural innovations – starting from Middle Eastern food and ending with wearing colourful clothes differently to Armenian in the Republic – which were perceived positively and with interest, according to interviews conducted and published research (e.g. Varshalomidze, 2017).

Finally, professional qualities of Syrian Armenians were usually very highly appreciated in the country – a component of host society perception, affecting the general attitude towards newcomers (Castles and Miller, 2003: 5; Guild, 2005: 101–112). During my interviews a number of such reviews were provided, highlighting friendliness, honesty and professional competence. For instance, one Armenian man in his 50s said: 'I've recently been to a hospital for blood analysis. My veins are very bad, but a nurse did it so neatly! I started talking to her. It appeared she was from Syria. She was very professional. It could be felt she knew her business' (Personal interview, Yerevan, 2015).

At the same time rare cases of negative attitude were found, even if on a very small scale. This would usually refer to the fact that Syrian Armenians came only because they had to, not by free will and so they should be quiet (Sargsyan, 2015a). In some interviews it was also said that occasionally people could say to Syrian Armenians that they did not speak proper Armenian (referring to their accent), which the newcomers found very insulting, considering it has been a source of pride for diaspora members that in spite of being a relatively small minority in a state of settlement they were able to preserve the language.

Cultural differences also emerged in working culture. One of the main related issues, discovered during the interviews, became that many Syrian Armenians were used to working for themselves and it was hard for many to accept the idea of being an employee. Another related problem emerged as a result of a combination of cultural differences and economic weakness of the Armenian market. Some, including youth, generally considered the opportunities available and the salaries paid for them too low-status and low-earning:[2]

> Some young people don't want to work for very low salaries or in certain jobs ... even if it proves to help them in the mid-term, as for example while working in cafes and restaurants they often meet their future employers there ... I tell them that they should use this opportunity. Today you receive 3000 drams. After one year 5000, then 10 000 and then you'll solve your problem. You have 4 people in your family (in general). If each member of your family works and receives 2–3000, then you definitely will be able to pay the rent. You won't have [a] luxury life, but you will be able to make a living. It's hard I understand. You had another life in Syria, but this is your reality now. If you are here, you should survive. But many of them aren't willing to do it. (Personal interview, NGO director, Yerevan, 2015)

This difficulty, at least at the time of the fieldwork, was especially noticeable for mid-age and elderly men, as such jobs were often perceived by them as degrading their social status and already shaken self-esteem. Additionally, it was not always only about the real opportunities, but also about the stress of change in conditions and the need to adhere to them (Pine, 2014: 100). It could be seen that Syrian Armenians tended to romanticize their economic and social past in Syria and psychologically refused to accept changes and to act accordingly. For months, or several years, many newcomers did not wish to integrate and start a business in Armenia, as they planned to return to Syria soon. According to Bonacich (1973) migrants who planned or thought of returning to the country of previous settlement (home country) found it more important to keep strong relations with representatives of their community, rather than build up new relations with members of a host society or to integrate in general. In case of Syrian Armenians, this factor noticeable slowed down their economic involvement and limited their opportunities of finding a job. As an NGO representative stated: 'According to our calculations around 75% of Syrian-Armenians are physically here, but their mind is still in Syria' (Personal interview, NGO director, Yerevan, 2015). This frequently led to absence of will to discuss with local business consultants how to organize business successfully in Armenia, which spheres are less monopolized or have better development opportunities, or, even in some cases, to come to a job interview. At the same time, the body of research suggests (Semyonov and Lewin-Epstein, 2011; OECD/EU, 2015: 21, 86, 109) that the longer they stayed in Armenia the better the chances were that they would have to consider economic integration in Armenia, as they would meet reality head on, unless they leave for a third country. The proof of this theoretical statement could already be seen in 2017–2018, when more Syrian Armenians started succeeding in private enterprise.

Another psychological factor slowing the process of economic and, to some extent, social integration was the exaggerated group favouritism and rise of emotional attachment to an ethnic group, while 'others' (non-Syrian-Armenians) were seen as 'inherently untrustworthy' (Lake and Rothchild, 1996: 41, 56). For example, the belief that 'Syrian-Armenians were fooled many times – by organizations, by the state' (Personal interview, anonymous, Yerevan, 2015) was widespread and often based on first-hand experience, disincentivizing the newcomers from investment or opening a business in a country.

Generally, the socio-cultural differences between Syrian Armenians and the host population were perceived positively by the latter. The most problematic area of such differences has been working culture, especially combined with economic difficulties in Armenia. The research, however, shows that although further understanding of the realities of the Armenian labour market has been essential for the newcomers, they have gained a highly positive professional image, which has increased the likelihood of positive integration in this sphere. Any minor hostility by the host population towards the newcomers, as well as the attitude of Syrian Armenian arrivals towards host society members, can both be taken as part of the process of adaptation to the new environment that is likely to be at least partly overcome with the passing of time.

Conclusions

The chapter demonstrated the high complexity of socio-linguistic aspects of Syrian Armenians forced migrants' integration in a perceived ethnic homeland, the Republic of Armenia. Language has two major impacts on the process. Firstly, command of host country language facilitates easier access to employment and public institutions and allows the establishment of social relations with members of the host society. Secondly, as language affects culture, values and general perception of reality, the ability to speak one language provides better opportunities for socio-cultural understanding between members of immigrant and host society groups. Both Syrian Armenians and Armenians in the Republic have a command of Armenian, but Western and Eastern respectively versions of it, thus providing relatively good chances understanding possibilities. The study demonstrated that overall verbal communication between the two groups represented a minor integrational issue, while written language was perceived as a more serious problem. To address this, free language courses were opened for the newcomers of school and university levels, as well as for adult migrants. These actions likely positively influenced linguistic integration, at least in the first two groups (i.e. pupils and university students), as significantly better results were reached in comparison with, for example, Iraqi Armenian forced migrants, who arrived in the country at the beginning of the 2000s. The main linguistic problem became the Russian language, which improves job opportunities in Armenia in general, and in Yerevan, in particular, due to a large number of Russian-speaking tourist and business visitors, as well as close cooperation between Armenia and Russia in various socio-economic fields where the working language is Russian. Additionally, as command of the language has been important in the country for almost two centuries, the local population tends to mix Russian words into conversations or even switch languages without noticing it, thus leaving the newcomers lost. Although Russian language courses were also opened to address the issue, the problem is likely to persist, as the language comes from a different source from Armenian or Arabic linguistic family and so learning it requires significant efforts.

In terms of socio-cultural integration and factors related to the forced nature of migration and to integration in a perceived ethnic homeland, factors analysed can be divided into two groups. Historical sites of Armenia, as well as integration among people of the same ethnic kin and religion are likely to have a positive influence on the process. The positive perception of the host society, based on appreciation of cultural and professional characteristics of Syrian Armenians by Armenians in the Republic, is also identified as a highly supportive element of the process. Finally, Syrian Armenians' historical ability to adapt in various societies and their experience of bilingual societies (Armenian and Arabic in Syria) and even usage of two versions of language in daily life (literal Arabic and Syrian dialect) mean they are likely to be able to adapt to life in Armenia, albeit relatively easily.

However, at the same time, significant socio-cultural differences between the newcomers and members of the host society, in combination with limited economic opportunities in Armenia, are likely to slow down the process. Psychological attitudes towards integration in a situation of forced migration and ethnic homeland integration, such as high levels of stress due to the forced nature of migration, worries about family members, friends and properties left behind, and uncertainties about the future, are also likely to mean integration taking longer. Still, as previous research demonstrates, the longer Syrian Armenians reside in the Republic of Armenia, the higher the chances of linguistic and cultural integration.

Notes

1　See, for instance, Remmenick 2010 in relation to ethnic Jews from the post-Soviet space.
2　According to the report of the European University Institute, salaries of Syrian Armenians in Armenia are considerably lower than they were in Syria.

References

AFP (2017b). *Armenia's Plans on Teaching Russian Raise Fears of Moscow Influence.* Available online: http://en.rfi.fr/wire/20171025-armenias-plans-teaching-russianraise-fears-moscow-influence (accessed 27 March 2018).

AFRa (2017). *Syria's Armenians Are Fleeing to Their Ancestral Homeland.* Available online: https://www.economist.com/news/europe/21724036-war-may-bring-end-christian-minoritys-century-long-story (accessed 30 November 2018).

Ben-Rafael (2010). 'Diaspora'. *Sociopedia.isa.* doi: 10.1177/205684601052. Available online: http://www.sagepub.net/isa/resources/pdf/diaspora.pdf (accessed 30 November 2018).

Berry, J. (1997). 'Immigration, Acculturation, and Adaptation'. *Applied Psychology* 46(1): 5–34.

Bonacich, E. (1973). 'A Theory of Middleman Minorities'. *American Sociological Review* 38(5): 583–594.

Bonvillain, N. (2011). *Language, Culture, and Communication: The Meaning of Messages* (6th ed.). Upper Saddle River, NJ: Pearson.

Brandist, C. (2011). 'Introduction'. In C. Brandist and K. Chown (ed.), *Politics and the Theory of Language in the USSR 1917–1938*, 1–16. London: Anthem Press.

Campos, N. M. (2016). *Historical Trauma and Refugee Reception: Armenians and Syrian-Armenian Co-Ethnics* (Unpublished master's thesis). University of San Francisco.

Castles, S., and Miller, M. (2003). *The Age of Migration: International Population Movements in the Modern World*. New York: Guilford Press.

Chubareva, M. S. (2017). 'Influence of Russian Language and Literature on the Student's Ethos (in Russian)'. *Концепт* 5: 141–145. Available online: http://e-koncept. ru/2017/770126.htm (accessed 30 November 2018).

Darieva, T. (2013). 'Homeland Tourism, Long-Distance Nationalism and Production of a New Diasporic Identity (Armenian case)'. *Kobe University*. Available online: web. cla.kobe-u.ac.jp/group/IReC/pdf/2012_darieva.pdf (accessed 27 March 2018).

Dietrich, A. P. (2005). 'Language Policy and the Status of Russian in the Soviet Union and the Successor States outside the Russian Federation'. *ASEES* 19(1–2): 1–27.

Duncan, A., and Mavisakalyan, A. (2015). 'Russian Language Skills and Employment in the Former Soviet Union'. *Economics of Transition* 23(3): 625–656. doi: 10.1111/ ecot.12075.

Gentner, D., and Goldin-Meadow, S. (2003). *Language in Mind Advances in the Study of Language and Thought*. Cambridge, MA: MIT Press.

Goebel, Z. (2010). *Language, Migration, and Identity: Neighborhood Talk in Indonesia*. Cambridge and New York, NY: Cambridge University Press.

Guild, E. (2005). 'Cultural and Identity Security: Immigrants and the Legal Expression of National Identity'. In Guild, E. and Selm, J. V. (eds), *International Migration and Security: Opportunities and Challenges*, 101–112. London: Routledge.

Hansen, A., and Oliver-Smith, A. (1982). *Involuntary Migration and Resettlement: The Problems and Responses of Dislocated People*. Boulder, CO: Westview Press.

Harutyunyan, A. (2014). 'School Barriers for Syrian Armenians'. *Global Voices Caucasus*. Available online: https://iwpr.net/global-voices/school-barriers-syrian-armenians (accessed 30 November 2018).

Hess, C. (2010). 'Post-Soviet Repatriation and Nationhood in Germany and Greece'. *Political Perspectives* 4(2): 25–48.

Home Office (2004). *Indicators of Integration: Final Report*. Available online: http:// webarchive.nationalarchives.gov.uk/20110218141321/and http://rds.homeoffice.gov. uk/rds/pdfs04/dpr28.pdf (accessed 30 November 2018).

Hürriyet Daily News (2012). Available online: from http://www.hurriyetdailynews.com/ armenia-establishes-school-for-syria-kids-32508 (accessed 15 April 2018).

Lake, D., and Rothchild, D. (1996). 'Containing Fear: The Origins and Management of Ethnic Conflict'. *International Security* 21(2): 41–75.

Lieberman, A. (2017). Lessons Learned as Syrian-Armenian Refugees Return to Armenia. DEVEX. Available online: https://www.devex.com/news/lessons-learned-as-syrian-armenian-refugees-return-to-armenia-90551 (accessed 30 November 2018).

Malek, A. (2012). Syrian Armenians Seek Shelter in Armenia. *The New York Times*. Available online: http://www.nytimes.com/2012/12/12/world/middleeast/syrian-armenians-seekshelter-in-armenia.html?_r=0 (accessed 27 March 2018).

Mangalam, J. J. (1968). *Human Migration. A Guide to Migration Literature in English, 1955–1962*. Lexington, KY: University of Kentucky Press.

Marinosyan, T. E., and Kurovskaya, Yu. G. (2015). 'Position of the Russian Language in Countries' Integration and Disintegration: Russia – Armenia'/'Положение русского языка в условиях интеграции и дезинтеграции стран: Россия – Армения'. *Отечественная и зарубежная педагогика*, 3: 83–93.

Maruyama, N., and Stronza, A. (2010). 'Roots Tourism of Chinese Americans'. *Ethnology* 49(1): 23–44.

Minasyan, S. (2013). Russian-Armenian Relations: Affection or Pragmatism? PONARS Eurasia. Available online: http://www.ponarseurasia.org/memo/russian-armenian-relations-affection-or-pragmatism (accessed 30 November 2018).

National Assembly of the Republic of Armenia (1993). *Law of the Republic of Armenia: On Language/Закон Республики Армения: О языке*. Available online: http://www.parliament.am/legislation.php?sel=show&ID=1793&lang=rus3 (accessed 30 November 2018).

OECD/EU (2015). *Indicators of Immigrant Integration 2015*. OECD and European Commission. http://www.oecd.org/els/mig/Indicators-of-Immigrant-Integration-2015.pdf (accessed 30 November 2018).

Olsson, E., and King, R. (2008). 'Introduction: Diasporic Return'. *Diaspora: A Journal of Transnational Studies* 17(3): 255–261.

Panossian, Razmik (2006). *The Armenians: From Kings and Priests to Merchants and Commissars*. London: Hurst & Company.

Personal Interview with a Syrian-Armenian Student, Yerevan, 2015.

Pine, F. (2014). 'Migration as Hope: Space, Time, and Imagining the Future'. *Current Anthropology* 55(S9): 95–104.

Remennick, L. (2003). 'What Does Integration Mean? Social Insertion of Russian Immigrants in Israel'. *Journal of International Migration and Integration/Revue de l'integration et de la migration internationale* 4(1): 23–49.

Safran, W. (1991). 'Diasporas in Modern Societies: Myths of Homeland and Return'. *Diaspora: A Journal of Transnational Studies* 1(1): 83–99.

Santrosyan, R. (2017). Sex vs. Gender through Linguistic Expression in Armenian. *EVN Report*. Available online: https://www.evnreport.com/arts-and-culture/sex-vs-gender-through-linguistic-expression-in-armenian (accessed 30 November 2018).

Sargsyan, G. (2015). 'Armenia or Turkey? Laklakian Family from Aleppo Faces Difficult Choice'. *Hetq*. Available online: http://hetq.am/eng/news/61016/armenia-or-turkey-laklakian-family-from-aleppo-faces-difficult-choice.html (accessed 30 November 2018).

Save the Children (2011). *Child Rights Situation and Issues of Children of Refugee Families in Armenia*. Available online: https://armenia.savethechildren.net/sites/armenia.savethechildren.net/files/library/REFUGEE%20CHILD%20RIGHTS%20SITUATION_SC_UNHCR.pdf.

Semyonov, M., and Lewin-Epstein, N. (2011). 'Wealth Inequality: Ethnic Disparities in Israeli Society'. *Social Forces* 89(3): 935–959.

Sen, K. (2011). 'The (Re)turn of the Native: Diaspora, Transnationalism and the Re-Inscription of "Home"'. In M. David and J. Muñoz-Basols (eds), *Defining and*

Re-Defining Diaspora: From Theory to Reality, 227–250. Oxford: Inter-Disciplinary Press.

Sindelar, D. (2013). *Does Language Influence World Perception?/Влияет ли язык на восприятие мира?* Available online: https://rus.azattyq.org/a/vliyaet-li-yazyk-na-vospriyatie-mira/24958054.html (accessed 29 November 2016).

Smith, M. G. (2011). 'The Tenacity of Forms: Language, Nation, Stalin'. In C. Brandist and K. Chown (eds), *Politics and the Theory of Language in the USSR 1917–1938*, 105–122. London: Anthem Press.

Sophocleous, A. (2006). 'Identity Formation and Dialect Use among Young Speakers of the Greek-Cypriot Community in Cyprus'. In R. Kiely, P. Rea-Dickins, H. Woodfield, and G. Clibbon (eds), *Language, Culture and Identity in Applied Linguistics: Selected Papers from the Annual Meeting of the British Association for Applied Linguistics, University of Bristol, September 2005*, 61–78. British Association for Applied Linguistics in Association with Equinox.

Spencer, S. (ed.) (2006). Refugees and Other New Migrants: A Review of the Evidence on Successful Approaches to Integration. *Compas.* Available online: https://www.compas.ox.ac.uk/2006/er-2006-integration_refugees_uk_ho/ (accessed 30 November 2018).

Tsuda, T. (2009). 'Introduction: Diasporic Return and Migration Studies'. In T. Tsuda (ed.), *Diasporic Homecomings: Ethnic Return Migration in Comparative Perspective*, 1–20. Stanford, CA: Stanford University Press.

UNHCR (2013). *A New Beginning: Refugee Integration in Europe.* Available online: http://www.unhcr.org/uk/protection/operations/52403d389/new-beginning-refugee-integration-europe.html (accessed 30 November 2018).

UNHCR (2018). *Syria Regional Refugee Response.* Available online: https://data2.unhcr.org/en/situations/syria (accessed 30 November 2018).

Van Hear, N. (1998). *New Diasporas: The Mass Exodus, Dispersal and Regrouping of Migrant Communities.* London: UCL Press Limited.

Vardanyan, G. (n.d.). Armenia in Russia's Zone of Influence. Retrieved from https://chai-khana.org/en/armenia-in-russias-zone-of-influence (accessed 30 November 2018).

Varshalomidze, T. (2017). *Syrian Refugees Improve Armenia's Social Fabric.* Available online: https://www.aljazeera.com/indepth/features/2017/12/refugees-improve-armenia-social-fabric-171214061224398.html (accessed 30 November 2018).

Vinokur, G. O. (2006). Culture and Language/*Культура и язык.* Moscow: Labirint.

Voevoda, E. V., Belogurov, A. Y., Kostikova, L. P., Romanenko, N. M., and Silantyeva, M. V. (June 2017). 'Language Policy in the Russian Empire: Legal and Constitutional Aspect'. *Journal of Constitutional History* (33): 121–129.

Whorf, B. (1956). 'The Relation of Habitual Thought and Behavior to Language'. In J. Carroll (ed.), *Language, Thought, and Reality: Selected Writings* of Benjamin Lee Whorf, 134–159. Cambridge, MA: MIT Press.

Yamskov, A. N. (1994). *The "New Minorities" in Post-Soviet States*. Available online: https://www.culturalsurvival.org/publications/cultural-survival-quarterly/new-minorities-post-soviet-states (accessed 30 November 2018).

Zetter, R. (2014). *Protecting Forced Migrants: A State of the Art Report of Concepts, Challenges and Ways Forward*. [online] Switzerland: Federal Commission on Migration. Available at: https://www.ekm.admin.ch/content/dam/data/ekm/dokumentation/materialien/mat_schutz_e.pdf (accessed 21 May 2017).

Integrating Intercultural Communication in Crisis-Affected Health Settings

Medical Translation in Crisis Situations

Vicent Montalt Resurreccio

Introduction

Crisis situations or disasters may occur at any moment anywhere in the world. They include such diverse events as epidemics and pandemics, wars, ethnic cleansing, terrorist and bioterrorist attacks, mass shootings and bombings, mass transport accidents, tsunamis, storms, hurricanes, droughts, cold and heat waves, insect infestation, land and mud slides, severe local storms, snow avalanches, wildfires, floods, earthquakes, volcanic eruptions, or nuclear, chemical and industrial accidents. These can be grouped in four areas: (a) armed conflict, (b) disasters triggered by natural hazards, (c) endemic and epidemic disease, and (d) social violence and healthcare exclusion (Purtle, Siddiqui, & Andrulis, 2010: 78). Many of these events force victims to migrate, seek asylum in other countries and become refugees – according to UNHCR, the figure was as high as 70.4 million people, figure as of 30 June 2018 (UNHCR, 2018).

Being prepared for and responding to them to help the victims is highly complex, and always involves communication – and very frequently translation. Their intensity and impact can range from events very localized in time and space affecting a few people – such as an explosion in a factory – to massive destruction affecting thousands – such as a hurricane or a war. Whatever their cause or intensity, they always have a negative impact on the health and well-being of the victims, and thus medicine and healthcare are always involved in a variety of ways, from prevention campaigns to emergency surgery.

From a translation angle, a few questions come to mind. What is the role of medical translators and translations in humanitarian crisis communication? How can medical translation contribute to facilitate healthcare provision efficiently? In which ways should medical translation evolve and expand to include relevant aspects of crisis situations that can help translators work more effectively and improve victims' lives, the ultimate goal of humanitarian aid and action?

This chapter offers a small contribution to what Federici has described as an 'urgent need to establish a concerted and multidisciplinary debate on the role of intercultural communication in international multilingual missions that respond to emergencies across the world' (Federici, 2016: 3). My aim is to start a dialogue between medical translation and crisis situations from which both can benefit. More specifically I set out to explore what medical translation can learn from crisis situations and what medical translation can contribute to improve communication in humanitarian crises. For this purpose, I will occasionally refer to Doctors Without Borders (DWB) and Translators Without Borders (TWB) as cases in focus that can serve as a starting point for further development in this under-researched area. The method is thus based on several types of sources: (1) content analysis of reports, videos, narratives, webpages and newsletters, mainly those published by Doctors Without Borders (DWB) and Translators Without Borders (TWB); relevant input from other NGOs (such as the World Health Organization) is also considered; (2) two interviews with DWB professionals; (3) apps relating to healthcare and well-being in crisis situations; and (4) a review of recent research in medical translation.

Mapping key concepts

Within the disaster sector, this chapter focuses on humanitarian aid and action in multilingual and multicultural settings, and more specifically on its medical and healthcare dimension, and the roles that medical translation and translators can play in fostering effective communication in them. Therefore, in this chapter translation and translators are situated mainly in the field of disaster medicine and healthcare in the context of non-governmental organizations such as DWB.

From the outset, two basic premises will be established. First, that translation is a vital activity in crisis situations in which the responders and the affected population do not share the same language or culture. This is especially the case in developing countries where foreign aid and professionals are needed (Bolton & Weiss, 2001). Humanitarian aid situations (HAS) are crisis situations in which humanitarian aid is provided to especially vulnerable populations, normally in countries other than the ones that provide it. Second, that survivors of disasters need information of all kinds, and they need it in their respective main language.

There are important reasons for these premises. The most obvious one is that patients in any health system normally communicate in their mother tongue because – whether or not they speak other languages – it is the language or language variety they most easily understand and in which they can express themselves best. Knowing what the mother tongues of the victims in different crisis situations are is a pre-requisite for any humanitarian action in any part of the world.

However, according to the report *Putting Language on the Map in the European Refugee Response* (TWB, September 2017), as recently as 2017, humanitarian organizations and policymakers are responding to complex crises without adequate information not only on which languages the affected populations speak, but also on how well they understand the languages used by responders, and on which formats and channels will be most effective for communicating complex information, such as medical facts, recommendations or warnings. As pointed out by TWB in the above-mentioned report, using the country of origin as proxy is misleading because many different languages and dialects may be spoken in that country or in the affected area. 'Lack of access to objective information – because it is not provided, or not available in the right language, format or channel – makes victims reliant on word-of-mouth and social media for [finding out about] decisions, and [makes them] potentially more vulnerable to rumour and misinformation' (2017: 3). The negative consequences of not receiving information in the language victims understand best are far-reaching, from basic sanitation issues to behaviour that could increase the risk of contracting a fatal disease, such as Ebola.

The situation is even worse when children in crisis situations are unaccompanied. According to REACH, 'Over 100,000 refugee and migrant children, of whom more than 33,800 were unaccompanied and separated children (UASC) (34 per cent), arrived in Europe in 2016' (2017: 2). When children do not receive information in a language they understand, it leads them to make high-risk choices, including dropping out of the formal reception system, out of ignorance of their rights and options (TWB, 2017: 3), or indeed not being treated for their illnesses or not being able to avoid risky behaviour for their health.

But there is yet another even more powerful reason for translation from a medical perspective: the effects of injury and trauma suffered during the disaster mean that patients may be unable to shift to another language which is not their own. Health professionals and translators care for and address people who are both survivors and victims. In disasters, survival means having witnessed chaos, destruction and quite often the death of relatives. Many of the victims are affected by acute illness or injury, and/or trauma. According to Peleg (2013: 2), 'Disasters have far reaching effects for the population. Psychological and behavioral support must be part of the medical support given to survivors *en route* to recovery [...] High percentages of injuries in MCIs [Mass Casualty Incidents] are people with Post Traumatic Disorders or Acute Stress Reaction.'

Members of the target audiences addressed by translations issued in crises are in situations of uncertainty, stress, anxiety, fear or panic. Owing to the emotional burden they carry, memory of past experiences and events, processing and comprehension of messages containing relevant information, recall of information provided to them and fluent interaction with translators and health professionals may very well be beyond them. Thus, in addition to linguistic and cultural barriers, translators have to cope with the distress of their target readers and interlocutors. Their ability to convey empathy is vital here. Cultural knowledge about how empathy and respect are understood, valued and expressed in different cultures and languages is highly relevant for crisis situation training of both medical translators and healthcare professionals. Recent research on empathy in doctor–patient interaction – both mediated and non-mediated – shows its importance in the improvement of communication and health outcomes (Howick et al., 2018). Likewise, a growing body of research indicates that cross-cultural competences in health professionals can improve migrant patients' health-related outcomes (Granero-Molina et al., 2019). In addition to this, translators must bear in mind that first responders themselves often suffer the effects of stress and trauma: 'All the complexities regarding the treatment of many injured patients at once can cause adverse effects on those treating them. The care for first responders and medical personnel is a field of growing importance' (Peleg 2013: 2).

Another key concept in HAS for the medical translator is Disaster Medicine (DM) – or Disaster Healthcare (DHC). Following Peleg (2013) disasters and MCIs occur out of the blue, usually without warning, and in a wide range of locations. Unexpectedness can be aggravated by unprecedentedness, that is, disasters which have never happened before and for which there is no accumulated experience and expertise. Even when they are not unprecedented, each disaster develops consequences and effects in a unique manner, thus affecting people in often unpredicted ways. Disaster medicine involves dealing with situations in which the immediate need for care is much greater than the resources available at a given location and time. Medical staff work in stressful conditions because a sudden concentration of casualties overwhelms existing medical facilities, equipment and personnel.

One of the main differences between ordinary healthcare and healthcare in crisis situations is that in the former the focus is on the individual patient, whereas in the latter individual care coexists with dealing with the population as a whole under time and organizational pressures. This is an ethical challenge for the translator affecting patient autonomy, confidentiality and privacy. This challenge involves important dilemmas regarding, for example, informed consent, which can often be impossible in life-or-death situations. Along these lines, Filmer and Federici (2018: 243) point out that forms of communication taking place in suboptimal conditions do not consider standard deontological practices. Undeniably, the operational conditions may increase power asymmetries not only between health professionals and patients, but also between health professionals and translators.

Disasters are complex for other reasons as well. They involve many participants – citizens, governments, non-governmental organizations, companies, international institutions, health authorities, the military and so on. Fredriksson, Olsson and Pallas (2014: 78) point out that crisis communication is 'an institutionally defined (and bounded) practice'. According to neo-institutional theory, organizational behaviour is situated in, and influenced by, other organizations and wider social forces – especially broader cultural rules and beliefs. Institutions shape the behaviour of participants in crisis situations, such as NGOs, victims, governments and translators. The disaster sector is huge, immensely varied and complex, and of growing importance worldwide.

According to Peleg (2013) disasters typically have several phases – preparedness, response, recovery, prevention – each requiring different approaches and actions. Preparedness focuses on planning, education and, if possible, prevention or at least damage limitation. Response is the immediate action taken following a disaster. The aim is to save lives. Recovery is the effort to return to normal life, which is completed by prevention. Purtle et al. (2010) report on language issues and barriers at each of these phases and highlight several aspects regarding translation. One of them is evaluating translated disaster preparedness materials as a promising practice for ensuring that resources are culturally and linguistically appropriate (2010: 2). They also underline the benefits of licensed medical interpreters in the response stage to reduce mortality, morbidity and other long-term consequences. However, 'fiscal constraints of emergency response agencies often limit the extent to which this strategy has been embraced' (Purtle et al., 2010: 3). According to these authors, the alternative, low-cost option of bilingual staff and volunteers does not work because of lack of linguistic and cultural diversity among them.

Therefore, in the following section, medical translation is looked at from the angle of crisis situations in order to highlight some of its most useful aspects in the above-mentioned phases as well as to point to some challenges.

Medical translation *vis-à-vis* crisis situations

In his review of the literature about crisis situations, Federici (2016: 5) points out that translation is 'the notable absentee' regarding 'planning, preparedness, training, resilience, and crisis management as they are considered among international and national bodies'. In reviewing recent research in the field (Montalt, Zethsen, & Karwacka, 2018), a similar conclusion can be reached from the opposite perspective: crisis situations can be called a notable absentee in medical translation literature.

Medical translation as a professional activity and an academic field has been conceptualized and shaped in the context of medicine and healthcare in developed economies. So far it has completely ignored needs beyond the traditional market (pharmaceutical laboratories, specialized publishers, medical manufacturers, national and international health organizations, and so on) and the opportunities offered by other, less visible and practically unknown realms of humanity, except for their superficial treatment and ephemeral presence in the media when a disaster of great magnitude takes place. One indication of this superficiality is that frequently the first (and, in fact, the only) thing that seems to matter the media in general is whether any national of the country has been involved in catastrophes that occur far away in remote places. Disasters have often become somewhat fictionalized shows and 'being a spectator of calamities taking place in another country [...] a quintessential modern experience' (Sontag, 2003: 16, cited in Federici, 2016). As pointed out by Federici, 'The fact that such calamities and their ensuing emergencies take place in other countries, other cultures, and to speakers of other languages is often underestimated' (16).

However, crisis situations offer rich opportunities for academic and professional development as well as for challenging long-established notions and premises in translation theory and practice regarding visibility, equivalence, comprehensibility, source and target contexts, the scope of translation – what counts as translation – the roles of translators and translations, ethics, translation *vs* multilingual communication, or the professional boundaries between translators, interpreters and mediators. Some of them will be pointed out in this section. In standard translation theory and practice, source and target communicative situations go hand in hand and are normally considered as parallel entities in a successive timeline: the target communicative situation somehow mirrors what happened in the source communicative situation. When a university textbook for medical students is translated say from English into Spanish, the translator's reasoning and imagination normally focus on the intention that the target context, participants and text should emulate what happened in the source context, participants and text as much as possible. The same can be said about a patient information leaflet, an informed consent or a clinical guide for doctors, to mention just a few examples.

Communicative situations that occur in the source context are somehow re-enacted in the target context by different actors, in a different language and in a different culture. The motivations for this re-enactment can be very varied: a new technique that needs to be shared with and applied by health professionals in another context; new advances in the treatment of a particular disease that patients in a given target context need to know about in order to manage their condition better. In the translation ethos, the notion of equivalence – formal, functional, pragmatic, etc. – is paramount. Translations' and translators' credibility and reliability are based on coherence or congruity between what is said in the source text and what is said in the target text.

In crisis situations, there is no original situation in the source language and culture that is somehow 'mimicked' in the target language and culture in order to achieve the same pragmatic effect. The target situation has no correlate. In the humanitarian ethos, aid comes from one side and travels to the other side, and not the other way around. In the same ethos, communication and translation seem to go from one side to the other side, and not the other way around. Just as medical help is transferred from A to B, medical information seems to be transferred from A to B in a unidirectional – and therefore asymmetric – communicative process. In the best cases, translation is still seen as a secondary, subordinate, instrumental tool to facilitate the transfer of factual information, to the extent that professional translators are often absent in the discourses and narratives of NGOs such as DWB, in which healthcare – and translation – are still doctor-centred.

In a crisis situation, communication is articulated in complex ways. The sender in the case in focus is DWB and the receivers are the victims. Communication does not take place in well-defined institutional contexts, such as a hospital or a health centre. It normally takes place in field conditions in a place devastated by natural or human-induced catastrophe. In these field conditions, different systems and institutional frameworks may coexist. Whatever is left of the health system – if indeed there was one – of the target country coexists with international agencies' human and material infrastructures. That is why traditional notions of contexts in translation studies are also problematic. In crisis situations, it is not so easy to construct the traditional dichotomy between source and target contexts. Rather we find a merging of provisional, ever-changing fragmented contexts. This is even more apparent when we think of displacement processes, refugee camps or tragedies at sea where the notion of a stable context is severely disrupted. This, of course, has an impact on communication and translation.

Among the different tasks of international organizations, governments, academic institutions and professional bodies devoted to medical preparedness, making sure that relevant research and technical knowledge is simplified, made accessible and 'translated' into practice is paramount. This metaphorical sense of 'translation as transfer of specialised knowledge' is, in fact, more literal and language- and culture-based than it would seem at first sight. Catastrophic events such as a nuclear detonation or the outbreak of a disease require all relevant information to be translated into protective actions for both responders and victims. This involves disseminating such information in a way that the final recipients will be able to access, understand and use. For example, a guide to key facts about Ebola such as the WHO's online Ebola virus disease is an intralingual simplified translation of a more detailed and technical guide, in this case 'Clinical care for survivors of Ebola virus disease. Interim guidance', addressed to health professionals (WHO, 2018). The guide to key facts is a derived version of a previous, more specialized text, and it is conceived of as a tool for prevention among the affected population. This use of translation is often overlooked in the crisis preparedness phase.

In the metalanguage of translation studies, the examples just mentioned would be cases of intralingual heterofunctional translation (García-Izquierdo & Montalt, 2013) – rewriting a text belonging to a specific genre into a text belonging to a different genre, normally less specialized, within the same language. Heterofunctional translation can also take place between different languages (interlingual heterofunctional translation). For example, medical translators may have to translate a research article in English into the form of a summary for patients in the target language. It may be that there is no single genre in the target culture that fulfils the needs of the target readers, in which case a more radical approach is required that consists of using attributes of different target or source genres, and combining them together into a creative unit which is a hybrid text.

Traditionally, medical translation's scope has been limited to expert–expert communication, focusing on biomedical discourse and technical registers, with terminological equivalence and accuracy being the cornerstones of the professional activity. Medical translators have thus concentrated on highly specialized genres used mainly in biomedical research, medical manufacturing, pharmaceutical production, regulatory activity, clinical practice and higher education. Expert–expert communication is the dominant pattern when DWB international medical teams from different countries gather and coordinate to provide the healthcare needed by the victims. According to our informants from the sources mentioned earlier, many of these expert–expert translation needs are often met by mediating languages, such as English or French, in the case of DWB.

If we look at written communication in the medical and healthcare contexts in industrialized countries, many of the genres are highly standardized, even internationalized. Think, for example, of how biomedical research is produced and communicated internationally: the Vancouver norms of style establish the structure, types of information, length, style, etc. of articles published in scientific journals, such as *The Lancet, British Medical Journal* or *New England Journal of Medicine*. Most forms of medical translation are currently genre-based. In preparedness, ready-made solutions and standardized language and communication can be relevant and useful before the catastrophe happens. But catastrophes are unpredictable and, once they happen, they force us to think in different, more creative *ad hoc* ways. We need to move beyond or away from thinking of discrete genres since clearly there are circumstances in which one-size-fits-all cannot apply. Translation needs to become transcreation, a creative hybrid which can respond to unpredictable situations in which ready-made solutions prepared in advance often fail to provide solutions for all cases and circumstances.

In recent years, expert–lay translation in healthcare has started to take centre stage. New social needs have given rise to new textual practices. In particular, patient-centredness – rooted in person-centred and client-centred therapy – is changing the way things have traditionally been done in healthcare and clinical communication. Biomedical and doctor-centred discourses coexist with more popular, patient-centred types of discourse and registers. In the medical field, expert–lay translation is particularly relevant in doctor–patient communication. In standard doctor–patient communication conceptual accuracy is of critical importance – in areas such as explanation of diseases, different synonyms for the same disease, different commercial names for the same drug, drug dosages and so on – but it is not sufficient on its own. Patients have specific information needs and relevance plays a key role in regulating interactions, in particular in crisis situations. The medical information provided to the patient may be very accurate but at the same time it may be totally irrelevant, both conceptually and/or culturally. In other words, some information might be missing that could help patients relate whatever information they are given with their own cultural experience and values. Or they could be overloaded with irrelevant or inopportune information. Framed in patient-centred healthcare, the notion of Patient Centred Translation (PCT) can be useful in crisis situations where different cultures and languages converge and coexist in any or all of the stages of humanitarian action.

In the transition from doctor-centred to patient-centred healthcare, lay–lay communication is becoming more important. Patients' narratives providing personal information, experience and perceptions about illness are shared with other patients, thus empowering those who write and those who read by exchanging non-biomedical perspectives on their individual therapeutic processes. In non-critical situations, patients are becoming the main stakeholders in healthcare and are starting to take a greater part in issues such as shared-decision-making.

In this patient-centred context, beyond highly technical texts, a plethora of new genres have emerged, from fact sheets or informed consents adapted for specific groups of patients to apps that are used by patients to monitor and manage their conditions. Comprehensibility together with cultural factors in medical communication is revolutionizing the task of the medical translator. As has been pointed out by TWB, comprehensibility is one of the crucial issues in crisis situations and depends on a number of factors, such as the profile of the readers – educational background, previous knowledge, needs for information, etc. – the broader context and specific situation in which they read and use the texts as well as the physical conditions of the reading process. Comprehensibility can be enhanced by combining different modes, formats and media effectively. Images, symbols, and other visual elements are often used to facilitate understanding in populations and situations where written verbal information is not enough. The use of images in medical communication has proved to be fruitful (Prieto-Velasco & Montalt, 2019): they may have different functions, from signalling the progression of a text to establishing a warning, etc. In low-literacy or illiterate patients, multimodality may offer effective solutions.

To be assessed accurately, comprehensibility must include not only linguistic, but also cognitive and communicative, issues. Readability formulae have traditionally been used to measure how easy or difficult texts are to understand. A number of critical voices have questioned their validity and usefulness and have proposed alternative methodologies, such as usability tests. Mixed-methods analysis combining readability formulae, experts' analysis and focus groups have also been proposed for assessing the comprehensibility of both original and translated texts addressed to patients (García-Izquierdo & Montalt, 2013). Comprehensibility tests for crisis situations can benefit from quantitative and qualitative research in this area in a limited way. The physical and emotional conditions of the reading process of victims of a disaster differ greatly from those of a reader in a normal, non-critical situation. More research is needed in the problem of comprehensibility and multimodality in critical, extraordinary circumstances.

The feedback that can be obtained by canvassing the opinions of patients in clinical settings or focus groups in stable conditions is clearly out of the question when victims of disasters have lost everything and are lucky if they have even the most rudimentary conditions in which to simply survive. So how can translators learn about the social and psychological impact of trauma caused by catastrophic natural or man-made disasters? How can they learn about the added suffering resulting from the breakdown of any semblance of organized society when lawlessness rules and it is everyman for himself, and when perhaps former neighbours take the opportunity to settle old scores which may have been festering for generations?

They can be encouraged to read eyewitness testimonies of helpers working on the ground, memoires written by survivors and first-hand accounts of dedicated journalists and broadcasters, men and women, who risk their own lives in war-ravaged zones and who themselves largely work through interpreters. Translators/interpreters can get initial experience of the later aftermath of humanitarian crisis in their own countries. In those countries providing health and social care to immigrants and refugees they can become aware of the many challenges such people face in managing their day-to-day affairs. These challenges may be cultural, linguistic, legal, medical, educational, practical, etc. When misunderstandings arise, translators may also gain insights into under-the-radar cultural values.

An often-disregarded source of information is fiction. Novels enable us to vicariously experience situations and conditions we rarely meet in real life and to observe the consequences of and reactions to the behaviour of fictional characters.

Novels, films and plays, both in the original and in translation, also offer a window on different cultural values, beliefs and expectations, and may sensitize us into appropriate modes of expression in unfamiliar territories. Emotions play a crucial role in human verbal and non-verbal interaction. And yet we know little about the way words and other types of symbols trigger certain emotions and how those emotions affect communication. The emotions arising from the devastating effects of humanitarian crises could be alleviated but might equally be exacerbated depending on how the message is conveyed to them. Language used appropriately can ease the emotional burden of victims. But this involves, first of all, being aware of how it will be received on an emotional level by victims. If used negatively, it could add an extra layer of discomfort on the sufferers. There is a further issue with emotions – in different cultures they are expressed in different ways. Translators need to be aware of issues such as these as well as cultural differences which might affect the expression and reception of language.

Translators are not only crucial in the target context where aid is received. Our informants say they are also instrumental in the source contexts where the resources come from. Awareness-raising campaigns in the media, information provided to members in the newsletters, webpages, videoed testimonies of DWB workers on YouTube, executive reports that are briefed to the media and governmental bodies, educational materials for school children, etc. all require translation to raise both awareness and money. Advocacy is another area in which translation plays an important role. Humanitarian action also takes place in the source contexts – that is, the countries where asylum seekers often wish to settle. NGOs such as Medical Justice or Doctors of the World advocate for universal health coverage and help detainees in need of interpreters to go to the doctor. Medical Justice offers independent medical advice and assessments to immigration detainees and writes medico-legal reports (MLRs) which can be used to support asylum claims and letters outlining significant medical concerns. In the case of refugee doctors living in the UK and receiving support from NGOs such as the Refugee Council, many of them have professional and humanitarian experiences that could be shared to provide cross-cultural awareness to future responders, including translators and interpreters.

In-the-cloud and on-the-ground medical translation

In this section, two complementary approaches of medical translation and communication in crisis settings will be presented. The first is based on digital technologies and distance translation and communication ('in the cloud'), in particular a number of apps that have been developed in recent times. The second is based on human, situated communication in specific locations ('on the ground'). These two approaches can be used to provide solutions for the different stages of crisis situations.

In-the-cloud

As pointed out by one of our informants, audiovisual formats, mobile apps and social networks are starting to be used by DWB in crisis situations. There are places where international personnel cannot reach and, in such cases, telemedicine can be very helpful. Human translators are sometimes used in telemedicine in critical situations. In addition to the barriers of distance and lack of physical access to the places where aid is needed, speed in the transmission of information is also a critical factor in crisis situations. In recent years, social networks like Twitter have been used successfully by humanitarian organizations. Empirical studies such as that carried out by Yoo et al. (2016) suggest that social media networks are effective at passing along information during humanitarian crises that require urgent information dissemination.

Mobile phone connectivity has been used as a tool to harness many different forms of data and provide practical solutions in the field (Federici, 2016: 15). Concepts such as mHealth (mobile health) and eHealth (electronic health) have been developed in the last few years thanks to technological innovations and in response to a growing need for Universal Health Coverage (UHC). According to a recent survey by the WHO (2016) more than half of WHO Member States had an eHealth strategy, and 90 per cent of eHealth strategies reference the objectives of UHC (Universal Health Coverage) or its key elements. This means that digital infrastructures are increasingly available for use in times of humanitarian crises.

The area of mobile health (mHealth) is particularly noteworthy in crisis situations because it provides a series of advantages in the transmission of vital information. Existing technologies currently used in mHealth can also be made available in crisis situations. This is the case of *mSehat*, an integrated, Android and web-based, multimedia-enabled mobile platform for frontline health workers, which includes accredited social health activists (ASHAs), Anganwadi workers (AWWs), auxiliary nurse midwives (ANMs) and health programme managers. *mSehat* was named after the Hindi word for health, 'sehat', and assists these workers via an integrated service-delivery platform accessible via smartphones, tablets and web-based dashboard reporting (WHO, 2016: 51). From a translation point of view, perhaps the most interesting feature of this technology is that it provides the information in several local languages and dialects. In addition, the content is visual and it includes voice for low-literacy or disabled users. The goal of the programme is to accelerate the reduction of maternal, neonatal and child mortality and lower the total fertility rate in Uttar Pradesh.

ReliefWeb – the leading humanitarian information source on global disasters, a specialized digital service of the UN Office for the Coordination of Humanitarian Affairs (OCHA) – has created *RW Crises*, an app which provides comprehensive coverage of over twenty crisis-affected countries. It provides the latest humanitarian updates, disaster trends and country overviews as well as links to in-country contacts, data sets, and jobs and training opportunities. Updates can be followed in real time and the content saved for offline use.

Another example of mHealth tools is *Show Me for Emergencies*. This has been designed for emergency staff and people with communication needs such as difficulty understanding English, hearing impairments and cognitive disabilities, and family members coping with intense stress. It uses easy-to-understand icons for two-way communication during an emergency.

Apps developed by non-governmental organizations, such as *The MSF Medical Guidelines app*, developed by DWB, aim to improve access to medical guidelines for field workers. *Red Cross Emergency* is an all-inclusive app that combines more than thirty-five different severe weather and emergency alerts from natural to man-made, giving users real-time information about incidents that are about to occur in their location. First Aid by American Red Cross provides free lifesaving first-aid instruction and disaster preparedness information, including videos, interactive quizzes and simple step-by-step advice.

There are apps that specialize in supporting responders to disasters triggered by natural hazards such as earthquakes, tornados, hurricanes, or floods, all provided by American Red Cross. They provide access to local real-time information, warning alerts, power outages, recommendations of what to do under certain circumstances or even customizable 'I'm safe' notification.

More victim-centred apps are being developed, such as MedlinePlus, that provide access to consumer-oriented health information on disaster topics in English and Spanish. Some apps, such as *PTSD* or *Provider Resilience*, offer mental and emotional aid, in particular information about post-traumatic stress disorder (PTSD), including educational resources, information about professional care, a self-assessment tool, opportunities to find support and tools to help manage the stresses of daily life with PTSD. This type of app can be used to address mental health issues in the recovery phase.

Other apps are more specialized and focus on specific fields, such as nuclear accidents, hazardous materials and biosafety in bioterrorism crises. For example, *REMM* (Radiation Emergency Medical Management) provides guidance about clinical diagnosis and treatment of radiation injuries during radiological and nuclear emergencies. It was developed by the US National Library of Medicine and the Office of the Assistant Secretary for Preparedness and Response, US Department of Health and Human Services. *WISER* (Wireless Information System for Emergency Responders) assists first responders in Hazmat incidents, in particular in identification support, containment and suppression advice, and medical treatment information. *TOXNET* from the National Library of Medicine covers toxicology, hazardous chemicals, environmental health and related areas. *The Laboratory Response Network Rule-Out and Refer* app provides easy access to critical information regarding six potential bioterrorism agents – Bacillus anthracis, Brucella species, Yersinia pestis, Francisella tularensis, Burkholderia pseudomallei and Burkholderia mallei.

If medical translators have a detailed knowledge of these and other digital resources in the cloud, they can develop an extremely useful expertise in crisis situations. In addition, many of these apps exist only in English, and translation into other languages may be needed. There is a potentially rich field of translation activity here.

On-the-ground

Many of the information and communication needs in a crisis situation cannot be covered by digital technologies. Here we consider *ad hoc* mediation at both the individual and population levels involving face-to-face interactions as well as printed means: for example, translating in the ward of a refugee camp, producing trans-semiotic messages (images, symbols, spoken words, written words in different languages, etc.) to warn against mines in a specific area walked through by refugees, communicating with victims on a boat at sea in the rescue process or writing and translating posters to prevent the spread of a communicable disease in a specific population where different dialects are spoken. Face-to-face interactions are critical in a number of contexts, such as (a) gaining access to the crisis, (b) responding on the ground initially and (c) providing healthcare in the aftermath of the disaster.

Without access to crisis locations, material and human aid does not reach the people and places where is needed. According to our DWB informants, gaining access is both vital and increasingly difficult, not only in cases of disasters triggered by natural hazards, but also in war zones where armies, organized guerrillas, insurgent groups and so on try to prevent any interference that might lead to their loss of control over the people and the territory. It is important that local leaders perceive the responders – in this case DWB – as neutral and independent as possible. Access to the crisis depends on their knowing the NGOs involved well, trusting them and accepting them. Respondents' safety and capacity for action depend on this initial stage. Interpreters play a crucial role in this negotiation process in which not only linguistic and cultural issues but also rhetorical, ideological and interpersonal ones matter. 'What is really important in negotiations is the contact with local leaders from both sides. The key of your work is in the ability to establish local networks of contacts and include the leaders of that particular territory' (227).

In the early stages of medical response on the ground, the translators who work together with health professionals are more than linguistic and cultural mediators. One of our informants defined them in this way: 'They are far more than translators; they are the door to the world.' They know the local populations well because often they are members of them – they normally translate into and from their language or dialect to English and have the key to unlock fully new systems of values, beliefs and ideas about life, health, and illness. Another informant defines translators as 'their teachers' because they provide the context and background information needed to make sense of communication with the victims.

In the relief and recovery stages, on-the-ground translation can be used in creative and innovative ways. In a project about AIDS and awareness about HIV, DWB offered an imaginative solution in which medical knowledge was combined with choral music and relevant messages were constructed and spread among the population at risk.[1] Some of the messages dealt with different types of treatments, consequences of the disease or people at risk: 'A person swallowed pills and the virus was no longer active', 'A young person has died. And others are sick to the point of death', 'In Zimbabwe we have a problem due to VHI-[in original for HIV] It has no cure. Promiscuous people put all the nation at risk', 'There are antiretrovirals, there are condoms, I cannot sit, I cannot rest while the virus is here', 'Look at us, the condom works, look at us, the pills work'.

Although the contents are simple, they are powerfully formulated and staged in a way that is fully embedded in the traditions and values of the target culture and relevant for the society that needs a greater individual and collective awareness of the fight against HIV. This campaign aims to change the habits of individuals and to mobilize the whole community. Instead of a top-down approach in which information is transferred from the specialist down to the citizens at risk, it is a bottom-up process where the citizens themselves engage in an appeal to and dialogue with their own neighbours through choral music and dancing. This formula empowers not only the citizens who receive the information but those who actively engage in the process of spreading it. Any such form of social staging of relevant medical messages is powerful and effective. Citizens themselves are the translators of medical knowledge into their own cultural scripts and resources, and thus become promoters of health in their communities.

Together with prepared solutions that have been created before-hand ready to be used – such as, for example, medical vocabularies in different languages or apps, there is plenty of room and need for *ad hoc*, context-bound, bottom-up, creative solutions.

Concluding remarks

In sharp contrast with other disciplines and professions, such as doctors, nurses or anthropologists, translators as scholars and consultants have no discernible presence in medical humanitarian situations. We need to find out how translators perceive medical humanitarian practice; which aspects should be seen as priorities for translation-oriented research; and how translators use translation, interpreting and mediation in humanitarian contexts. More research, training programmes and critical thinking are clearly needed in many areas regarding medical translation in crisis situations, some of which have been briefly pointed out in this chapter. They can be summarized in a model based on the three dimensions of Aristotelian rhetoric: *logos, ethos* and *pathos*. They are inter-related and coexist in more or less conscious and visible ways in medical translation in crisis situations.

Logos. When applied to systematized medical knowledge, *logos*, in the classical sense of intelligent and rational thinking and speaking, fulfils a critical function. The accuracy and reliability of the medical content and the terminology of the messages are paramount. Here clarity and comprehensibility are particularly important. Logos also refers to logistics, and, more particularly, language and translation logistics, that is, the rational organization and distribution of relevant information, the creation of effective messages and coordinated communication, using the most appropriate on-the-ground and in-the-cloud formats, genres, channels, modes and technological tools. Crisis situations often require crises exercises in which crisis management team competences are performed through simulations. In 'A New Method and Tools to Scenario Design for Crisis Management Exercises', Limousin et al. (2016) deal with a method created to help those who design scenarios for crisis functional exercises and point out the importance of dramaturgy in simulation. Using professionally trained role-players in simulated interactions can also contribute to a better understanding of communication and translation in crisis situations, and to reflective practice of the responders.

Ethos. I use ethos to refer to the values and practices that distinguish one person, profession, institution, organization or society from others. The humanitarian sector has generally adopted the four principles of humanity, impartiality, independence and neutrality, commonly referred to as humanitarian principles. NGOs such as DWB have their own ethos as actors playing in the international arena of crisis situations. They struggle to be perceived and recognized as having a specific set of defining values – such as respect for human life, dignity, compassion and impartiality. Likewise, translators and interpreters have their own professional and personal ethos. They can position themselves in a range of ethical roles from mere conduit of medical information to facilitator of comprehension or victim advocate. A third level of ethos pertains to the medical profession's own ethical codes that regulate their activities – including the way they use language and communication. Last but not least, ethos also refers to the values of the target culture, the social practices in which the victims involved in crisis situations take part. Both culture and social practices in the target population determine their values about health and illness, and have an impact on the way information is received and messages are understood or misunderstood. Professional and non-professional translators need support in the form of useful resources of all kinds, ethical principles that combine medical ethics and translation ethics, social visibility and a supportive translation-centred discourse that empowers their active role in interdisciplinary teams. One of the worrying impressions when analysing documentary materials published by MSF is the lack of visibility of translators, not only in institutional discourse found in the webpages, but also in personal narratives of its humanitarian workers.

Pathos. I here use pathos in the classical way to mean both experience and suffering. Victims in crisis situations go through the fear and trauma of displacement, terror, disease and abuse. Personal and collective suffering is what really defines victims in these situations. Feelings and emotions cannot be overlooked and cannot be removed from the logos and ethos dimensions. Hence empathy is a critical component. Both patients' narratives and humanitarian workers' narratives can shed light into how communication and translation take place in crisis situations. Giving them a voice, making it audible and listening to them are important steps forward. *Pathos* is not restricted to the victims but also includes the responders, including health professionals, translators and other professionals and non-professionals. From a multilingual and multicultural perspective, *pathos* poses the challenge of how feelings and emotions are expressed in different languages and cultures or how certain messages can trigger different emotional responses in given individuals and cultural groups. In Aristotelian rhetoric, *ethos* is very much focused on the source's credibility, the speaker's/author's authority. *Pathos* rebalances this monological, unidirectional view of communication and translation, and takes the victim as a person centre stage on equal terms with the rest of participants. This dialogical shift is perhaps one of the key challenges in medical translation – and in communication in general – in the endeavour to offer truly humanitarian, victim-centred aid.

Acknowledgements

This chapter presents the findings of research carried out with the financial support of Universitat Jaume I, Spain, and the Spanish Ministry of Economy and Competitiveness.

Note

1   The example can be retrieved from the following online clip: https://www.youtube.com/watch?v=wripQUIRBac.

References

Bolton, P. A., and Weiss, W. M. (2001). 'Communicating across Cultures: Improving Translation to Improve Complex Emergency Program Effectiveness'. *Prehospital and Disaster Medicine* 16(4): 252–256.

Federici, F. M. (2016). Introduction: A State of Emergency for Crisis Communication. In F. M. Federici (ed.), *Mediating Emergencies and Conflicts. Frontline Translating and Interpreting*, 1–29. New York, NY: Palgrave Macmillan.

Filmer, D., and Federici, F. M. (2018). 'Mediating Migration Crises: Sicily and the Languages of the Despair'. *European Journal of Language Policy* 10(2): 229–253.

Fredriksson, M., Olsson, E. K., and Pallas, J. (2014). 'Creativity Caged in Translation: A Neo-Institutional Perspective on Crisis Communication'. *Revista internacional de relaciones públicas* 8(4): 65–84.

García-Izquierdo, I., and Montalt, V. (2013). 'Equigeneric and Intergeneric Translation in Patient-Centred Care'. *Hermes. Journal of Language Communication in Business* 26(51): 39–51.

Granero-Molina, J., Jiménez-Lasserrrotte, M. d. M., Fernández-Sola, C., Hernández-Padilla, J. M., Sánchez Hernández, F., and López Domene, E. (2019). 'Cultural Issues in the Provision of Emergency Care to Irregular Migrants Who Arrive in Spain by Small Boats'. *Journal of Transcultural Nursing* 30(4): 371–379. doi: 1043659618803149.

Howick, J., Moscrop, A., Mebius, A., Fanshawe, T. R., Lewith, G., Bishop, F. L., Mistiaen, P., Roberts, N. W., Dieninytė, E., Hu, X. Y., and Aveyard, P. (2018). 'Effects of Empathic and Positive Communication in Healthcare Consultations: A Systematic Review and Meta-Analysis'. *Journal of the Royal Society of Medicine* 111(7): 240–252.

Limousin, P., Tixier, J., Bony-Dandrieux, A., Chapurlat, V., and Sauvagnargues, S. (2016). 'A New Method and Tools to Scenarios Design for Crisis Management Exercises'. *Chemical Engineering Transactions* 53: 319–324.

Montalt, V., Zethsen, K. K., and Karwacka, W. (2018). 'Medical Translation in the 21st Century-Challenges and Trends'. *MonTI. Monografías de Traducción e Interpretación* 10: 27–42. Available online: //www.e-revistes.uji.es/index.php/monti/article/view/3684/3012 (accessed 22 March 2019).

Peleg, K. (2013). 'Disaster and Emergency Medicine – A Conceptual Introduction'. *Frontiers in Public Health* 1(44). doi: 10.3389/fpubh.2013.00044.

Prieto-Velasco, J. A., and Montalt, V. (2019). 'Encouraging Legibility and Comprehensibility through Multimodal Patient Information Guides'. *Linguistica Antverpiensia, New Series–Themes in Translation Studies* 17. Available online: https://lans-tts.uantwerpen.be/index.php/LANS-TTS/article/view/476/423 (accessed 22 March 2019).

Purtle, J. P., Siddiqui, N. J., and Andrulis, D. P. (2010). 'Language Issues and Barriers'. In K. B. Penuel and M. Statler (eds), *Encyclopedia of Disaster Relief*, 379–382. Thousand Oaks, CA and London: Sage.

Sontag, S. (2003). *Regarding the Pain of Others*. New York, NY: Penguin Books.

TWB (2017). *Putting Language on the Map in the European Refugee Response*. Available online: https://translatorswithoutborders.org/wp-content/uploads/2017/04/Putting-language-on-the-map.pdf (accessed 22 March 2019).

UNHCR (2018). *Mid-Year Trends 2018*. Geneva: United Nations High Commissioner for Refugees. Available online: https://www.unhcr.org/statistics/unhcrstats/5c52ea084/mid-year-trends-2018.html (accessed 22 March 2019).

WHO (2016). *Global Diffusion of eHealth: Making Universal Health Coverage Achievable: Report of the Third Global Survey on eHealth*. Retrieved from Geneva; New York, NY: https://apps.who.int/iris/bitstream/handle/10665/252529/9789241511780-eng.pdf; jsessionid=58E8C6F4ED8C632395B1A6A0B4B50100?sequence=1 (accessed 22 March 2019).

WHO (2018). *Ebola Virus Disease*. World Health Organization. Available online: https://www.who.int/en/news-room/fact-sheets/detail/ebola-virus-disease (accessed 22 March 2019).

Yoo, E., Rand, W., Eftekhar, M., and Rabinovich, E. (2016). 'Evaluating Information Diffusion Speed and Its Determinants in Social Media Networks during Humanitarian Crises.' *Journal of Operations Management* 45: 123–133.

6

Intercultural Mediation in Healthcare: Thematic Analysis, from the Interpreters' Perspective

Izabel Emilia Telles de Vasconcelos Souza

Medical interpreters have an important role in the provision of culturally competent care. Cultural differences in intercultural communication are often a barrier to high-quality healthcare. Providing culturally and linguistically appropriate services is gaining adherence worldwide as part of an effort to eliminate health disparities, minimize risks and thus increase patient safety (Angelelli, 2004, 2015; Angelelli & Baer, 2015). How intercultural mediation affects patient outcomes, patient satisfaction and patient compliance is still not very well understood by healthcare providers or the public at large (though some studies exploring the issue are emerging, for instance Cox & Gutiérrez, 2016; Ryan et al., 2017). In healthcare settings, interpreters mediate language and culture. The data presented in this chapter were obtained in a doctoral study carried out between 2011 and 2015, exploring the professional medical and healthcare interpreters' opinions about addressing cultural issues in healthcare. As they provide culturally and linguistically appropriate interpreting services, this chapter will focus on the advantages and disadvantages of intercultural mediation (Souza, 2016).

Overall the study adopted a qualitative/quantitative mixed-method approach (Brannen, 2005; Cresswell et al., 2003) in order to facilitate the triangulation of data. The eighteen semi-structured interviews lasted approx. 45–60 minutes. The interviews took place in the United States, Israel, Australia, New Zealand and Japan. The interviews in Israel and Japan were conducted with a professional medical interpreter and included confirmation of meaning of each response. The interviews were complemented by a focus group held in June 2015. The focus group allowed data to flow from the interaction of participants and provided an environment for a deeper discussion of the topic at hand. Last, the opinions and perspectives of 423 healthcare interpreters, working in 25 countries, were collected by means of an online survey. The online survey was designed by utilizing phraseology of the responses from the interviews, allowing for the initial data responses to be quantified and compared to the initial data set, and for there to be enough response distribution to make comparisons by country of practice. One interpreter requested to send in an essay on the subject as dada, and therefore the study produced four data sets. The sections that follow focus on the presentation, and analysis of the interpreters' professional opinions about the advantages and disadvantages of their cultural work. The themes emerging from their answers seemed to cluster around medical concepts, and will be grouped into two main areas: (1) the reasons behind cultural interventions, and (2) the difficulties encountered when doing this work. The subthemes showcase how intercultural mediation is experienced by these professionals.

Reasons for cultural intervention

Interviewees had very enlightening responses to the question regarding the benefits and advantages of intercultural mediation. They gave the reasons for their intervention, as well as the positive results, which acted as motivators for their actions. These reasons go beyond interpreting, and beyond asking for clarifications. The reasons listed explain the mindset of the interpreter in practice, and the specific tasks medical interpreters undertake in a healthcare environment to achieve the objectives and results they are looking for.

Checking for Understanding

The first reason for intervening, according to one of the interviewees, is described it as follows:

> There are more advantages than disadvantages. I only intervene if I see there is a gap in understanding. If I get the sense that it is due to culture then I pause and intervene and explain what the cultural issue means, to both parties so both parties are on the same page (transparency and impartiality). It dissipates frustrations or fear especially in the case of the client (patient), like when they are expecting the diagnosis. It increases clarity and peace of mind.

First, we must take note that the interpreter states that he/she intervenes 'only' when there is a gap in understanding. That may reflect the fact that interpreters do not have to intervene regularly, or often. They intervene when needed. The interpreter describes her concern for the patient's right to meaningful communication, which can happen only when both parties understand each other. Meaningful communication is an important concept in the provision of equitable healthcare services. According to this participant, a gap in understanding requires interpreter intervention. This comment relates to a task in addition to 'interpreting' from one language into another. In some more restrictive settings, interpreters need to limit themselves to strict linguistic interpreting. However, medical interpreters, also called healthcare interpreters, 'check for understanding' as part of their standard of practice (IMIA and EDC, 2007). The premise here is that without understanding, there is no communication, only the transmission of information. In healthcare, accurate diagnosis or treatment is not possible without accurate and clear communication and understanding. The only way the interpreter can check for understanding is by stepping out of the conduit role of interpreting messages, so the interpreter will then speak on his/her own behalf as a professional to seek clarification of some issue that may be cultural, or not.

Dissipating fear, stress and frustration

The participant also alludes to the fact that understanding provides clarity and peace of mind to the patient. This demonstrates his/her concern for how the patient is receiving the information and how it affects the patient emotionally. Seeking medical attention is a stressful endeavour. Whenever a patient has a different cultural background and does not speak the language of service, it is safe to assume that the level of stress may be greater. Stress can even affect the level of understanding in one's primary language. The participant describes how she is attempting to dissipate a certain level of frustration and fear, mostly by the patient, about his or her diagnosis. Increasing clarity and peace of mind are the intangible benefits to the patient. Most people, who have not experienced requiring care in a language one does not speak, cannot imagine the level of stress and discomfort this can cause a patient. Another participant touched on the same point:

> The advantage for the patient is that he is at ease, and can get comfortable. They feel included, it's very important for them to feel included and respected. They feel that their culture is being taken into account, it is important.

Ensuring cultural inclusiveness

It seems that in addition to providing comfort and ease (diminishing stress) to patients, these cultural services help the patient feel culturally included and respected (Weech-Maldonado et al., 2012). Inclusion can go a long way in improving patient trust levels and can ease collaboration in treatment plans simply by being understood. Trust in the provider increases patient compliance (Rolfe et al., 2014). Understanding how to incorporate patient cultural preferences is an important move towards a culturally competent patient-centred system. The patient-centred care model of shared decision-making between providers and patients is based on a partnership of equals (Wenger, 1995). Patients who do not adhere to physician instructions or recommended follow-up treatment plans are difficult to manage, and often present significant risk management concerns for the physician (Bontempo, 2012). Compliance increases if patients are given clear and understandable information about their condition and progress in a sincere and responsive way. How patients feel about the message and the messenger may be a factor in their compliance (Segal, 2007). Cultural inclusion is a component of the provision of culturally competent services.

Educating providers and patients

Survey participants mentioned other benefits of addressing cultural issues, focusing on the educational component of intercultural mediation:

1. Providers learn about the variety of cultures.
2. One of the immediate advantages is clarification to one or both parties, who are then better informed. Awareness for medical staff of things that they will probably deal with if they continue to serve LEP (Limited English Proficient) communities of that particular ethnicity.
3. The provider can understand more and it can open his mind, his horizons, to understand the patient, where they are coming from, from a cultural aspect. There are no disadvantages; I can't think of one. Discussing the cultural issue helps the provider and the patient. First, Western medicine is exposed to our traditions and then they can understand the patients better and give them what they want.

Clarifications and culturally relevant information produce better-informed providers and staff as they continue to serve patients who are culturally and linguistically diverse. It seems that medical interpreters, through their interventions, may have a significant role in educating providers at the moment where learning is most relevant. When engaging in informing providers or patients about certain cultural issues, it seems interpreters act as cultural educators. According to Jalbert (1998), these would be the roles of *cultural informant*, when enquiring or explaining a cultural concept to the provider, or *healthcare professional*, when enquiring or explaining a medical practice to the patient. Explaining a medical practice to a patient is not the same but can be confused to the giving medical advice. It can be a statement that explains some medical protocol in the country of service, such as, for example, that in Japan prescriptions expire in four days, or that in the United States all patients are asked whether or not they drink alcoholic beverages. Providers have access to cultural training at different levels, but the best learning moment is when the specific cultural issue in question takes place. In addition, no cultural training can predict all of the cultural situations that will ensue. Providers learn the appropriate cultural information as needed, and, with that information at hand, they can decide whether or not to culturally adapt their service. The reality is that cultural competency program needs to include micro adaptations on a case-by-case basis.

Enhancing the patient experience

Another statement from an interviewee discussed her role as intercultural mediator:

> The providers feel that they get more than linguistic help. For the role of bridging, the staff knows me well, after 15 years; even some patients know me well. We are staff interpreters and are allowed to advocate, we are part of the healthcare team, and are much more than a voice (the patient's voice). We are part of the healthcare team. Helping with even a smile, making the patients appreciate those things. It's an ambassadorship, so the patients know that you are there to make their experience better. When there is this trust, then they will tell you. For example, the patient may tell me 'I didn't mention but I used this herb.' They feel more comfortable stating this to us rather than someone else. I never presume that I have any answers, but I want the patients to communicate in the manner that they feel comfortable. Well, certainly they have a better understanding of how the healthcare system works in the U.S. so they can adjust themselves to receive good care in the U.S.

Above, the interviewee explains that the institution she works for sees her as more than a voice, or a mouthpiece for the patient. In the case of staff interpreters, they are treated as healthcare professionals (not clinical) but nonetheless as members of the healthcare team. In a humanitarian setting, such as healthcare, the ultimate goal is for all to work together to treat the patient, so collaboration for a positive health outcome for the patient is the ultimate goal. This means that the interpreter may be seen as an integral piece of the puzzle of providing intercultural healthcare. She speaks about being an ambassador for the institution, and that part of her task is to make their (the patients) experience better. It seems intercultural mediation would be one of the means to improve the patient experience. An interpreter who comes to a hospital for the first time as the 'outside contracted' linguist may not have the full context or latitude to act in such a manner, but will nonetheless have interactional tools to ensure that both parties are satisfied.

Her use of the word *advocate* is broad, as she refers to it as any action that involves more than being a voice for the patient or provider. She is not speaking of representing the patient in any position against the healthcare team, as she is part of that healthcare team. The term *advocacy* is used loosely in English, with many connotations, as it can mean simply 'promoting an idea', as in advocating for clear communication and a positive patient experience. In other languages, the term *advocacy* has a more legal connotation, which often generates confusion even within the interpreting field. Interpreters are impartial mediators, and, as such, do not 'represent' either party at any time.[1]

Ensuring patient safety

One of the focus group participants explains another guiding force in cultural interventions:

> The first thing I think of is patient safety. If we can intervene and help the patient and provider stay on track, great. The focus needs to be on the medical reason why we're all there. Cultural competence, and emotional, or other issues are secondary. This is the standard use: The patient safety model. It trumps everything else.

All the focus group participants agreed with this statement and stated that patient safety, through improved effective and safe communication, was actually the primary driver and benefit of addressing cultural issues. Here, the focus was on the medical goals and ethics or interpreting goals. This may sound surprising to readers who see interpreters solely as linguists, and who do not necessarily see the *healthcare* interpreter as a healthcare professional. This participant's assertion showcases the importance of the medical goals of the encounter, and ultimately of the patient's safety. The Latin motto *Primum non nocere*, also known as the Hippocratic oath, when translated into English, means *first, do no harm*. It is the highest guiding ethical principle for healthcare providers all over the world. Accurate communication will assist in ensuring no patient harm takes place, therefore ensuring patient safety is maintained. This may be the most important benefit from the perspective of the patient's health. This also showcases that, when medical interpreters are treated as integral members of the healthcare team, they seem to internalize the same goals as the rest of the healthcare team. Another participant describes this safety issue:

> [cultural intervention] could help a safety issue or even prevent an issue due to a misinterpretation of a behaviour that is being construed when it is common in that culture, such as coining, or, in Somali communities, the burning of the hands, etc.

As the participant describes above, cultural interventions can prevent a sentinel event, or legal impact or liability, as the newsworthy Willie Ramirez case which cost the hospital $70 million due to an interpretation error (Price-Wise, 2015) that left the patient a quadriplegic. There are other lawsuits that have been brought about by patients related to interpretation errors (IMIA, 2018), so it is not surprising that medical interpreters worry about preventing errors that may cause sentinel events. In both cases, the linguistic goal of interpreting seems to be secondary to the medical goals of ensuring patient safety as an interpreter, by addressing any issue that may affect clear communication, including the cultural ones.

Improving the therapeutic rapport

Another theme in the interpreted communicative event (IMIA & EDC, 2007) was the effort of improving the provider–patient therapeutic rapport, which has a direct relationship to patient compliance of treatment. Why would the therapeutic rapport require improvement or enhancement? As stated by respondents, the fear and distrust can be lower in a linguistically and culturally concordant interaction. Language and culture discordant providers and patients may be unfamiliar with each other and may even feel frustrated with the need to communicate with a third party. Several interpreters discuss the presence of frustration and their efforts to dissipate frustration and fear, as well as their efforts to increase the peace of mind for the patient. One even mentions that with his/her assistance the staff and providers can take care of the patients calmly, without being upset. Other responses included the following:

1. [addressing cultural issues] dissipates frustrations or fear, especially in the case of the client (patient), like when they are expecting the diagnosis. It increases clarity and peace of mind.
2. Hospital staff members, including healthcare providers, dieticians, etc., can take care of foreign patients calmly, not upset.
3. A connection is made that wouldn't be made without it. Patients are able to communicate and know that they are being understood.
4. The providers feel that they got more with that help. To give better treatment, to give more peace of mind to the patient. The doctor can understand his/her patient better.
5. One of the immediate advantages is clarification to one or both parties, who are then better informed. Awareness for medical staff for things that they will probably deal with if they continue to serve these communities of a particular ethnicity. It could help a safety issue or even prevent a legal issue, due to a misinterpretation of a behaviour that is being construed when it is common in that culture, such as coining, or, in Somali communities, the burning of the hands.
6. Everyone is learning from each other, so the differences are diminishing.
7. The provider can understand more and it can open his mind, his horizons, to understand the patient, where they are coming from, from a cultural aspect.
8. Providers learn about the variety of cultures.

Three other participants spoke of the provider–patient rapport and the relation between facilitating this relationship and addressing cultural issues:

1. It is important that we support the patient–provider relationship, to facilitate that relationship. Anything the medical interpreter does not understand or identifies as a cultural barrier we must ask for a clarification and ask the patient to explain, we can't make the assumption that the patient can't.
2. Sometimes the relationship between the provider and the patient can be difficult. In the case where the patient cannot trust the provider, for example.
3. We help create bonds (between provider and patient). If they do not discuss it [the cultural issue], it will affect the communication (negatively).

The fact that the provider and patient are from different cultures and cannot communicate creates a wider separation or gap than a more culturally and linguistically congruent provider and patient would have. This means that improving the provider–patient rapport is one way to close this intercultural gap.

Addressing patient comfort

Focus group participants also discussed how addressing cultural issues is a way to address patient comfort, which is a task for medical interpreters in the IMIA Standards of Practice (IMIA & EDC, 2007). A participant stated the following: 'We don't do it only for patient safety reasons, but also because the patient is not comfortable. Then the staff will understand it is due to the patient's culture, and not something else.' This standard relates to the patient's comfort in all of its forms: the physical, mental, emotional and spiritual. One participant commented on how he believes telephonic interpreting affects intercultural mediation:

> There is really no relationship over the phone but in person the provider gets it that they need to partner up with the interpreter and that brings satisfaction to our work.

It appears that the participant above discusses the need to partner, or work with, the provider, and that the lack of physical presence of the interpreter on the phone may make this more difficult.

Online results quantify agreement with themes

The online survey participants were given eight examples of possible advantages, as summarized in Table 6.1. These cover three main themes: (a) improving the therapeutic rapport of the patient and provider, over the rapport with the interpreter (1,2,3); (b) improving understanding in intercultural communication (4); and (c) educating participants to a more culturally competent environment.

In medical interpreting standards of practice, the medical interpreter promotes the provider–patient therapeutic rapport (IMIA, EDC, 2007). According to the survey participants, the top advantage of addressing cultural issues from this list was the improvement of the rapport between the provider and the patient, with 70.90 per cent level of agreement. This figure supports the qualitative data, where interviewees and focus group participants discussed

Table 6.1 Advantages of addressing cultural issues ($n = 423$)

	Answer Choices	%
1	The rapport between the interpreter and the provider improves.	37.30%
2	The rapport between the interpreter and the patient improves.	31.97%
3	The rapport between the provider and the patient improves.	70.90%
4	There is a better understanding of the reasons behind the participant(s) [sic] ideas and opinions.	66.53%
5	There is an opportunity for the provider to adapt the services to the patient's cultural preferences.	64.46%
6	There is an opportunity for the patient to adapt better to the healthcare system serving him/her.	57.44%
7	The delivery of services is more culturally competent when we are able to address these issues.	68.80%
8	The parties I interpret for learn something new about teach other's culture.	42.56%
9	Other	6.61%

the importance of improving the rapport of the provider and the patient. The data reaffirm the practice of improving provider–patient rapport by addressing cultural issues. It is important to note that the improvement of the rapport between the medical interpreter and the provider (37.30 per cent), and likewise of the interpreter and the patient (31.97 per cent), was secondary in importance when compared to the therapeutic rapport between the provider and the patient, as encouraged in all the standards of practices for medical interpreters. This means that although it is tempting for both parties (provider and patient) to work with the interpreter who speaks their language, the interpreter uses his interactional, linguistic, diplomatic and cultural skills to minimize his/her presence, or direct relationships with either party, so that the main parties can forge a therapeutic relationship between themselves, as if they are communicating with each other, and not with the interpreter.

The second ranked advantage with 68.80 per cent agreement, related to the increased understanding of context for each party. Without understanding there can be no communication, so it seems that the participants are very aware of the importance of ensuring understanding that includes the cultural context, when necessary, in order to improve the communication between the two parties. When the medical interpreter is viewed as an invisible conduit, these important healthcare-related goals and tasks are not taken into account. The interpreter feels a responsibility to ensure accurate and complete communication (for patient safety reasons) through a variety of subtasks in addition to that of consecutive or simultaneous interpretation. This can include, according to participants, requests for clarification, confirmation of understanding or reformulation of messaging in the same language, or into the other language. The interpreter is constantly working to improve the provider–patient therapeutic rapport and that is an important task in an interpreted communicative event. Without the interpreter's constant subtle interventions, miscommunication could ensue, even with a flawless linguistic interpretation in both directions. What is most interesting here is that these intercultural interventions are not for cultural reasons, per se, but to improve the quality of healthcare services.

The third advantage with the highest level of agreement (68.44 per cent) was the benefit of a service delivery that is more culturally respectful, competent and responsive. It seems that participants are keenly aware of their overall responsibility of healthcare organizations in providing culturally and linguistically appropriate services to patients. While this is not a healthcare policy in all countries, it has become the norm in countries with a high incidence of patients who do not speak the language of service. It is important for healthcare organization to create a corporate environment that allows and encourages all parties, including medical interpreters, to engage in providing services that are culturally competent. This enhances the ability of the provider and organization to bridge not only the language barrier but also the cultural barriers.

There were two items that discussed the possibility of a positive side effect or advantage of the provider knowing how to adapt to the patients' cultural needs (64.75 per cent), or for the patient to know how to adapt to the healthcare system (57.79 per cent). It seems that participants may believe that even though adaptations need to happen on both sides, healthcare providers (including the institution) have the highest burden to adapt in order to truly provide culturally and linguistically competent services to their patients. These adaptations can make it easier for the patient to comply with the treatment and medications prescribed. Upon review of the written comments to this question about advantages, participants stated the following:

1. The communication is clear between the client and the Non-English speaker.
2. Better care and better results.
3. It is done when there is an issue that will affect treatment and outcome.
4. The interpreter must always intervene to provide better health outcomes/ overview to the provider.

5. Communication needs to be clear so that medical services can be provided appropriately. Rapport is secondary; I am more interested in things that will affect a person's safety or health.
6. With our interventions, the patient and hospital staff can engage in the most appropriate treatment, based on a better understanding of the patient and the patient has a better understanding of why things are the way they are and is more likely to be compliant. Everybody rubs along better.
7. Delivery of services is just more satisfactory to the patient and the provider, and is successful.
8. Patient care and health outcomes improve.
9. Saving money and saving patients.
10. The patients evaluate the doctor based on how they were treated, rather than on their skills as a healthcare provider. The more comfortable they feel, the more they will follow up and do what they need.
11. To avoid behaviour or language that could be offensive to either party.

These responses showcase the interpreters' preoccupation with how this intercultural communicative work affects providers, patients and ultimately error-free and quality healthcare. It is true that interpreters provide linguistic services, which involves interpreting consecutively and simultaneously, as well as providing sight translation, as required. However, based on the results, they are also using their skills to engage in many other tasks and activities before, during and after a communicative event that go beyond their linguistic domain. The cultural and health-related domain considerations are also within their scope of work, and require their professional judgement and skills.

The data up to this point demonstrate how the patient, provider and healthcare system may benefit from the interpreter intercultural mediation interventions. The patients benefit from meaningful communication, which lowers their risk of a misdiagnosis or non-compliance or mis-compliance that could happen due to a misunderstanding. Intercultural mediation also allows the patient to feel culturally included, and, in this way, is respected as an individual, where his/her cultural background, values or traditions are not ignored. The patient's comfort needs are also being addressed by the interpreter, to ensure a more pleasant experience for the patient. It is not hard to extrapolate that a patient will have a higher satisfaction with a communication that is more understandable and inclusive to the patient's cultural needs, than one that is not (Weech-Maldonado et al., 2012).

Providers benefit indirectly from the interpreter's assistance to provide the patient with a positive experience, by ensure understanding, educating the client and being aware of the patient's comfort needs. They benefit directly from the interpreter's efforts to improve the therapeutic rapport despite the differences, to clarify issues for the provider, and, ultimately, to educate the provider on the cultural issues taking place, improving the provider's cultural competency. Healthcare organizations benefit from this cultural work which is taking place in the interactions and situations where it is needed. These cultural adaptations can be used by the organization to make immediate, temporary or systemwide adaptations to patient care.

Barriers to addressing cultural issues

It is important to look at the difficulties of addressing cultural issues, according to interpreters, in order to see how these barriers or difficulties affect this practice and to learn how they can become more effective. The answers of focus groups clustered around a number of core issues. Interviewees had greater difficulty addressing the disadvantages, as if they had not thought of them before. There were hesitations in their answers, and several stated they didn't know at first. However, when probed, several of them mentioned five difficulties: (a) time, (b) disrupting the flow of communication, (c) inaccurate interventions, (d) difficulty of patient or provider to explain cultural issue and, (e) over-reliance on the interpreter. Let's explore each one separately.

Lack of time to address cultural issues

The participants' responses below illustrate the significance of time as a deciding factor in mediating cultural issues:

1. The amount of time the provider has to stay with a patient. They are always in a rush. I keep interpreting and remain on point by conveying the message, and it doesn't allow the interpreter much room for intervening.
2. It will take more time for understanding each other, so that the consultation time becomes longer, which is sometimes difficult for other patients who are waiting for a long time. And for the doctor, it takes more time to see one patient. However, those are small matters, as I believe both sides usually appreciate the intervention.

For both participants (giving answers 1 and 2), time is a measurable entity. Time is also disadvantage, as consecutive interpreting requires all utterances to be stated, and then interpreted after the speaker has stopped speaking, roughly doubling the time of the encounter. Most communicative events take anywhere from 10 minutes to an hour. Doubling the time for patients who do not speak the language of service is not a feasibly possible in most healthcare organizations. This means that the provider must accomplish the same discussion with culturally and linguistically diverse patients, regardless of the presence of a healthcare interpreter, in half the time.

One can extrapolate that this provides a definite difficulty for the provider and patient time wise. In order for the provider not to run behind, he/she has several options. The provider must either (a) cut out some of the contents of the conversation that would be had in order to make up for that time or (b) speak very fast. The patient may feel rushed, only adding to the intercultural gap in the therapeutic rapport. Intervening at any moment can delay the time of the appointment and make it difficult for the health provider to finish on time. It is worth mentioning that this is a barrier for any type of interpreter intervention, and not only cultural interventions. Further study is needed to explore up to what level time affects an interpreter-mediated communicative event. It is worth mentioning that if the time factor is a constant, it may add stress to any intercultural and interlinguistic intervention, regardless of whether it is cultural or not. Lack of appropriate time with patients with special linguistic needs may have a negative effect on the ability of providers as well as medical interpreters to provide a customized service that is culturally and linguistically appropriate.

Disrupting the flow of communication

Medical interpreters are very cognizant of their task to avoid disrupting the flow of communication (IMIA & EDC). In interpreter-mediated communicative events, the flow of communication is laboured, as each party has to listen to communications in a language that he/she does not understand until the interpreter utters a message that is understandable. Regardless, interpreters have strategies and skills to do their best to render an interpretation that has as much flow as possible. Interpreters are very cognizant of their responsibility to maintain a flow of communication that is conducive to accurate communication (IMIA & EDC, 2007). Below are two comments that reflect this concept.

1) It seems that there is no way to intervene without breaking the flow of communication between the provider and the patient, although the concept of 'flow' may be a misnomer given that each party only understands half

of what as an interpreter says. Having stated this, the interpreter works to create an interpreted-communication flow. I think if you as an interpreter are not able to control it, and do it in a professional way, it could definitely hinder the flow and the professional development of an interpretation. What I mean is that it can become like a show where the interpreter becomes the star, and he/she will continuously interject and really destroy the flow, which should be the patient–provider interaction.

2) Like I said, the interpreter may be green and have the tendency to stop the session and say, 'Doctor, my experience with patients from Guatemala … '. I think the interpreters are too quick to want to help, out of a good heart, I'm not saying it's bad, but it is not our role as interpreters. Communication may not be clear and then, obviously yes, you do have to get clarification. A lot of times we are too quick to stop and interrupt the dialogue. The interpreter loses the focus as a facilitator of communication.

Maintaining the flow of communication is one of the goals and tasks of the interpreter (IMIA & EDC, 2007). At the same time, interventions interrupt the flow of communication. The first medical interpreter to make a comment mentions the need to resume the flow, but invariably a speaker may still have difficulty returning to the point in question before the interpreter's intervention. This showcases how certain tasks may be in opposition of others, making the work of the medical interpreter more complex than originally assumed.

Inaccurate cultural interventions

What if the communication becomes even more confusing? This participant below speaks to the fact that sometimes a cultural intervention may have the opposite effect:

> If the interpreter is not correctly informed about a particular practice or tradition in a culture. For example, I am from Central America, and if I assume that all Central Americans behave the same way as I do in Costa Rica, I could easily give the wrong explanation for the particular behaviour, tradition or whatever. Someone may think they know what they are doing but it may create a huge obstacle in the communication.

Inappropriate interventions may upset the party that feels an assumption was made of them, or have other negative consequences, such as eroding the trust the parties have on the medical interpreter. An interpreter should know not to generalize or stereotype, but as in all professionals, there will be some that are more or less competent in the area of cultural intervention. Lack of training in this area may also affect the ability of an interpreter to intervene appropriately. When an interpreter asks for clarification on the issue with the patient or provider first, it avoids confusion or assumptions. Asking the party in question to confirm and explain the possible cultural issue, before deciding to provide any intervention, also avoids confusion. It is standard best practice to enquire about an issue first, versus assuming a particular cultural issue is the culprit of the miscommunication or cultural gap.

Difficulty of patient or provider to explain cultural issues

A focus group participant explained how the patient is the one who needs to explain their cultural issue: '*The patient needs to be the one to explain.*' This relates to the fact that interpreters want the provider and patient to be the most active party, as the agent of the communicative messages. In order to achieve that, interpreters will ask the provider or patient, to explain what he/she means. Sometimes it is all the interpreter needs to do. Other times, however, the patient or provider may be hesitant to speak up and may ask the interpreter to explain. If this happens, the interpreter should verify the information to avoid providing inaccurate information. Four focus group participants brought up the fact that there are times when the patient is not able to speak up, for several reasons:

1. Here's a situation. The patient didn't know his date of birth and the nurse got very upset. I had to explain that this was common for this person's culture, so then she understood.
2. For some cultures, it is not possible to speak up about all that is culturally relevant. It is impossible as it is something that is not supposed to be spoken but be understood. We also have to act as to not lose the trust of the patient or provider on the interpreter. The interpreter should not interject personal bias, but the rules for the provider are different. The provider can allow himself or herself their cultural issues.
3. I empathize before sharing, I check with the patient, to correct or to make sure that they are comfortable. I don't want to, but sometimes they want me to, so I clarify with the patient if it is ok to go ahead. I will tell the provider that the patient is afraid to share. It is their (providers) responsibility to make it a safe space to disclose cultural information.
4. The patient is embarrassed about admitting to using or preferring a traditional home remedy, and may not want the interpreter to tell the provider.

In the first response, the patient didn't even know to explain that in her country it is common not to know their date of birth, as she probably didn't find that at all odd. In this scenario, the patient would have no idea why the nurse was so upset. Cultural beliefs and values are also often difficult to explain. As the second participant explains, culture is not something commonly discussed or compared. For example, one cannot explain one's cultural belief or practice in relation to another culture if one does not know the other cultural belief or practice. Only those who understand the two beliefs or values to be compared can offer a comparative explanation.

Often, cultural values are believed to be absolute (believed by all) unless challenged. In some of these situations, the interpreter may interject, not due to an overt miscommunication, but due to other goals: (1) improve provider–patient rapport, (2) mitigate the nurse's response due to lack of knowledge about that culture (3) or educate the nurse about this issue, so that when she or he encounters other patients who respond in the same way, the nurse will know why and will not doubt the patient. In the case of not knowing one's birth date, the medical interpreter explained that she was observing not only the patient's non-verbal communication, but also the nurse's non-verbal communication, and made the decision to intervene without the permission or clarification of the patient. When the interpreter was asked during the focus group why she did not ask the patient first if she could explain that, in the patient's culture sometimes patients did not know their date of birth, the interpreter answered that she did not want to embarrass the patient and that the patient may not understand why she is asking this.

It seems that interpreters have their professional reasoning for requesting permission, or not. These are professional decisions interpreters need to make in each unique scenario based on their professional judgement. The last comment about this clearly suggests that sometimes the patient may not feel comfortable or empowered to explain a cultural issue. Many interpreters are very skilled at empowering the patient to speak, when necessary. However, the interpreter cannot force the patient to speak. Also, if a patient requests the interpreter to explain a cultural concept, the interpreter may feel obliged to do so and will not refuse.

Over-reliance on the interpreter

There is another disadvantage stated by a participant that can occur when interpreters address cultural issues:

Hospital staff members may depend on interpreters too much. We may have to take care of everything for patients sometimes. It's a big burden for the U.S.

When asked about this statement, the interpreter explained that sometimes the provider will simply work with the patient by communicating directly with the interpreter, avoiding eye contact (non-verbal communication) with the patient, and communicating in the third person, as in '*Tell him* that he needs to take his medications', instead of '*You* need to take your medications'. This is a burden for interpreters. The interpreter stated that the provider would ask her the questions that he should be asking the patient. This comment, within a real work experience, does not seem to be related specifically to addressing cultural issues, but to the tendency of some providers to believe that they may not need to learn how to work with the patient, so long as they have an interpreter present who will be the one who knows how to work with the patient. The International Medical Interpreting Standard for medical interpreters (IMIA & EDC) dictates the need for a professional interpreter pre-session, with both parties, in order to set the rules of an interpreted communicative event. The interpreter will explain, for example, to both parties, that it is important that they speak to each other directly using the first person, in order to have a direct therapeutic rapport with each other; and that the interpreter is there to help as the interpreter.

Results of online survey aligned to other data sources

Online survey participants were given six disadvantages to rate, based on the qualitative responses of interviewees. Survey responses are presented in Table 6.2.

As can be seen by the online responses, similarly to the interviewees, online survey participants listed the delay of time (55.37 per cent) as the primary

Table 6.2 Disadvantages of addressing cultural issues ($n = 423$)

Answer Choices	%
Sometimes it delays the time of the encounter.	55.37%
Sometimes it causes more confusion than clarity, as the parties really cannot conceptualize or accept the ideas being put forth about the other culture.	41.74%
I can end up being reprimanded for getting too involved with the patient and healthcare provider interaction.	19.01%
The provider may not want me to address cultural issues, and if I do, the provider may get upset with me.	23.55%
Other	19.83%

difficulty of addressing cultural issues. Time with the patient is a very substantial component to any quality services and this obstacle should be further evaluated in the quest to provide equitable care to linguistically and culturally diverse patients. This has not been discussed in any interpreter study and merits further research.

The second disadvantage, with a 41.74 per cent agreement, is that this is a complex issue and if the parties cannot conceptualize or accept the ideas being put forth about the other culture, the communication can be challenging. Intercultural mediation requires a high level of diplomatic skills. Confusion can ensue and clarity is not always attainable. This is a risk that medical interpreters need to weigh in every time they are considering addressing a cultural issue, and address when confusion ensues.

The third disadvantage, with a 23.55 per cent agreement, relates to the provider not wanting the medical interpreter to address intercultural issues. The provider may get upset with the interpreter, for delaying the appointment, or for discussing issues the provider does not believe are relevant or important. There is the potential for this factor to act as a strong deterrent for interpreters to address cultural issues. If the healthcare interpreter does not feel that the provider will appreciate the cultural information, the interpreter may feel he or she will be not be able to intervene. Some interpreters are being erroneously trained to intervene only with the provider's authorization, even if the provider is unaware of the importance or relevance of addressing cultural issues. This is contrary to the directives of several healthcare organizations to provide culturally and linguistically competent healthcare services. The comments section of this question online presented a few interesting responses (parenthesis by author):

1. Every time you intervene as an interpreter, you enter into a conversation that is not yours and you can impact the way the patient and provider relate to each other. You can become the center of attention and you can derail the flow of the encounter and interfere with what the actual speakers are trying to say to each other (flow of communication and invisibility of interpreter).
2. I don't see any disadvantages if the interpreter takes the approach of having the provider and the patient work through the cultural issue and the interpreter supports that process (invisibility of interpreter).
3. I risk frustrating either patient or provider if I reveal that I need clarification on a possibly culture-based confusion (flow of communication).
4. Delaying the time is a consequence, but that can happen with any other clarification the patient could need (delay).

5. It takes more time in a crowded hospital when many patients are waiting (delay).
6. I don't think any disadvantage overrides the importance of cultural sensitivity.
7. None. Because they mostly involve medication, it would be dangerous not to intervene (patient safety first).
8. It may cause confusion if the interpreter does not know how to address cultural issues effectively. Many times providers believe that interpreters are the culture experts, when in reality it is the patient who is expert in his/her own culture (confusion and training).
9. It may upset and confuse the patient even further (confusion).

The first two comments speak of how an intervention puts the interpreter at the forefront of the discussion and how this is uncomfortable for an interpreter who has the conflicting goals of (a) remaining in the background and (b) supporting the provider–patient relationship. The other statements above reiterate some of the primary dangers of an intervention, such as (a) causing a delay, (b) breaking the flow, and (c) causing confusion. It is important to state here that twenty-three participants responded in the Other section of the questionnaire stating that they did not see any disadvantage in addressing cultural issues, as 'no disadvantage' was not listed as a sub-item. This may signal that there is a portion of medical interpreters who believe that there may be no disadvantage to addressing cultural issues, just challenges. The essay participant also did not mention any disadvantages.

Upon reviewing all four data sources, there seems to be a consensus among participants that there are fewer disadvantages than advantages in addressing cultural issues. The main disadvantages were clearly the time delay, the interruption of the flow of communication and the possibility of the intervention itself causing confusion to either party. The time issue is not one under the interpreters' or the providers' control. However, there are other demands, or challenges, that can be controlled by the interpreter with skills and strategies that are specific to each case. The interviewee data expressed disappointment at the fact that some providers are not culturally competent, and that these providers are the ones challenging the interpreters' intercultural role. Interpreters understand their role as one to assist providers in their work with diverse populations. The providers with lower cultural competency usually have greater difficulty in handling diverse patients and may require more help. Unfortunately, they may also be the ones that do not value cultural competency or intercultural interventions.

The more culturally competent a provider is, the easier it is for the interpreter, as fewer interventions are required. However, no matter how culturally competent providers become, they will never be as versed as a medical interpreter in the culture(s) of the patients they serve, due to a variety of reasons. Unless they were born or raised in the patient's culture, for example, or speak the patient's language, they will not be able to identify verbal and non-verbal cues and cultural nuances to the level of a healthcare interpreter. Healthcare interpreters who are not raised in the cultural groups they interpret for may also lack certain specific knowledge and therefore cannot assume to know the patient's culture. In the end, every patient has his or her unique cultural makeup. Culture is also much more than the country they were born in or the religion they practice. Last, communicative events between Western and Western cultural groups will require less intercultural mediation than those of religious differences or East–West encounters. Often, minority languages and cultures are also less understood, and may require greater intercultural enquiry and mediation (Verrept, 2008). The requirement that patients achieve a level of understanding before agreeing to a proposed treatment ultimately may require mediators to reconcile fundamentally different and sometimes incompatible concepts of illness and healing (Kaufert et al., 1996).

Interpreters, as with any other profession, while trained in reading non-verbals and checking for communication in intercultural interactions, will vary in their ability to provide intercultural mediation services. Their abilities will vary depending on their own cultural backgrounds and experiences, and the professional training they receive. However, the fact remains that medical interpreters will continue to be the ones, within an intercultural communicative event, who understand both cultures and languages to the greatest extent.

One of the challenges given by a participant included the following:

> If we're looking at staff providers who are ethno-centric and have a view of defence or that everyone has to be treated the same, I know who they are and don't do it because it can create a more hostile environment and not one of mutual understanding.

This participant indicated that sometimes providers show with their verbal and non-verbal behaviour that they simply do not want to take part in any cultural intervention or adaptation. The fact that this participant chooses to interject only with providers that are ethno-relative (Bennett, 1993) means that the interpreter is not always being given the space to address both linguistic and cultural issues taking place. The provider–patient space of healthcare communication becomes void of intercultural understanding, and of cultural competency.

It is important to note that the reasons for the providers not to want cultural intervention may be varied, and that further study is needed to better understand all the reasons why some providers are not welcoming cultural interventions. Some may be ethno-centric, as this participant describes, with a lack of understanding that equal service is not the same as equitable service. Others may simply have other reasons to avoid interjections, such as being worried with the amount of time they have to address the medical issue at hand.

Conclusions

The older paradigm of patient assimilation, that demanded the minority cultures adapt to the majority culture and services, is being replaced by the new paradigm of cultural competency and patient-centred care (MFH Project Group, 2004). It requires providers to be mindful to adapt to patient preferences in order to ensure quality healthcare. Because of this, the cultural educator and intercultural mediator roles of medical interpreters seem to be growing in relevance, not only to improve the cultural competency of all stakeholders involved in the patient care, including the organization that provides the service, but also to ensure that cultural misunderstandings do not affect the quality of care or patient safety (Flores, 2005). Further research is needed to ascertain the perspectives of patients and providers on the effects, benefits and difficulties of addressing cultural issues with professional medical interpreters.

It is ironic that a profession that gives a voice to patients and providers has not had a prominent voice on this subject in research, since most research involves the observation of interpreters at work. This study focused on documenting the professional opinions of medical interpreters regarding their cultural work. Most studies have focused on discourse analysis or observation, which are valid, yet are not viable methods to get into the interpreter's thinking process. These practitioners bring much more to the table than the act of providing accurate consecutive or simultaneous interpretation of healthcare messages from one language into another language. Medical interpreters are addressing the intercultural dimension of health-related communicative events in order to ensure patient safety. They remain the most qualified professionals to ensure culturally competent care for culturally diverse patients. However, this does not mean that interpreters are familiar with all the cultural nuances that they will encounter, or the specific cultural makeup of an individual patient. They don't need to know so long as they have the skills and abilities to properly identify and engage in cultural enquiry.

Their professional intercultural input, at any moment, is essential to the provision of culturally competent and patient-centred healthcare services (Putsch, 1985). As the voice of the practitioner is heard louder and louder, a better understanding, recognition and support for this cultural scope of work will evolve. Medical interpreters are beginning to distinguish themselves as a unique specialization in their own right, with certain characteristics, leeways and objectives that are uncommon to all other interpreter specializations. These characteristics are specific to the context of the provision of healthcare services. These include professional responsibilities and tasks related to the ethical concerns of ensuring patient safety, the therapeutic rapport and the provision of culturally competent healthcare services. The need for this intercultural role is a reality of practice, of interpreters responding to the unique demands of the culturally diverse patients and providers within the healthcare context. This chapter attempted to offer through the participants' voices a broader understanding of the cultural scope of work of interpreters in this specialization. Ultimately, this work enables all in healthcare to become more culturally competent for the benefit, well-being and safety of the patient.

> The cultural differences are as important as the linguistic differences in communication. Practically, we are unable to know all of the cultures in the world. However, we can exercise humility to continue learning new things from each other and working as a team to provide the best possible healthcare for our patients. (Essay participant, United States)

Note

1   Editors' Note. The idea that interpreters, especially in the health sector, are impartial mediators is an extreme oversimplification. In community interpreting, especially in healthcare interpreting for culturally and linguistically diverse communities that could represent ethnic minority or marginalized groups, the ethical and deontological debate on advocacy is extremely rich. The debate pertains to Anglophone as well as other traditions of interpreting and is in fact very well known in the United States and Australia – see the works of Angelelli and Ozolins, among many. The contributor of this chapter was asked to address the issue of advocacy and took a very superficial approach to dismiss the debates; it is important to mention it here *exactly because* it pertains to the very core of intercultural mediation practices, which in crisis situations do not rely on professionals trained on restricted views of advocacy but on a range of operators. Such operators carry extreme values in terms of advocacy.

References

Angelelli, C. V. (2004). *Revisiting the Interpreter's Role: A Study of Conference, Court, and Medical Interpreters in Canada, Mexico, and the United States*. Amsterdam and Philadelphia, PA: John Benjamins.

Angelelli, C. V. (2015). *Study on Public Service Translation in Cross-Border Healthcare: Final Report for the European Commission Directorate-General for Translation*. Available online: https://publications.europa.eu/en/publication-detail/-/publication/6382fb66-8387-11e5-b8b7-01aa75ed71a1/language-en (accessed 30 November 2018).

Angelelli, C. V., and Baer, B. J. (2015). 'Exploring Translation and Interpreting'. In C. Angelelli and B. J. Baer (eds), *Researching Translation and Interpreting*, 5–13. London and New York, NY: Routledge.

Bennett, M. J. (1993). 'Towards Ethnorelativism: A Developmental Model of Intercultural Sensitivity'. In R. M. Paige (ed.), *Education for the Intercultural Experience*. 2nd edition, 21–71. Yarmouth, ME: Intercultural Press.

Bontempo, K., and Malcolm, K. (2012). 'An Ounce of Prevention Is Worth a Pound of Cure'. In L. Swabey and K. Malcolm (eds), *In Our Hands: Educating Healthcare Interpreters*. Washington, DC: Gallaudet University Press.

Brannen, J. (2005). 'Mixing Methods: The Entry of Qualitative and Quantitative Approaches into the Research Process'. *The International Journal of Social Research Methodology,* Special Issue 8(3): 173–185.

Cox, A., and Gutiérrez, R. L. (2016). 'Interpreting in the Emergency Department: How Context Matters for Practice'. In F. M. Federici (ed.), *Mediating Emergencies and Conflicts*, 33–58. Basingstoke and New York, NY: Palgrave Macmillan.

Cresswell, J. W. (2003). *Research Design: Qualitative, Quantitative and Mixed Method Approaches*. Thousand Oaks, CA: Sage.

Flores, G. (2005). 'The Impact of Medical Interpreter Services on the Quality 3 of Healthcare: A Systematic Review'. *Medical Care Research Review* 62(3): 255–299.

International Medical Interpreters Association & Education Development Center (2007). *Standards of Practice*. Available online: http://www.imiaweb.org/uploads/pages/102.pdf (accessed 30 November 2018).

International Medical Interpreters Association (2018). *Lawsuits Listing*. Available online: http://www.imiaweb.org/resources/legal.asp (accessed 30 November 2018).

Jalbert, M. (1998). 'Travailler avec un interprète en consultation psychiatrique'. *Prisme* 8(3): 94–111.

Kaufert, J., Lavallée, M., Koolage, W., and O'Neil, J. (1996). 'Culture and Informed Consent: The Role of Aboriginal Interpreters in Patient Advocacy in Urban Hospitals'. *Issues in the North* 1(34): 89.

MFH Project Group (2004). *Amsterdam Declaration towards Migrant Friendly Hospitals*. Available online: http://www.mfh-eu.net/public/files/european_recommendations/mfh_amsterdam_declaration_english.pdf (accessed 30 November 2018).

Price-Wise, G. (2015). *An Intoxicating Error: Mistranslation, Medical Malpractice, and Prejudice*. Pennsauken, NJ: Baby Book Publishing.

Putsch, R. W. (1985). 'Intercultural Communication, the Special Case of Interpreters in Healthcare'. *Journal of American Medical Association* 254(23): 3344–3348.

Rolfe A., Cash-Gibson L., Car J., Sheikh A., McKinstry B. (2014). 'Interventions for Improving Patients' Trust in Doctors and Groups of Doctors'. *Cochrane Database Sys. Rev.* 4(3): 7.

Ryan, J., Abbato, S., Greer, R., Vayne-Bossert, P., and Good, P. (2017). 'Rates and Predictors of Professional Interpreting Provision for Patients with Limited English Proficiency in the Emergency Department and Inpatient Ward'. *INQUIRY: The Journal of Health Care Organization, Provision, and Financing* 54, 0046958017739981. doi: 10.1177/0046958017739981.

Segal, J. Z. (2007). '"Compliance" to "Concordance": A Critical View'. *Journal of Medical Humanities* 28(2): 81–96.

Souza, Izabel E. T. de V. (2016). *Intercultural Mediation in Healthcare: From the Professional Medical Interpreters' Perspective*. Bloomington, IN: Xlibris.

Verrept, H. (2008). 'Intercultural Mediation: An Answer to Health Care Disparities?' In C. Valero-Garcés and A. Martin (eds), *Crossing Borders in Community Interpreting: Definitions and Dilemmas*, 187–201. Amsterdam and Philadelphia, PA: John Benjamins.

Weech-Maldonado, R., Elliott, M. N., Pradhan, R., Schiller, C., Hall, A., and Hays, R. D. (2012). 'Can Hospital Cultural Competency Reduce Disparities in Patient Experiences with Care?' *Medical Care* 50: S48.

Wenger, A. F. (1995). 'Cultural Context, Health and Health Care Decision making'. *Journal of Transcultural Nursing* 7(1): 3–14.

7

Interpreting for Refugees: Empathy and Activism

Marija Todorova

We are witnessing increasing numbers of refugee crises around the globe and the need for trained interpreters who would work alongside humanitarian personnel is significant. This chapter looks at the special position interpreters have in emergency situations arising from violent conflicts, especially in working with refugees directly at the border or in refugee camps. I will argue that, in these particular situations, interpreters are not just enablers of communication by transferring content from one language into another but are active partners, alongside the humanitarian personnel, in the process of advocacy for people who are in a vulnerable position, such as refugees are for longer or shorter periods of time. This chapter grounds its findings in ethnographic approach to data collection and the analysis of interviews with three interpreters and an introspective report of the author/interpreter who have all been directly involved in interpreting during the last twenty years on the territory of Macedonia.

At a first glance, interpreting for these vulnerable groups and individuals might seem to be similar to interpreting for asylum seekers in the countries that they see as their final destination. However, beyond the initial similarities it must be said that when working at the border or in large refugee camps, the interpreters face the situation more directly and immediately. The vulnerable person has not been safely removed from the sensitive situation and is strongly affected by it. Sometimes the perpetrator, or the cause of fear, might still be present at the site. These circumstances additionally require empowering the victims so that they can find their voice. The interpreter can assist in the creating empowerment for the vulnerable party during the mediation process by providing cultural knowledge; the interpreter can do this by being a strong advocate for the refugees when needed, that is when the context makes them vulnerable. This activity is highly dependent on the interpreters' ability to empathize with the vulnerable groups of refugees.

Empathy and interpreting

For the purposes of this study of the interpreter-mediated interaction with refugees, empathy will be defined as 'a perspective-taking capability, entailing: awareness of both self and the other (and of self as distinct from the other); understanding of the other's situation; and a degree of concern for the other, communicated through a range of carefully selected affective displays in compliance with the aims and overall objective of the specific institutional activity' (Merlini and Gatti, 2016: 143). Additionally, even when formal training is provided to interpreters in emergency situations, such training is not specifically designed to reflect the work requirements of such interpreters but rather uses standard training materials. Empathy is generally understood to mean 'putting yourself in another person's shoes' or 'seeing things through someone else's eyes'. A formal definition of empathy includes the ability to identify and understand another person's situation, feelings and motives. The English word 'empathy' is in itself a translation from the German words *Einfühlung* and *Mitgefühl* introduced into the English language in 1909 (Lanzoni, 2012: 302–303). The concept initially was used in the field of psychology and aesthetics to represent the ability for 'images, sensations, and affects running through the mind while observing, listening to stimuli, or imagining objects in the laboratory' (Lanzoni, 2012: 302). Nowadays, empathy as a term is used in various disciplines: from medicine (see for instance the discussion in Chapter 5 in this volume), and more specifically in psychology (Hardy, 2017), to international relations and conflict transformation (Head, 2012).

Empathy seeks to apprehend another person's particular frame of reference. Drawing on Batson (2009), Naomi Head makes a distinction between intersubjective, dynamic, cognitive and emotional processes which characterize empathy (2016a: 174–175). Cognitive empathy can be explained as the capacity to put oneself into other's shoes, to understand other's perspective (Batson, 2009). Cognitive empathy understood in the most general sense can be said to mean 'imagining or grasping another's thoughts, feelings and perceptions; affective empathy involves sharing another's feelings' (CEIA, 2016: 3). Defining empathy as a 'process' rather than a 'state', Rogers maintains that 'to be with another in this way means that for the time being you lay aside the views and values you hold for yourself in order to enter another world without prejudice' (1975, 4). It is essential to appreciate the experience of the other, as if walking in their shoes, while also having the capacity to step in and step out of them so as not to lose oneself in the process (La Corte and Jalonen, 2018: 82). The feeling of empathy is demonstrable in that a person will know that they are being attentively and caringly listened to and understood if an accurate representation of what they are experiencing is reflected back to them. Richard Ned Lebow has written that '[e]mpathy in turn encourages us to see others as our ontological equals and to recognize the self-actualizing benefits of close relationships with others' (2005: 42). In its essence empathy means acknowledging others as human beings (Head, 2016b).

In the field of peacebuilding and conflict transformation studies empathy has recently witnessed an increased interest (Morrell, 2010; Baron-Cohen, 2011; Monroe, 2012; Crawford, 2014). Empathy is seen as important to mediators helping them understand what others are feeling, and why are they reacting to situations in a certain way, helping them create relationships of trust, and in informing and guiding their decisions. As the capacity to recognize the concerns other people have, empathy is especially valuable in the process of mediation as a peacebuilding and conflict resolution method. When employing empathy, 'rather than suppressing their sense of self, some mediators try to reach into themselves to find some part of their character or experience that resonates with the other' (CEIA, 2016: 3). For mediators, empathy can implicate 'finding something within themselves that enlarges their capacity for understanding and connection' (CEIA, 2016: 3). The lack of empathy on the side of the mediator can pressurize parties and even further marginalize vulnerable parties (Grillo, 1991; Pavlich, 1996) because the mediator is preoccupied with the form, rather than the parties, their participation and needs. Adequate mediation 'should also allow people's emotions to be part of the process, allow their values and principles to matter in the discussion' (Grillo, 1991: 1610). Mediation cannot always protect the weaker party and depends on the skill and knowledge of the mediators to effectively recognize power imbalances among parties and address them. In order to address the imbalances, the mediator is actively engaging in advocacy using an 'activist' approach to transformative mediation (Harper, 2006).

Empathy is a skill that is required in the area of activism, too. Pérez-González defines activists as '[h]ighly critical individuals whose personal narratives fail to align, totally or partially, with public narratives at a given point in time and space and who, consequently, set out to bring one or more aspects of their personal narrative to bear on the collective ones' (2010: 262). Hoffman (1989) identifies empathy as one of the essential elements that prompts what he defines as 'prosocial activism'. For Hoffman 'prosocial activism' is 'sustained action in the service of improving another person's or group's life condition either by working with them or by trying to change society on their behalf' (1989: 65). In doing this, empathy is directed towards both the individual and the collective, understanding the collective narratives of others, their beliefs, identities and feelings as a group (see Baker, 2006; 2008). This implies acknowledging the possibility of a different interpretation of events by another group.

Lynne Cameron makes the connection between empathy and the communicative practices (2011). Most often empathy has been studied in the field of medical communication. In her research of empathy among physicians Hardy situates the reasons for lack of empathy in 'the distrust of affective practices, the fear of risky personal connections, and the need for a coping strategy to avoid professional burnout' (2017: 246). In a similar fashion, young medical interpreters are trained and reminded by professional codes of conduct to stay objective and refrain from emotional connection with the speakers. They should be unbiased and be capable of objectively rendering the statements. Avoiding empathy secures the professional distance that interpreters are advised to maintain. However, '[e]mpathy is beneficial, leading to a greater amount of shared information, perceive care, trust, and empowerment for the patient, as well as a greater sense of fulfilment and lower chance of professional burnout for physicians' (Hardy, 2017: 246). Among the personal qualities of aspiring interpreters Setton and Dawrant (2016: 66) list the capability of empathy, especially cognitive empathy that helps interpreters put themselves into the target audience's shoes.

Building on the current research in community interpreting, Martin and Valero-Garcés rightfully note that regardless of the level of professionalization, community interpreters will continue to work in 'circumstances in which it would be difficult for any human being to remain unperturbed' (2008: 2). Defining an ethical and efficient community of interpreters, Zhang (2016) maintains that they are 'impartial yet empathetic, which presents an obvious contradiction at face value: being impartial implies distance, whereas empathy denotes a connection'. The work of a community interpreter is unique in its context: they often have the privilege of seeing people at their most vulnerable. Their ethics training guide them as they seek a right course of action, and they navigate between their roles as conduits, clarifiers, cultural brokers and advocates. Decisions are made swiftly, and adjustments are made based on moment-to-moment dynamics. The distinction between an 'impartial' interpreter and an 'advocate' one is a simplification which may carry some theoretical value but has little applicability to the practice of community interpreting having in mind the very different contexts in which it takes place.

Interpreters are sometimes described from the perspective of mediation theory as active participants in a mediation process (Todorova, 2017; 2016). In conflict situations they often performed duties that are similar to those of mediators. While mediation scholars mainly describe mediation as impartial, some claim that it can be an empowering process for the less powerful party. Interpreters are also involved in creating and maintaining a relationship of trust in the conflict setting. The role occupied by the interpreters in humanitarian emergency situations as the ones who are from the onset positioned well inside the conflict situation, belonging to one (or more) of the parties to that conflict allows them to empower the vulnerable party in the mediation process.

Although connected in many ways to medical and legal interpreting, interpreting in emergencies does have its own distinctive characteristics arising from the iterative and prolonged contact with individual refugees, as well as the highly emotional content of the mediated communication resulting from the trauma of conflict and forced migration. Empathy is a vital foundation for establishing a working relationship of trust between the interpreter and the refugee, and in this it is a significant predictor of a positive interaction. In addition, many people working as interpreters within refugee emergencies are non-professionals and former refugees themselves. They are dedicated staff members, but often without adequate training for dealing with emergency situations when compared with humanitarian workers operating. In the section that follows we will look at the work of four interpreters working with refugees focusing on their exercised empathy towards the refugees as a group, and minority vulnerable groups within the refugee group.

Interpreting for refugees

According to UNHCR there are currently over 25 million refugees throughout the world.[1] Refugees are defined as people who are forced to live outside their country of origin due to a well-founded fear of persecution based on race, religion, nationality, political opinion or membership in a particular social group.[2] All these reasons imply that refugees have experienced some kind of traumatic event in their place of origin that lead to forced migration. These 'pre-migration traumas, combined with traumas experienced during flight, such as danger and life in refugee camps, and traumas during resettlement, such as acculturative stress, combine to form what is referred to as the triple trauma paradigm' (Baker, 1992: 83–106). Having this in mind, empathy is an important tool needed for interpreters working in refugee-related emergencies. The use of empathy enhances interpreters' effectiveness in helping refugees receive better protection of their human rights.

Macedonia has served as a host country to refugees since its early independence in 1991. In the early 1990s Macedonia took in tens of thousands of refugees from both Bosnia and Herzegovina fleeing the Bosnian War (1992–1994). They were accommodated in collective centres, often repurposed children recreation centres, throughout the country. However, the first big influx of refugees that required international assistance took place in 1998 and 1999 as a result of the conflict in Kosovo. During the Kosovo conflict, refugees fleeing Kosovo were crossing the Macedonian–Kosovo border at Blace in huge numbers. Within about two months, a total of 344,500 refugees entered Macedonia, and more than 100,000 accommodated in refugee camps (UNHCR, 2000). The Kosovo refugees entering Macedonia included mainly ethnic Albanians, but also Roma and Ashkali populations, taking temporary refuge in Macedonia, or seeking asylum in other countries. The languages involved in this emergency situation were Albanian, Serbian and Macedonian, as well as mainly English as the language of the international organizations, as UNHCR was managing several refugee camps, one of which on the very border crossing in Blace.

Another similar situation was created during the so-called European Refugee Crisis in 2015 when Macedonia has become the host of an increasing number of refugees and asylum seekers mainly coming from Afghanistan, Pakistan, Somalia and Syria (UNHCR, 2015b – see also the effects of this crisis in Croatia, as described in Chapter 2 in this volume). Refugees from these countries were crossing the Mediterranean Sea looking for safety in Europe, first arriving in Greece or Italy, and then continuing their journey through the Western Balkans and Eastern Europe towards other European Union (EU) member states in Western and Northern Europe, predominantly Germany and Sweden (UNHCR, 2015a). The refugees were mainly crossing the Greek–Macedonian border near the town of Gevgelija and passing through Macedonian territory to reach the Serbian border on their way to EU. Only a small number of refugees decided to permanently settle in the territory of Macedonia. With the rise of the European refugee crisis, which significantly affected Macedonia as a transit country with more than 50,000 refugees taking shelter in two refugee camps, UNHCR again increased and strengthened its presence in Macedonia. Their operation, as well as the work of the Macedonian border police and humanitarian organizations, depended on interpreters with mainly Arabic language skills, but also Farsi and Urdu. After the borders with Greece and Serbia were closed to refugees on 7 March 2016, the number of refugees in Macedonia was significantly reduced. Today there are about 1,500 people left in the two transit centres in Tabanovce and Vinojug, mainly families with small children or people with few resources. With the outbreak of the European refugee crisis, which significantly affected Macedonia as a transit country, UNHCR increased and strengthened its presence in Macedonia again. Interpreters from Arabic who were able to provide this service were in short supply and UNHCR tapped insider sources to get to interested people with the relevant skills to perform the job, contacting embassies, universities and other organizations.

The four interpreters interviewed for this study were individuals engaged for more than a year for their language skills in emergencies involving refugees. They were employed to work in Macedonia for humanitarian organizations, primarily UNHCR, providing immediate assistance to refugees at border crossings or large refugee camps and collection centres. Two of the interpreters have been engaged during the 2015 refugee crises to interpret between Macedonian–English–Arabic. Two other interpreters were part of a UNHCR Blace border team in 1999/2000, to interpret between English and their native language, Albanian and Macedonian respectively. Both interpreters were fluent in Serbian as well. Two of the four interpreters were engaged to work outside of the border of Macedonia, in Greece and in Kosovo respectively.

All participants in this study were asked to share their experiences by using semi-structured interviews developed for the purposes of this study. The interview examined the background of the interpreter in terms of their experience and education, their views of the role interpreters play in the refugee assistance process, the availability of institutional support for their work, the emotional impact of interpreting for refugees on their own well-being, the most challenging and rewarding aspects of their work, and the areas in which they believed refugee interpreters should receive training. As some of the participating interpreters in this study lived in geographically distant regions, it was necessary to conduct the interviews online (by Skype), which proved to be a good substitute for an on-location face-to-face interview. All interviews were conducted in Macedonian language and translated for the purposes of this chapter by the author.

As little research currently exists on the work of interpreters in emergency settings, and in particular on interpreting for refugees, the most effective way would be to examine issues identified from the researcher's personal experience and discover other potentially important issues not previously discussed by interpreters. Semi-structured interviews are a valued method used in research on topics about which relatively little is known (Banyard and Miller, 1998). Listening to their stories of how they perform their day-to-day duties (Allen, 2012) the author would like to change the common situation where 'even on those occasions when their presence is mentioned, interpreters working in conflict zones are rarely referred to by name or singled out for detailed description or comment' (Ruiz Rosendo and Persaud, 2016: 2).

At this point I will have to acknowledge that one of the latter two interpreters is the author of this research. My personal experience is analysed to inform the roles and positioning of the interpreters working with refugees in emergency situations – a form of self-reflective ethnographic narrative was used as the interview. In this attempt the author follows the position that 'the mythology of "hygienic" research, with its mystification of the researcher and the researched as objective instruments of data production must be replaced by the recognition that personal involvement is more than dangerous bias — it is the condition under which people come to know each other and admit others into their lives' (Oakley, 1981: 58).

Interpreters' background, self-perceptions and emotional reactions

The interviews shed light on the fact that the interpreters who worked with the refugees in emergency situations have all had some shared background with the group they interpreted for. Although they have not been through the same experiences as the refugee groups, they were committed to helping the refugees receive assistance and were capable of engaging with their emotions. This established trust between the interpreter and the refugee, in a situation when the capacity to trust was diminished. It also helped to better understand their needs, but also motivated the interpreters to provide direct assistance. All interpreters showed a strong self-perception as not only enablers of communication but also assistants in the effort to bring vulnerable groups to safety.

Adelina Ajdaraga and I worked alongside an international UNHCR officer in the same team engaged to assist them at the Blace border crossing between Macedonia and Kosovo. Adelina is an ethnic Albanian from Macedonia who trained to be a physiotherapist and to work in the healthcare system. However, with the beginning of the crisis in Kosovo she felt compelled to help the people with whom she shared the same cultural background, and even family relations. In her accounts of working as part of the UNHCR Blace border team she remembers often times feeling required to make direct individual contact with the refugees due to the fact that she was the first point of contact for most of the refugees, creating strong relationships with the people she was interpreting for. The very fact that the day-to-day political events were dictating the speed and scale of field activities at the Blace border crossing often made her the only contact with a UNHCR staff that some of the refugees had time to establish. Describing the scope of her work she explains:

> At times the refugees came in huge numbers, but they were immediately organized for transportation towards other camps in the country. Other times, they were waiting for hours at the no man's land, in the sun or in the rain, without any information how long they will need to wait or not knowing the reason why they are left to wait. Sometimes they were accommodated in the temporary camp at the border crossing, which was the worst option in terms of their acceptance in the country. The nature of the needs and the problems of the refugees who arrived at the border every day, with smaller or bigger intensity, was mainly identical for all: they were tired, scared, hungry, etc. The intensity of what was happening taught me to recognize their priority needs at the very first contact.

Adelina points out that she soon learned how to recognize the needs of the refugees and this motivated her to offer help or information independently (e.g. how to reach a certain camp, where to look for medical support or where to look for information on other refugees from the same region, village or town). She often explained to the refugees what their basic rights as refugees were. Also, she became quick at distinguishing with ease between groups of refugees who left their homes in a hurry and headed immediately towards the border, and those who had sheltered at other places before arriving at the border (in the woods, in improvised shelters, with relatives or neighbours). The first group was visibly anxious and feared the unknown enfolding of the events, but happy to be have escaped. They were in a better physical condition as well. The latter were tired and dishevelled, physically and mentally exhausted, very often with empty looks in their eyes.

Another group of people Adelina had contact with were not the refugees, but people from the country who came to the border to enquire about the arrival of refugees, often expecting relatives. Although these people were not immediate concern and within the remit of responsibility of UNHCR, Adelina took it upon herself to 'patiently explain the procedure of refugee registration and what are the responsibilities of different institutions' to these people, so that they could trace the whereabouts of their relatives.

The advantage during this situation was the fact that the refugees were travelling in groups, often big families, and it was easier to identify the individuals leading the group and representing the interests of the others in the group. This helped Adelina better identify if there was a specific problem, a sick person or a pregnant woman. Based on her immediate evaluation of the situation, she was then able to ask for a quicker intervention when required by the field medical teams or, in some cases, she personally, as a trained medical care person, tried to meet the more modest requirements of the refugees.

When asked about a specific incident when she feels her presence was most valuable, Adelina recounts a situation at the Blace border in 1999 when she identified a group of forty refugee women, young and older, with young children from the same family. She was already familiar with stories that there were attacks against civilians and victims. This led to her approaching the group separately, and without the company of the International Officer. According to their account they were all internally displaced for several months before crossing the border; during these months, they had been intercepted by paramilitaries and witnessed killings. All male members of the family, and male children above the age of fourteen, had been rounded up, several of them killed immediately, and others taken away. The women felt they could trust another woman, who shared same ethnic background and language, with their story. In this and previously described instances Adelina acted on behalf of vulnerable refugees and their relatives even when that was not necessarily in the description of her duties.

Similar to Adelina, I joined UNHCR in 1999 immediately after the airstrikes in Kosovo and Serbia, leaving my job as a field-interpreter for the OSCE mission in Skopje. I felt that working for the UNHCR would have put me in a position to offer help where it was most needed. As I did not speak the language of the refugees, I was specifically assigned to work closely and liaise with the Macedonian border police. However, this work enabled me to act on behalf of the refugees who were trapped in the no man's land and who were negotiating with the border police possibilities to help the most vulnerable people among themselves as identified by the other interpreter.

After the repatriation of the Albanian refugees from Macedonia back to Kosovo, I was invited to join the UNHCR Prishtina team to offer language support to the team working with Serbian-speaking isolated and internally displaced people within the city of Prishtina with restricted movement due to fears for security or disability. I was deployed in Prishtina as UNHCR interpreter for almost a year; during this time, I personally felt responsible to visit individuals and small minority communities of the Serbian-speaking ethnic Serbs, the Gorani and the Roma population, making sure they received their much-needed living supplies and medical attention. Although employed as a local interpreter expected to work alongside an international officer, I was expected to perform this task individually, with the support of a local driver with knowledge of the local area. My objective was to identify their needs and connect them with the humanitarian organization responsible to cater for the specific needs, most often medical supplies and assistance, but also provisions of food, baby supplies or family reunion. After a day spent in the field, I would prepare written reports about the situation identified and the mitigation activities I had conducted. Due to the fact that the international organization strongly accused the Serbian politics in Kosovo, and Serbia was bombed by NATO forces, the Serbian-speaking population in Kosovo felt increasing distrust towards all the international organizations. However, by providing them with an interpreter, as a first contact, who did not belong to any side of the conflict, they were given a voice to freely express their needs and fears. As the first point of contact, the interpreters were able to develop a relationship with the refugees before they even met with the humanitarian workers, allowing them to establish a connection based to empathy, support and trust.

Hana Habahbeh and Simona Alavi were both engaged to work with the refugees because of their knowledge of and language skills with Arabic, Macedonian and English. However, they both also share cultural background with the refugees that were trapped at the Macedonian–Greek border. Simona Alavi's father is Syrian; her mother is Macedonian. She was born and lived with her family in Syria; however, the war made her family flee Syria and resettle in her mother's homeland, Macedonia. Although a dentist technician by vocation, she was engaged as a Field Assistant in three UNHCR-managed refugee camps and at the train station in Gevgelija. Apart from UNHCR, she was assisting as interpreter for the Red Cross and the Macedonian police. She stresses that she 'felt close to the refugees and could best understand and translate their stories' as she had Syrian background herself and had personally experienced life in the Syrian war zone.

Another specific aspect related to interpreting for refugees in emergency situations is the fact that the interpreters often feel close connection and identify with the refugees for whom they interpret. This situation is most obvious in the case of Simona Alavi, who was advised to just interpret what was said, and she followed those instructions. However, she soon learned that she was not only a language broker, but also found herself having to explain cultural or religious sensitivities. She says that she could not 'feel like any other UNHCR employee and wait for cases and come to their office'; rather, she was proactive in going around and asking refugees if they had any needs, whilst identifying the vulnerable cases herself. She also felt responsible for the refugees, especially when taking a shift as the only representative of the UNHCR in a refugee camp. As previously mentioned, although interpreters stated they agreed they should indeed remain invisible, at the same time most of them reported having a proactive role in taking action, working independently and suggesting remedial activities. This position 'would indicate that while they may be intuitively aware of their agency in the process, the dominant education narrative still works to cancel that out' (Todorova, 2016: 238). To be thoroughly effective in their work, conflict interpreters should 'perceive their role as powerful and visible' and they should 'acknowledge the agency they possess' (Angelelli, 2004: 3; see also Inghilleri, 2005).

Simona was reportedly employed to work primarily with women refugees. Refugee women who needed special attention, were pregnant or had been victims of sexual assault preferred to talk to women interpreters rather than men. When the border between Macedonia and Greece was closed in the period February–March 2016, Simona spent a month interpreting for the refugees stranded on the Greek side. Simona particularly stresses the difficulty she experienced while interpreting for sexually assaulted women during her mission in Idomeni, Greece, reporting cases of assaulted minors. While working with women and girls who were sexually assaulted by other refugees, her being a woman from the same community proved to be helpful in providing refugee women with a voice to report the assaults and making sure that their needs were being adequately met. Similar to Hana, Simona also claims that she has 'helped everyone regardless of their background and situation'; however, she believes that working with vulnerable women and girls 'gave her the opportunity to be where she was needed most and to make the highest impact in supporting the refugees'.

Another group of refugees needing special attention were the unaccompanied minors. They were primarily accommodated separately than other adults. These refugees require special attention due to their vulnerability and limited capacity to make decisions for themselves.

Hana Habahbeh has been working for UNHCR since the beginning of the European Refugee Crisis, first as an Assistant Interpreter, and later as Field Assistant, using English, Macedonian and Arabic. She was one of the three UNHCR interpreters employed to work during the emergency response to the increasing numbers of refugees at the Macedonian–Greek border. Born and raised in Macedonia, Hana learned Arabic from her Palestinian father, and uses Arabic at home as her second native language. Having been using it to communicate with family and friends, she never imagined having a career in translation or interpreting since the Arabic language is rarely used in Macedonia. Therefore, she chose to work in the area of law instead. Hana was invited for an interview, where she was tested for her skills to use spoken Arabic, and after two days she was invited to join UNHCR.

The two vulnerable groups that Hana experienced as an interpreter at the Macedonian–Greek border were the Yazidis and the members of the LGBT population. Both of these groups used the Arabic language but required special protection needs of accommodation and transportation in separate groups. Hana states she 'never made any distinction between different people' and maintained during our conversation that 'she cannot take sides'. However, she has also reported having a proactive role in the process of providing refugees with the necessary assistance. Hana says she 'feels responsible for the people she is interpreting for since there may be terrifying consequences if you do not interpret properly, especially in medical situations'.

One of the most rewarding and most problematic instances of interpreting that Hana described during her two years' employment at the UNHCR in Macedonia happened at the Greek–Macedonian border, at Gevgelija. The border was temporarily closed for a day or two when the authorities started sorting refugees at the border based on their origins, in order to give priority to people from Syria, Iraq and Afghanistan. During this day there were about 5,000 people at the border impatiently waiting to enter Macedonia. UNHCR staff was ordered to stay away from the border-crossing zone due to security reasons. The Macedonian border police was trying to establish order, but since they had no interpreters available the communication with the refugees was difficult. Hana decided to act on her own and after two hours of 'shouting and persuasion' she managed to persuade everyone to line up and created some order. During this event, and many other events, Hana performed her work independently, not accompanied by any member of the UNHCR international staff. She felt that she needs to act on behalf of the refugees.

Training and support

Ruiz Rosendo and Persaud point out that 'despite the position the interpreter has played in conflict scenarios, no provision has been made for training interpreters specifically to work in those settings, with few exceptions' (2016: 28). Apart from one trained interpreter, the other three interviewed interpreters were trained in different fields. The interpreters working in the refugee settings are more often non-professional interpreters, who have not received significant amounts of training due to the urgency of the situation. During the early stages of the response, there was no training provided for Hana's to perform her interpreting duties, and she was bound to learn from her own daily experience. Later on, there were two training sessions conducted by UNHCR international staff from Geneva and Budapest. The training incorporated topics related to interpreting methods and techniques, including the use of body language. Additional training was also provided by UNICEF. However, Hana found that the UNHCR 'rule book' (cf. UNHCR, 2009) offered the best guidance as it provided advice on 'how to behave and that you are not the one who will determine who lies and who tells the truth'. Languages that were still lacking interpreters were Farsi and Urdu in particular, as there were far less speakers who could interpret these languages. One or two were eventually found; however, refugees also used English as a relay language.

Interpreters working in emergency situations, and those who want to specialize to work with refugees in humanitarian emergencies, should be provided with appropriate training which will draw not only on the most recent development in interpreting studies, but also on conflict resolution, peacebuilding, and crisis management studies. This training should prepare interpreters to develop their empathic reactions, being able to identify the most vulnerable groups and individuals providing them with a voice.

In these situations, interpreters who belong to or can identify with the refugee group can not only provide the required rare language skills but can also serve as cultural connections between the refugee and the humanitarian worker. Additionally, many refugees are afraid that they will not be adequately understood by foreigners who have no connection with what they have experienced (Miller, 1998). Communicating with an interpreter from a refugee background may create a sense of trust in the refugees in need of interpreting, thus ensuring that the refugees see the interpreter as an ally who is wiling to help in voicing their experiences and feelings.

Empathy is something humans do and is not something that they have. Oftentimes empathy comes spontaneously, like when we see someone hurt or laughing, but it can also be controlled and learned. Controlled empathy comes after a process of thinking and reasoning, and is about taking the perspective of the others, understanding how they feel. Controlled empathy takes longer to handle than automatic empathy and, often, it needs support. Empathy plays a significant role in the reduction of prejudice and new research in medicine claims that if it is specifically targeted in education it can lead to promoting understanding and changing the attitudes of towards the vulnerable and marginalized groups (Batson et al., 2002). Attempts have been made in the field of medicine to teach empathy using various methods through communication and mindfulness. One of the most recent experiential simulations where learners are asked to 'literally stand in the patient's shoes' has proven to be very effective for teaching empathy (Baerman et al., 2015).

Conclusions

Empathy is what makes us human. It is something that can never be automatized, and therefore 'the ability to imagine yourself in someone else's position, to imagine what they are feeling, to understand what makes people tick, to create relationships and to be caring of others' makes human interpreters indispensable in emergency multilingual encounters. Being empathic helps you to work with people and situations different from yourself; it enables you to communicate effectively in these moments, and build relationships of trust in extreme situations.

Bringing together interdisciplinary research on empathy in fields as activism, conflict transformation and heath studies offers additional tools for understanding these concepts within the context of translation studies, especially in the area of interpreting in emergencies, and opens up previously underexplored possibilities for investigation. As in any study, it can be argued that it is problematic to ascertain whether the data collected presents an accurate reflection of participants' actual beliefs, feelings and experiences (Miller, 2004). However, the interpreters involved in this study expressed a high degree of enthusiasm to participate in the project coming from the opportunity to present their perspectives and have their narratives documented, which usually remain excluded from historical accounts. This demonstrated enthusiasm on the part of the participating interpreters, coupled with the highly personal and emotionally charged content of their narratives, serves to validate the thus collected data as an authentic representation of the participants' actual thoughts, feelings and experiences (Miller et al., 2005).

Interpreters who work with refugees in humanitarian situations come from diverse educational backgrounds, as reflected in this study. Sometimes interpreters are former refugees themselves, as with Simona Alavi, who was hired for her linguistic skills, but also for her ability to empathize with the refugees because she shared similar experience with them. Others, like Ajderaga and Habahbeh, were hired for their linguistic skills and knowledge of the culture of the refugees. However, this study suggests that these interpreters showed another important skill that helped them in effectively conducting their job and in addition helping others in need. Empathizing with the others they have been able to assist the humanitarian workers and work with them in a team in order to maximize the assistance provided for the large numbers of refugees in the described emergency situations. Exploration into the two situations that served as the bases for this study showed ways for looking at the interconnectedness of trust, empathy and communication which can be further explored in other similar situations, in both refugee and disaster emergencies.

Interpreters were also involved in creating and maintaining a relationship of trust in the conflict setting. This trust allows them to empower the vulnerable groups, as the interviews reveal. In all these situations, interpreters were engaged to enable communication between the refugees and the organizations providing humanitarian and legal protection. These were both professional and non-professional interpreters. Very often they only had knowledge of the languages involved, but came from different professions, from engineers to medical doctors (Baker, 2010). Regardless of whether they were trained or untrained interpreters, these language brokers were expected to perform duties in situations that were neither clearly defined nor explained in formal or informal interpreting training. In fact, these situations often demanded a response contrary to any instruction and preparation the interpreters had received primarily regarding their neutrality, impartiality and invisibility (Todorova, 2016; 2017).

Notes

1   UNHCR. Figures at a glance. Available from http://www.unhcr.org/en-us/figures-at-a-glance.html.
2   United Nations. *Convention relating to the Status of Refugees*. Geneva; 1951.

References

Primary Sources

Ajdaraga, A. (2017). 23 November. Interview.
Alavi, S. (2017). 26 October. Interview.
Habahbeh, H. (2016). 12 December. Interview.

Secondary Sources

Allen, K. (2012). 'Interpreting in Conflict Zones'. *NAJIT*. Available online: http://najit. org/blog/?p=229 (accessed 30 November 2018).

Angelelli, C. V. (2004). *Revisiting the Interpreter's Role: A Study of Conference, Court, and Medical Interpreters in Canada, Mexico, and the United States*. Amsterdam and Philadelphia, PA: John Benjamins.

Baerman, M., Palermo, C., Allen, L. M., and Williams, B. (2015). 'Learning Empathy through Simulation'. *Simulation in Healthcare* 10(5): 308–319.

Baker, R. (1992). 'Psychological Consequences for Tortured Refugees Seeking Asylum and Refugee Status in Europe'. In M. Basoglu (ed.), *Torture and Its Consequences, Current Treatment Approaches*, 83–106. Cambridge: Cambridge University Press.

Baker, M. (2006). *Translation and Conflict: A Narrative Account*. London and New York, NY: Routledge.

Baker, M. (2008). 'Ethics of Renarration – Mona Baker Is Interviewed by Andrew Chesterman'. *Cultus* 1(1): 10–33.

Baker, M. (2010). 'Interpreters and Translators in the War Zone: Narrated and Narrators'. *The Translator* 16(2): 197–222.

Banyard, V. L., and Miller, K. E. (1998). 'The Powerful Potential of Qualitative Research for Community Psychology'. *American Journal of Community Psychology* 26: 485–505.

Baron-Cohen, S. (2011). *Zero Degrees of Empathy*. London: Penguin.

Batson, C. D. (2009). 'These Things Called Empathy: Eight Related but Distinct Phenomena'. In J. Decety and W. Ickes (eds), *The Social Neuroscience of Empathy*, 3–15. Cambridge, MA: MIT Press.

Batson, C. D., Chang, J., Orr, R., and Rowland, J. (2002). 'Empathy, Attitudes, and Action: Can Feeling for a Member of a Stigmatized Group Motivate One to Help the Group?' *Personality and Social Psychology Bulletin* 28: 1656–1666.

Cameron, L. (2011). 'Empathy in Talk: A Model and Some Methodological Considerations'. Working Paper 3, Living with Uncertainty. Available online: http://www.open.ac.uk/researchprojects/livingwithuncertainty/sites/www.open. ac.uk.researchprojects.livingwithuncertainty/files/pics/d127577.pdf (accessed 30 November 2018).

CEIA – Center for Empathy in International Affairs (2016). 'Empathy in Conflict Resolution: If, How and When'. Available online: http://www.centerforempathy.org/ wp-content/uploads/2016/06/CEIA-Empathy-in-Conflict-Resolution.pdf (accessed 30 November 2018).

Crawford, N. C. (2014). 'Institutionalizing Passion in World Politics: Fear and Empathy'. *International Theory* 6(3): 535–557

Grillo, T. (1991). 'The Mediation Alternative: Process Dangers for Women'. *Yale Law Review* 100: 1545–1610.

Hardy, C. (2017). 'Empathizing with Patients: The Role of Interaction and Narratives in Providing Better Patient Care'. *Medicine, Health Care and Philosophy* 20: 237–248.

Harper, C. (2006). 'Mediator as Peacemaker: The Case for Activist Transformative-Narrative Mediation'. *Journal of Dispute Resolution* 2(10): 595–611.

Head, N. (2012). 'Transforming Conflict: Trust, Empathy, and Dialogue'. *International Journal of Peace Studies* 17(2): 33–55.

Head, N. (2016a). 'Costly Encounters of the Empathic Kind: A Typology'. *International Theory* 8(1): 171–199.

Head, N. (2016b). 'A Politics of Empathy: Encounters with Empathy in Israel and Palestine'. *Review of International Studies* 42(1): 95–113.

Hoffman, M. L. (1989). 'Empathy and Prosocial Activism'. In N. Eisenberg, J. Reykowski, and E. Staub (eds), *Social and Moral Values: Individual and Societal Perspectives*, 65–85. Hillsdale, NJ: Lawrence Erlbaum Associates, Inc.

Inghilleri, M. (2005). 'Mediating Zones of Uncertainty: Interpreter Agency, the Interpreting Habitus and Political Asylum Adjudication'. *The Translator* 11(1): 69–85.

La Corte P. C., and Jalonen A. (2018). *A Practical Guide to Therapeutic Work with Asylum Seekers and Refugees*. London: Jessica Kingsley Publishers.

Lanzoni, S. (2012). 'Empathy in Translation: Movement and Image in the Psychological Laboratory'. *Science in Context* 25(3): 301–327.

Lebow R. N. (2005). 'Reason, Emotion and Cooperation'. *International Politics* 42(3): 42.

Martin, A., and Valero-Garcés, C. (eds) (2008). *Crossing Borders in Community Interpreting: Definitions and Dilemmas*. Amsterdam and Philadelphia, PA: John Benjamins.

Merlini, R., and Gatti, M. (2016). 'Empathy in Healthcare Interpreting: Going beyond the Notion of Role'. *The Interpreters' Newsletter* 20: 139–160.

Miller, K. E. (1998). 'Research and Intervention with Internally Displaced and Refugee Children'. *Peace and Conflict: Journal of Peace Psychology* 4: 365–379.

Miller, K. E. (2004). 'Beyond the Frontstage: Trust, Access, and the Relational Context in Research with Refugee Communities'. *American Journal of Community Psychology* 33(3–4): 217–227.

Miller, K. E., Martell, Z. L., Pazdirek, L., Caruth, M., and Lopez, D. (2005). 'The Role of Interpreters in Psychotherapy with Refugees: An Exploratory Study'. *American Journal of Orthopsychiatry* 75(1): 27–39.

Monroe, K. R. (2012). *Ethics in an Age of Terror and Genocide*. Princeton, NJ: Princeton University Press.

Morrell, M. E. (2010). *Empathy and Democracy: Feeling, Thinking, and Deliberation*. Pennsylvania, PA: Pennsylvania State University Press.

Oakley, A. (1981). 'Interviewing Women: A Contradiction in Terms'. In H. Roberts (ed.), *Doing Feminist Research*, 30–58. Boston, MA: Routledge & Kegan Paul.

Pavlich, G. (1996). 'The Power of Community Mediation: Government and Formation of Self-Identity'. *Law and Society Review* 30(4): 707–734.

Pérez-González, L. (2010). '"Ad-hocracies" of Translation Activism in the Blogosphere: A Genealogical Case Study'. In M. Baker, M. Olohan, and M. Calzada (eds), *Text and Context in Honour of Ian Mason*, 259–287. Manchester: St Jerome.

Rogers, C. R. (1975). 'Empathic: An Unappreciated Way of Being'. *Counseling Psychologist* 5(2): 2–10.

Ruiz Rosendo, L., and Persaud, C. (2016). 'Interpreting in Conflict Zones throughout History'. *Linguistica Antverpiensia* 15: 1–35.

Setton, R., and Dawrant A. (2016). *Conference Interpreting: A Complete Course*. Amsterdam and Philadelphia, PA: John Benjamins.

Todorova, M. (2016). 'Interpreting Conflict Mediation in Kosovo and Macedonia'. *Linguistica Antverpiensia* 15: 227–240.

Todorova, M. (2017). 'Interpreting at the Border: 'Shuttle Interpreting' for UNHCR'. *CLINA* 3(2): 115–129.

UNHCR (2000). 'Kosovo Emergency'. In *UNHCR Global Report 1999*. Available online: http://www.unhcr.org/3e2d4d5f7.html (accessed 4 November 2018).

UNHCR (2009). 'Self-Study Module 3: Interpreting in a Refugee Context'. Available online: http://www.refworld.org/docid/49b6314d2.html (accessed 19 December 2016).

UNHCR (2015a). 'Global Trends: Forced Displacement in 2015'. Available online: http://www.unhcr.org/576408cd7.pdf (accessed 28 December 2016).

UNHCR (2015b). *Поранешната југословенска Република Македонија како земја на азил: Забелешки за состојбата со барателите на азил и бегалците во поранешната југословенска Република Македонија* [*Former Yugoslav Republic of Macedonia as a Country of Asylum: Comments on the Situation of Asylum Seekers in Former Yugoslav Republic of Macedonia*]. Geneva: UNHCR.

Zhang, T. (2016). 'Empathy and Interpreting: The Curious Case of Healthcare Interpreting'. Available online: http://www.interpreterslab.org/single-post/2016/04/21/Empathy-and-Interpreting-The-Curious-Case-of-Healthcare-Interpreting (accessed 4 November 2018).

8

Voices of Refugee Doctors in the United Kingdom: An Exploration of Their Linguistic and Cultural Needs and Aspirations

Ceri Butler and Khetam Al Sharou

The National Health Service (NHS) across the United Kingdom (UK) has had a historical reliance on international medical graduates. These graduates need to develop the same understanding and knowledge of the health system and key concepts and approaches in the delivery of patient care in order to successfully practice medicine in the UK. The UK also has a proud (albeit recently more mixed) history as a country of refuge for individuals fleeing persecution, war and in fear of their own safety. Some of these individuals have been medically qualified doctors who need assistance to return to practice medicine in the UK. These doctors often have extensive experiences in their own countries of origin but can have linguistic and cultural challenges when seeking to work in the UK NHS (General Medical Council, 2011). This chapter discusses the outcomes of a specific project aimed at supporting refugee doctors to improve their linguistic and cultural skills and assist them in their journey to practice medicine in the UK.

Background context

Before moving on to explore the project that was devised for this group of individuals and the outcomes of that project, it is important that we take a few moments to expand on the context that sits and directly impacts on the lives of refugees and international medical graduates in the UK. Without wishing to digress into a detailed analysis of contemporary asylum and immigration legislation, in this chapter, a 'refugee' is defined as an individual who has been determined by the UK as being a refugee under international, regional or national law or who has been granted leave to remain as in response to fear of persecution in their country or origin. A 'doctor' in this chapter is defined by an individual who has primary medical qualification that is recognized by the World Directory of Medical Schools.[1] Thus a 'refugee doctor' is someone who has a primary medical qualification (usually from outside the UK) who has been granted refugee status or leave to remain in the UK.

The UK NHS has been reliant on international medical graduates historically. In 2015, 26 per cent of all doctors registered with the General Medical Council (GMC) had qualified outside the UK or European Union (EU) (General Medical Council, 2016). Current estimates indicate that there are significant shortages for doctors and nurses across the health system. In December 2015, data obtained by the British Broadcasting Corporation (BBC) from a Freedom of Information request found that 69 per cent of UK health trusts were actively recruiting doctors and nurses from overseas in an attempt to fill 23,443 nursing vacancies (representing a 9 per cent vacancy rate for nurses) and 6,207 doctor vacancies (representing a 7 per cent vacancy rate for doctors) across England, Wales and Northern Ireland (BBC, 2016).

The number of vacant posts in the NHS has continued to increase in recent years. A disclosure by NHS Improvement in May 2018 indicated that the NHS in England was short of nearly 93,000 staff during the 2017–2018 financial year (representing an 8 per cent vacancy rate overall) including 35,794 nurses and 9,983 doctors (Campbell, 2018). With increasing concerns and uncertainty over the future employment of European health professionals in the UK due to the UK's exit from the European Union in 2019, it is feared that this situation will continue to worsen.

While the precise number of refugee doctors currently residing in the UK is unknown, the BMA have historically had around 2,000 doctors registered on their voluntary database of refugee doctors. There are no current official figures of the number of medical professionals who managed to return to practice. Work undertaken by Butler and Eversley to explore the number of refugee doctors in London in the mid-2000s found nearly 800 refugee doctors in London, of whom almost 300 were working (Butler and Eversley, 2006).[2]

Support for refugee doctors has been provided through a range of organizations in the last two decades. While there were several individual voices raising concerns about the ability of refugees who have been medically trained to regain their professional identities and contribute to the UK, it was an article in the *British Medical Journal* in 1997 that brought broader attention to the issue of refugee doctors and the potential 'wasted resource' they represented (Berlin et al., 1997). Since then and following the work of a number of key individuals, organizations, charities and local communities as well as a number of Universities, Royal Colleges, Regulatory Bodies (such as the General Medical Council), Health Education England and NHS Trusts have been involved in the design and delivery of services for health professionals in the UK. Several initiatives have been devised in the UK more generally (The BMA[3] Refugee Doctors Initiative (RDI)) as specifically in London,[4] Scotland[5] and Wales. However, these services are dependent on funding that has fluctuated with public and media concerns around refugees and asylum seekers influencing government spending patterns.

Regardless, many refugee health professionals want to resume the career they practiced before leaving their countries as a result of oppression, persecution and/or civil unrest and war (Building Bridges Report, 2011–2013). However, to date, only a small number of refugee doctors, dentists, pharmacists and other health professionals have managed to meet the requirements and returned to clinical practice (Building Bridges Impact Report, 2014–15).

The pathway to employment

All internationally qualified doctors with a recognized degree need to satisfy a number of conditions prior to gaining registration with the General Medical Council or employment in the UK. A three-step process regulates access to the medical license to practice for non-UK-trained doctors. Firstly, they need to take and pass the International English Language Testing System (IELTS) test (or the Occupational English Test (OET) since 2018); secondly, they need to pass the two-part Professional and Linguistic Assessments Board (PLAB) test; and finally, they need to go on a clinical attachment or placement, which is 'designed to provide a sample of the NHS experience for international doctors' (GMC). The clinical attachment is unpaid work experience that aims to familiarize doctors with the NHS and UK practice at an NHS hospital for around ten to twelve weeks.

The PLAB test consists of two parts which test doctors' competence and includes PLAB 1, a written test, and PLAB 2, a practical test with different scenarios to test doctors' competence in settings such as a mock consultation or an acute ward (The British Medical Association (BMA), 2018). Once they have passed through the three-step qualification process, international doctors can apply to the GMC for their license to practice medicine and then apply for jobs as a doctor in the UK (BMA, 2018).

Internationally qualified doctors who arrived as refugees in the UK need assistance to return to practise medicine. They already have the skills, experience and specializations that could benefit the NHS workforce. The inclusion of refugee health professionals in the NHS workforce is essential to strengthen the ability of NHS bodies to achieve 'their equality and diversity goals and deliver high quality services to their patients and the wider community' (Refugee Healthcare Professional Programme, 2009: 1). This aim is imposed onto the NHS – with just and right purpose – and is not backed up by additional resources, or so it seems; therefore, an already overstretched system cannot necessarily deal with these rightful goals. As any refugee doctor will tell you: *Medicine is medicine.* Going through the PLAB tests enables all internationally qualified doctors to revise, refine and enhance their medical competences and skills within the context of the UK NHS. However, the most arduous obstacles come from the linguistic and cultural challenges when seeking to work in the UK NHS.

The process to integrate into the UK medical system is challenging, financially demanding for refugees, their families and the UK social benefit system. Refugee doctors may feel the license to practice is unattainable due to financial constraints and other practical obstacles. Due to this situation, some of them are often forced to rely on social security benefits instead of contributing their skills and knowledge to the NHS (see Wales Deanery Website 2016). Instead of becoming a potential resource for the UK health system, they are often forced to become a demand on the wider budgets on social welfare.

Concerns around refugee and international medical graduates working in the UK

Concerns around the ability of international medical graduates to adapt to working in the UK are not new. However, specific incidences or 'never events' involving internationally qualified doctors working in the UK (such as the Ubani case[6]) have resulted in louder calls for more work in this field and to ensure that all doctors seeking to work in the UK are competent in the English language. In particular, concerns have been articulated around internationally qualified doctors' linguistic skills, clinical communication skills and their awareness of medico-legal frameworks.

In 2011, the GMC summarized these concerns as three main 'difficulties' faced by internationally qualified doctors starting work in the UK as:

- Unfamiliarity with UK systems
- Communication and cultural issues
- Proficiency in English language. (General Medical Council, 2011)

Unfamiliarity with UK systems

A lack of familiarity with the organizational structures and processes of the healthcare system in the country of practice creates practical difficulties for the internationally qualified doctors (Slowther et al., 2009). In particular, there are significant differences in the ethical and legal frameworks for practicing medicine between the UK and their country of qualification, specifically around the model of the doctor–patient relationship and patient autonomy (Slowther et al., 2012). These differences are the result of a lack of awareness of, or reference to, the ethical and professional standards required of doctors working in the UK while being trained and preparing to practice independently.

Communication and cultural issues

Doctors new to the UK need to understand the subtleties of medical English and to identify vital verbal cues to communicate with patients and colleagues once in practice (GMC, 2011; NHS Employers, 2015). Communication skills are a key part of clinical practice. Doctors also need to manage communication effectively with colleagues and patients in a variety of contexts (Illing et al., 2008). Effective communication with patients is vital in gaining informed consent, discussing diagnoses and negotiating treatment options (Slowther et al., 2009).

Several studies show that effective communication is a challenge for internationally qualified doctors. These challenges relate to not only straightforward language barriers but also more subtle issues regarding being aware of non-verbal cues, concerns about different cultural protocols and the lack of communication skills teaching in their original country of qualification (see Fiscsella, 1997). Good communication skills are vital for handling sensitive situations where doctors need to deal with the natural and unplanned expressions of emotion and anger that might be part of supporting a patient and their relatives – there is growing evidence of the impact of these issues when *interpreters* need to be involved in medical communication (see for an overview Hsieh, 2016). These skills do not always have the time to develop *while practicing*, and so are better developed well in advance (Illing et al., 2008).

Doctors need to make sure that they communicate efficiently and effectively with their patients. In a study done by Tongue et al. (2005), 75 per cent of the orthopaedic surgeons surveyed thought that they communicated satisfactorily with their patients. This finding was not paralleled with the responses of their patients where only 21 per cent of the patients reported that they felt they had satisfactory communication with their doctors. Tongue et al. (2005) illustrate with several examples on how doctors need to communicate with their patients.

Studies of the role of cultural factors in doctor–patient communication usually focus on differences between individual doctors and patients. The wider the cultural divide, the less satisfied patients tend to be (Saha et al., 1999; Ramirez, 2003; Haviland et al., 2005). Studies carried out in Western settings have shown that open and clear communication between health providers and patients can facilitate the optimal delivery of healthcare (Maguire and Pitceathly, 2002).

For better and efficient communication between clinicians and patients, health practitioners need to take into account patients' cultural and religious beliefs and practices (Ministry of Health, 2013). Doctors need to familiarize themselves with the cultural and religious beliefs and practices of their colleagues and patients particularly where patients with different cultural backgrounds may have different approaches to, and experiences of, illness, health issues and disabilities (Ministry of Health, 2013).

Proficiency in the English language

Taking into consideration the fact that some of the refugee doctors trained outside the UK have studied in a language other than English, they may be inclined to use literal translation, technical clinical terminology or jargons when treating patients. When practicing, doctors need to communicate in a way that is understood by their patients. Even if a doctor and his/her patients speak and understand the same language, the variation in the use of some terms and expression may be different. For example, in Syria the term 'gums' has different names, formal and colloquial ones, and so doctors need to understand the background of his/her patients and use the suitable term accordingly.

Beyond Medical Practice: Project for refugee doctors

Previously published studies in this field mainly examine the impact of UK employment policies and international recruitment schemes on internationally qualified doctors, including refugee doctors and dentists in the UK and the obstacles they face to requalify in the UK (Sandhu, 2005; Butler and Eversley, 2006; David and Cherti, 2006; Stewart, 2007). Another set of materials on refugee doctors in the UK are reports and guides issued by organizations which are responsible and trying to help them integrate into the UK NHS (such as Building Bridges Impact Report, 2014–15-2011–2013; NHS Employers, 2015). The issues of integrating refugee doctors in the UK are also highlighted by different news articles often presenting stories of individual doctors or cohorts of doctors on a specific project and how they manage their life while working on their linguistic and cultural skills in order to be qualified and return to practice (Agerholm, 2017; Eco-business, 2017; Kirby, 2017; Nedelman, 2017; Nye and Furst, 2017).

Building on previous research and work undertaken by one author (CB) at the national and regional policy levels with refugee health professionals and interest in how we might best support the linguistic development of refugee doctors from the other author (KA), a new interdisciplinary project, 'Beyond Medical Practice' (BMP), was developed. This project brought together two doctoral students from distinct parts of University College London: the Centre for Translation Studies and the Research Department of Primary Care and Population Health.

A successful bid to the UCL Grand Challenges Doctoral Students' Small Grants Scheme[7] enabled the project to be delivered in the 2017/18 academic year – see overview in Box 1. Beyond Medical Practice delivered training and

---

Box 1   Beyond Medical Practice Project summary

Beyond Medical Practice
Cultural and Linguistic Training of Refugee Health Professionals for Integration and Employment in the UK

Project Aim
To deliver training and support to refugee doctors on the linguistic and cultural communication skills needed to facilitate their transition to into employment in the UK

Project Objectives
To deliver training and support to refugee doctors on:

- The language of medical practise in the UK: Verbal cues in communication and consultation skills
- The culture of the NHS; key concepts including a focus on patient-centred care and UK medical ethics and law.

support to refugee doctors on the linguistic and cultural communication skills needed to facilitate their transition into employment in the UK. This project was seen as an additional resource to complement existing provision for refugee health professionals in London. By bringing together practical advice and teaching from UCL faculty involved in the education of undergraduate and postgraduate doctors within UCL Medical School alongside the provision of support for academic English, this project offered a new, interdisciplinary approach to supporting refugee doctors drawing on the most up-to-date resources offered within a top-tier UK Medical School.[8]

Participants

This project was aimed at refugees and asylum seekers with permission to work in the UK with a primary medical qualification from outside the UK. It was aimed at doctors that had passed IELTS or those who had achieved a minimum average of 6.0.[9] The project grant enabled us to offer travel expenses and refreshments to fifteen participants per session. However, our initial budget meant that we could offer only £10 per participant per session. This restricted our focus and ability to fund participants only to people living within London.

Our initial call for participants was made through existing networks with refugee projects and groups operating in London. We received interest from more than fifteen eligible refugee doctors and dentists, including some living as far away as Manchester and Coventry (outside our area of focus). The interest expressed by dentists was also unexpected but reflected the lack of support available for dentists outside London and the complex and costly pathway to employment for them in the UK. We also received interest from a number of ineligible individuals who were at earlier stages in their English language learning. Given the interest of refugee dentists in London to participate in the project, we made a decision to allow two dentists to join the eight eligible doctors, as they would be able to benefit from the doctor-focused sessions.

Our main group of ten refugee doctors and dentists included participants predominantly from Syria, Afghanistan, Pakistan and Iraq who had entered the UK in the last two to three years. This is reflective not only of the ongoing wars and troubles in those regions but also of the UK Home Office's reported country or origin for asylum applications. The most significant factor was that the majority of participants spoke Arabic which enabled them to communicate and support each other as well as to communicate with one of the project leads, KA, during the sessions in a familiar language.

All participants had sat the IELTS English language test and all, apart from one participant who was awaiting his results, had not yet met the level required to progress to the next stage in their pathway to employment, the PLAB tests. The number of attempts made at IELTS ranged from one to fifteen amongst the participants with the writing paper proving to be the most difficult to secure the required 7.0. The level of concern and frustration naturally rose with the number of attempts made at IELTS. The doctor that had made the most attempts at IELTS was even discussing options for moving to Australia, where the required score was lower than that required in the UK. Overall, the key aspirations cited by participants for the BMP project were for them to:

- Improve their communication skills
- Improve their English language skills and pass IELTS
- Learn more about NHS environment in the UK
- Have a better cultural understanding about working in the UK.

Methods

The project initially aimed to deliver six sessions over a six- to eight-month period in the 2017/2018 academic year. In the first workshop, participants were invited to make suggestions as to what they would they would like to focus on. They were enabled to jointly develop their own programme of activities as part of a task-based approach (see Kiraly, 1995, 2000; González Davies, 2003, 2004, 2005; Hurtado Albir, 2007). The list of activities was drawn from evidence of what works with refugee health professionals drawn from the literature (Butler and Eversley, 2007; HENCEL, 2015), from the recommendations of external collaborators, and from the experiences of the researchers. In line with the participants' overall aspirations for the project, their primary focus was to learn:

- How to pass the English language test
- After prompting this was refined as a focus on academic English, in particular academic writing to enable participants to improve their English writing skills
- How the NHS works
- How you care for patients in patient-centred system
- The key medical ethical and legal framework in which a doctor (or health professional) must work in the UK.

Delivering the Sessions

- From the list above a series of five seminars and interactive workshops were devised and delivered focusing on:
- Workshop 1: Academic English and Writing with practical examples
- Workshop 2: Medical Ethics and Law (with a guest lecturer from UCL Medical School)
- Workshop 3: Practising Medical Ethics and Law scenarios
- Workshop 4: Clinical Communication and Consultation Skills (with a guest lecturer)
- Workshop 5: Practising Clinical Communication and Consultation Skills scenarios

Materials for these workshops were drawn from work undertaken by author CB in her work as a member of academic staff within UCL Medical School teaching and supporting undergraduate and postgraduate students as they progressed through their studies, particularly with regard to academic writing for Medicine. She also sought advice from UCL and external language teachers and resources in devising a session on English language and academic writing. In addition, guest lecturers were able to provide materials devised specifically for this group of doctors building on their own extensive work with UK students and qualified doctors.

Clinical scenarios and simulations were drawn from materials generated in part for a previous Grand Challenges Funded project (Berlin, Butler, and Smalldridge, 2018) along with scenarios selected by CB from existing stocks of clinical scenarios and examinations used in undergraduate and postgraduate medicine in the UK.

Project outcomes

Participants' views and experiences of the project were gathered using a mixed-methods approach incorporating a semi-structured survey (see Saldanha and O'Brien, 2013; Zohrabi, 2013) and focus group discussions (see Noaks and Wincup, 2004; Barbour, 2008; Rwegoshora, 2014). These were carried out at a midway point to provide formative feedback which could be integrated into the remaining project and at the end as part of a summative evaluation. Project members were invited to participate and provided with a Participant Information Sheet setting out why we were seeking to collect the information, how it was going to be used, that participation was voluntary and that their participation or non-participation in the formative or summative evaluation would not affect their ability to participate in the broader project.

Following the completion of an Informed Consent Form, a paper-based survey in the form of a questionnaire was distributed and completed anonymously. This questionnaire was divided into three sections: the first set of questions aimed to collect demographic information about the respondents (their age, sex, country of origin, year of arrival in UK and main language(s) spoken); the second section collected information about their medical qualifications and experiences (previous attempts at IELTS, previous attempts at PLAB, their experience working in the UK, and the support they received while in the UK); and the last section was mainly concerned about their linguistic skills and cultural skills and perceived challenges to employment in the UK as a doctor.

The focus group discussions were held after the questionnaires had been distributed and collected so it was a continuation where the questions in the questionnaire operated as triggers to set off the discussion and rephrased when the discussion moved off-topic in order to draw more comments from a new angle, which in turn would trigger new questions and reflections. In total, seven participants participated in the formative and summative evaluation. Discussions in the focus group enabled us to make an assessment of the perceived benefits of BMP: what participants had learned, what they feel more confident and/or competent about in terms of cultural communication, English language and the medico-legal framework. It also allowed us to identify the areas in which participants felt they needed more support or training which have implications for future projects. Overall, participants reported feeling more confident and articulated specific benefits of the project including:

1. The project's focus on specific aspects of English language;
2. Combining the benefits of working in the UK with the project to help them study for the IELTS/OET exam;
3. Improvements in consultation and communication skills following the project;
4. Learning more about the NHS and key concepts to help future working practises.

The majority of participants received English language support and teaching from recognized IELTS course providers in London. They also sought additional support in other areas including gaining work experience or placements in the health sector while two had already secured employment as a phlebotomist and healthcare assistant which they hoped would help them to improve their communication skills and understanding of how the NHS works. Overall, the participants' main focus remained firmly fixed on passing the immediate hurdle and barrier to progression: the English language test. Shortly before the end of the project, we heard that three participants had successfully passed their English language tests. One participant, a recent graduate from medical school in Syria, had passed the IELTS test on his first attempt while two participants, including one who had previously attempted IELTS thirteen times, had been successful at the newly approved OET test.

In response to questions around what additional support they would like in this or any future project, participants identified a range of topics to focus on:

- Additional clinical scenarios
- More detailed feedback on their language, communication and clinical skills
- More around the ethical/medicolegal framework in the UK
- Research methods
- Sessions on the new English language test approved by the GMC, the OET
- More academic English writing support.

Looking forward

This project was never intended to meet all of the needs that participants had. It was intended as an introductory project to allow participants to gain an awareness of the topics covered and to encourage them to undertake further self-directed studies in these fields. This project was also intended to act as a pilot project to allow its leaders to assess what size and type of demand there was for specific topics and, more importantly, whether we felt we might be able to meet that demand in a future, larger and more substantially funded series of seminars and workshops drawing in a larger number of participants and guest lecturers and experienced personnel. This project also enabled us to undertake some further research into the needs and aspirations of this, albeit small, group of refugee health professionals. What is clear is that more targeted and intensive training is needed to help the refugee doctors to acquire the linguistic and cultural competencies required to work in the UK.

Most refugee doctors are still struggling with achieving the required scores in the English language test. At the beginning, a considerable number of doctors expressed their wishes to join the project but failed to meet the IELTS score criterion. Perhaps we should consider a further exploration of those projects that are delivering English support to refugees more widely and refugee doctors specifically to assess where we might be able to help. In the context of systemic cuts to English language teaching, this may prove to be a challenging objective but would be in line with Casey's recent calls for more English language provision in the UK to enhance integration prospects for refugees.[10] In 2018, the GMC decided to accept the Occupational English Test (OET) in addition to the IELTS as proof of a doctor's language skills (Rimmer, 2018). Further research is needed in this field and additional work is underway articulated by Butler in her recent presentation at the OET conference at the Royal College of Nurses in August 2018 (Butler, 2018).

Some refugee doctors showed a lack of awareness of the importance of the understating of cultural differences and that it is an essential part of their career as doctors in the UK. They think that such skills can be attained during practice which is not always possible. A considerable number of these refugee doctors are actually very experienced and expert in their specialization. They can feed back into the system their own medical experiences. For example, as pointed out by CB in the first session of the project, refugee doctors especially who come from a country where there is war can help in treating cases which occur only in war time such as dealing with knife attacks and weapons injuries. Also, doctors who come from country where they had to operate in an under-resourced working environment with limited access to technology tend to depend more on their own knowledge and experience in examining and diagnosing their patients. As phrased by doctor Vural Özdemir (cited in Eco-business (2017), 'empowering refugee doctors to help address the needs of fellow refugees will help overcome entrenched dogmas toward refugee diversity and social identities.'

Conclusions

The refugee doctors and dentists who participated in Beyond Medical Practice reported benefits from their participation. This project has also allowed the authors to explore a range of other opportunities to support refugee health professionals using new or existing mechanisms.

Projects such as Beyond Medical Practice have a role in plugging gaps in existing provision for refugee health professionals. The topics covered in this project form part of existing undergraduate medical, dental and nursing curricular across the UK. The English language support is also available across UK Further and Higher Education. UK universities have vast resources and, while these resources are always on demand, there are opportunities for them to offer similar training to refugee health professionals seeking to return to clinical practise. With the correct guidance, direction and support they could link up with other initiatives across UK Higher Education to support refugee learners and make a real difference.

Notes

1. See https://www.wdoms.org (accessed 30 November 2018).
2. This was found by matching databases held by organizations in London delivering support, information, advice, guidance or specific training and employment to refugee doctors at that time.
3. The BMA Refugee Doctors Initiative (RDI) is a special package of free benefits, available to refugee and asylum-seeking doctors as they seek to establish their careers in the UK (The British Medical Association (BMA, 2018). The RDI works with other refugee groups to give financial help and support with IELTS and PLAB tests and assistance with finding a clinical attachment. By joining this initiative, eligible refugee doctors will get the following benefits: free weekly subscription to BMJ accessing NHS jobs, free weekly subscription to BMA News, use of the BMA Library (BMA, 2018). The BMA is the trade union and professional organization for UK doctors.
4. In London, the Building Bridges programme (of which Butler was an architect) is an NHS-funded partnership for all refugee health professionals living in London and is made up of three organizations: London Met's Refugee Assessment and Guidance Unit (RAGU), Glowing Results and the Refugee Council. RAGU offers trainings on the NHS including workplace communication and culture for health professionals for all health professionals and at all IELTS levels, to support them into work prior to IELTS.
5. The NHS Education for Scotland (NES) Refugees Doctors Programme is designed to assist asylum seeking and refugee doctors living in Scotland to achieve registration with the General Medical Council via the PLAB examinations in order to be in a position to compete for posts in the NHS in the UK. Support leading to successful completion of IELTS is also available to dentists and pharmacists. Refugee Doctors Programme, funded by the Scottish Government, is supporting medically trained and qualified refugees to achieve medical registration and contribute their skills to NHS Scotland.
6. See https://www.theguardian.com/society/2010/feb/04/doctor-daniel-ubani-unlawfully-killed-patient (accessed 30 November 2018).

7. UCL Grand Challenges Doctoral Students' Small Grants Scheme enabled the project to be delivered in the 2017/18 academic year. For information about the scheme, see https://www.ucl.ac.uk/grand-challenges/.

8. UCL Medical School is currently ranked 9th in the world for Medicine in based on the QS World University Rankings by Subject 2019 (see, https://www. topuniversities.com/university-rankings-articles/university-subject-rankings/ top-medical-schools-2019; accessed 5 July 2019) and 14th in the world for Medicine (behind Oxford, Cambridge, and Imperial College) based on the Times Higher Education's World University Rankings data for 2019 (see https://www. timeshighereducation.com/world-university-rankings/2019/world-ranking#!/ page/0/length/25/subjects/3141/sort_by/rank/sort_order/asc/cols/stats; accessed 5 July 2019).

9. Where the level required to register with the UK General Medical Council is an overall score of 7.5 with minimum scores of 7.0 in speaking, listening, writing and reading: https://www.bma.org.uk/advice/employment/immigration/english-testing (accessed 15 March 2018).

10. For example, see https://inews.co.uk/news/uk/english-common-language-says-former-tsar/ (accessed 15 April 2018).

References

Agerholm, H. (2017). 'Refugee Doctors Set to Fill NHS Staff Shortages'. *The Independent*, 6 September. Available online: http://www.independent.co.uk/news/uk/home-news/nhs-shortages-refugee-doctors-to-fill-gaps-staff-a7933176.html (accessed 30 November 2018).

Barbour, R. (2008). *Introducing Qualitative Research: A Student Guide to the Craft of Doing Qualitative Research*. London: Sage.

BBC News (2016). 'Thousands of NHS Nursing and Doctor Posts Lie Vacant'. *BBC*, 29 February. Available online: https://www.bbc.co.uk/news/health-35667939 (accessed 30 November 2018).

Berlin, A., Gill, P., and Eversley, J. (1997). 'Refugee Doctors in Britain: A Wasted Resource'. *British Medical Journal* 315(7103): 264–265.

Berlin, A., Butler, C., and Smalldridge, A. (2018). 'Refugees, Vulnerable Migrants and Health: Implications for Primary Care'. Conference Symposium presented to the Society for Academic Primary Care ASM, London, 11 July 2018.

Butler, C. (2018). 'Integrating Refugee Healthcare Professionals into Host Countries'. Paper Presented to the OET Forum. London, 29 August 2018.

Butler, C., and Eversley, J. (2006). *Ready and Waiting: Refugee Doctors in London, UK*. London: Refugee Doctor Programme Evaluation Network.

Butler, C., and Eversley, J. (2007). 'Guiding Their Way: Assisting Refugee Health Professionals'. *The Clinical Teacher* 4: 146–152.

Campbell, D. (2018). 'NHS in England Facing Deepening Staffing Crises, Figures Show', *The Guardian*, 26 July. Available online: https://www.theguardian.com/society/2018/jul/26/nhs-in-england-facing-deepening-staffing-crisis-figures-show (accessed 30 November 2018).

David, N., and Cherti, M. (2006). *Losing Out Twice? Skill Wastage of Overseas Health Professionals in the UK*. The COMPAS Annual Conference in 2006, London. Available online: https://migrantsorganise.org/wp-content/uploads/2012/09/MRCF-Report-on-Experiences-of-Migrant-Medical-Professionals-in-the-UK.pdf (accessed 30 November 2018).

Eco-business (2017). 'Refugee Doctors for Refugee Health'. *Eco-Business*, 7 December. Available online: http://www.eco-business.com/opinion/refugee-doctors-for-refugee-health/ (accessed 30 November 2018).

Fiscella, K., Roman-Diaz M., Lue, B. H., Botelho, R., and Frankel R. (1997). '"Being a Foreigner, I May Be Punished If I Make a Small Mistake": Assessing Transcultural Experiences in Caring for Patients'. *Fam Pract* 14(2): 112–116.

González Davies, M. (ed.) (2003). *Secuencias. Tareas para el aprendizaje interactivo de la traducción especializada*. Barcelona: Octaedro-EUB.

González Davies, M. (2004). *Multiple Voices in the Translation Classroom: Activities, Tasks and Projects*. Amsterdam and Philadelphia, PA: John Benjamins.

González Davies, M. (2005). 'Minding the Process, Improving the Product: Alternatives to Traditional Translator Training'. In M. Tennent (ed.), *Training for the New Millennium: Pedagogies for Translation and Interpreting*, 67–82. Amsterdam and Philadelphia, PA: John Benjamins.

General Medical Council (2011). *The State of Medical Training and Practice in the UK: 2011*. London: GMC.

General Medical Council (2016). *The State of Medical Training and Practice in the UK: 2016*. London: GMC.

Haviland, M., Morales, L., Dial, T., and Pincus, H. (2005). 'Race/Ethnicity, Socioeconomic Status and Satisfaction with Health Care'. *American Journal of Medical Quality* 20: 195–203.

Health Education North Central and Eastern London (HENCEL) (2016). *Building Bridges: Impact Report 2014–15*. London: HENCEL. Available online: https://www.refugeecouncil.org.uk/assets/0003/6701/BuildingBridges_ImpactReport2014-15.pdf (accessed 30 November 2018).

Hsieh, E. (2016). *Bilingual Health Communication: Working with Interpreters in Cross-Cultural Care*. London and New York, NY: Routledge.

Hurtado Albir, A. (2007). 'Competence-Based Curriculum Design for Training Translators'. *The Interpreter and Translator Trainer (ITT)* 1(2): 163–195.

Illing, J., Morrowand, G., Kergon, C., Burfordand, B., Spencer, J., Peile, E., Davies, C., Baldauf, B., Allen, M., Johnson, N., Morrison, J., Donaldson, M., Whitelaw, M., and Field, M. (2008). *'How Prepared Are Medical Graduates to Begin Practice? A Comparison of Three Diverse UK Medical Schools, Final Report to GMC April 2008.' Project Report*. London: GMC. Available online: https://www.gmc-uk.org/

FINAL_How_prepared_are_medical_graduates_to_begin_practice_September_08. pdf_29697834.pdf (accessed 30 November 2018).

Kiraly, D. (1995). *Pathways to Translation: Pedagogy and Process*. Kent, OH: Kent State University Press.

Kiraly, D. (2000). *A Social Constructivist Approach to Translator Education: Empowerment from Theory to Practice*. Manchester: St. Jerome.

Kirby, E. J. (2017). 'NHS Pilot Scheme Taps into Skills of Refugee Doctors'. *BBC*, 18 July. Available online: http://www.bbc.com/news/health-40442848 (accessed 30 November 2018).

Maguire, P., and Pitceathly, C. (2002). 'Key Communication Skills and How to Acquire Them'. *British Medical Journal* 325(7366): 697–700.

Ministry of Health (2013). *Refugee Health Care: A Handbook for Health Professionals*. Wellington: Health. Available online: https://www.health.govt.nz/system/ files/documents/publications/refugee-health-care-a-handbook-for-health-professionalsv2.pdf (accessed 30 November 2018).

Nedelman, M. (2017). 'Why Refugee Doctors Become Taxi Drivers'. *CNN*, 9 August. Available online: https://edition.cnn.com/2017/08/09/health/refugee-doctors-medical-training/index.html (accessed 30 November 2018).

NHS Employers (2015). *Working and Training in the National Health Service: A Guide for International Medical and Dental Graduates Thinking about Working or Training in the UK*. London: NHS Employers. Available online: http://www.nhsemployers. org/~/media/Employers/Publications/Working-training-NHS-guide-for-IMGs.pdf (accessed 30 November 2018).

Noaks, L., and Wincup, E. (2004). *Criminological Research: Understanding Qualitative Methods*. London: Sage.

Nye, C., and Furst, J. (2017). 'The Refugee Doctors Learning to Speak Glaswegian'. *BBC*, 6 September. Available online: http://www.bbc.com/news/health-41160013 (accessed 28 November 2018).

Ramirez, A. (2003). 'Consumer-Provider Communication Research with Special Populations'. *Patient Education and Counseling* 50: 51–54.

Refugee Healthcare Professional Programme (2009). *The Case for Working with Refugee Healthcare Professionals: An Equality and Diversity Perspective*. London: NHS Employers. Available online: http://www.nhsemployers.org/~/media/Employers/ Documents/Recruit/the_case_for_working_refugee.pdf (accessed 30 November 2018).

Rimmer, A. (2018). 'Doctors' Language Tests: Five Minutes with Ceri Butler'. *British Medical Journal* 360(k806). https://doi.org/10.1136/bmj.k806.

Rwegoshora, H. M. M. A. (2014). *A Guide to Social Science Research*. 2nd edition. Dar es Salaam: Mkuki na Nyota Publishers Ltd.

Saha, S., Komaromy, M., Koepsell, T. D., and Bindman, A. B. (1999). 'Patient-Physician Racial Concordance and the Perceived Quality and Use of Health Care'. *Arch Intern Med*. 159: 997–1004.

Saldanha, G., and O'Brien, S. (2013). *Research Methodologies in Translation Studies*. London and New York, NY: Routledge.

Sandhu, D. P. S. (2005). 'Current Dilemmas in Overseas Doctors' Training'. *Postgraduate Medical Journal* 81: 97–82.

Slowther, A., Hundt, G. L. Taylor, R., and Purkis, J. (2009). *Non-UK Qualified Doctors and Good Medical Practice: The Experience of Working within a Different Professional Framework: Report for the General Medical Council.* London: GMC. Available online: https://www.gmc-uk.org/FINAL_GMC_Warwick_Report.pdf_25392230.pdf (accessed 30 November 2018).

Slowther, A., Lewando Hundt, G. A. Purkis, J., and Taylor, R. (2012). 'Experiences of Non-UK-Qualified Doctors Working within the UK Regulatory Framework: A Qualitative Study'. *Journal of the Royal Society of Medicine* 105: 157–165.

Stewart, E. (2007). 'Addressing the Challenges Facing Refugee Doctors in the UK'. *Local Economy* 22(4): 409–417.

The British Medical Association (BMA) (2018). *Are You a Refugee Doctor Who Wants to Work in the UK?* London: MBA. Available online: https://www.bma.org.uk/advice/work-life-support/life-and-work-in-the-uk/refugee-doctors (accessed 30 November 2018).

Tongue, J. R., Epps, H. R., and Forese, L. L. (2005). 'Communication Skills for Patient-Centered Care: Research-Based, Easily Learned Techniques for Medical Interviews That Benefit Orthopaedic Surgeons and Their Patients'. *Journal of Bone and Joint Surgery American volume* 87: 652–658.

Wales Deanery (2016). *Refugee Doctors.* Cardiff: HEIW. Available online: https://psu.walesdeanery.org/refugee-doctors (accessed 30 November 2018).

Zohrabi, M. (2013). 'Mixed Method Research: Instruments, Validity, Reliability and Reporting Findings'. *Theory and Practice in Language Studies* 3(2): 254–262.

Section 3

Integrating Cross-National Representations of Local Crises

On France, Terrorism and the English Press: Examining the Impact of Style in the News

Ashley Riggs

On the night of 14 July 2016, just after thousands of residents and tourists had finished watching a fireworks display in celebration of Bastille Day, a violent attack took place in Nice, France. The perpetrator, Mohamed Lahouaiej-Bouhlel, drove a lorry through the crowds, killing 86 people and injuring 434 others. This attack came relatively soon after two other very serious attacks in France in January and November 2015, similar for their high number of fatalities – the so-called Bataclan and *Charlie Hebdo* attacks – which were still etched in people's minds and which had also determined security policies, such as a state of emergency, that were still in place.

I chose to study the way this event was portrayed in the British news[1] because a number of factors had coalesced after the tragically momentous attacks of 2015. The immigration 'crisis' continued, with the accompanying debate on open borders, security and jobs. Nationalism was on the rise across Europe. The Brexit vote had taken place just a few weeks before the Nice attack and was followed by an increase in hate crime in the UK, in particular against Muslims. Donald Trump, who is known for extreme positions on Muslims and immigrants and who would soon fuel an international focus on 'fake news', was campaigning to become president of the United States. Terrorist attacks in the UK and elsewhere seemed to be growing more frequent. At the same time, as the media landscape continued to evolve rapidly, there were many questions about the future of news, with journalism (appropriately or not) described as 'in crisis'. News seemed to be politically biased, sometimes bigoted and often alarmist. Where did this come from, and what could be done? Close analysis of news language was a good place to start.

Terrorism and crisis communication

In line with Canel (2012), Canel and Sanders (2010) and Federici (2016), terrorist attacks are instances when crisis communication occurs, as they involve 'extreme conditions' (Federici 2016: 2), risk and uncertainty, 'an important communication dimension, and [...] the reputation of organizations' (Canel, 2012: 215). I maintain that reporting on terrorist attacks qualifies as crisis communication: communication occurring during a crisis which provides information about the events and/or organizational responses to them.

Importantly, depending upon how it is conducted, reporting on terrorist events abroad may participate in the 'permanent *sense of a state of emergency* in the ways the world is *represented*' (Federici, 2016: 1; emphasis in the original). Zelizer's (2015: 892) critique of the concept of crisis serves as a reminder about the power the press wields in its role as crisis communicator: 'Though crisis is a phenomenon with material dimensions—factories close, people die, infrastructures collapse—it is shaped too by discourse: We name it, we flesh out its details with words, we give it identity through comparison and analogy and metaphor.' Zelizer also provides insight into how the press may play a better role in crisis communication. One way is by questioning our assumptions about crisis situations. For instance, '[i]s a crisis that ensues following long periods of neglect as sudden as we make it out to be? Why is disruption more deserving of attention than what precedes it?' Are 'noncrisis moment[s]' always the most valuable ones? (890). With regard to terrorism reporting specifically, Philip Seib (2017) highlights related questions that he believes the media is failing to ask as it reports on terrorist attacks:

> [I]t became clear that for all the breathless headlines about IS-inspired terror attacks, many know little about the complexities of terrorism and Islam. Who are these people who murder so wantonly? Why do they do it? And, most importantly, how might such attacks be stopped?

Journalists can and should ask key questions like Zelizer and Seib's about terror-related events and about how they themselves approach reporting on such events. In doing so, they will fulfil their role as cultural mediators (d'Hulst et al., 2014; van Doorslaer, 2012). Furthermore, as Zelizer highlights, they need to think carefully about the intricacies of their language, and its likely effects.

Style

The role journalistic style plays in conveying information and portraying events and cultures has been much overlooked and, I claim, its impact underestimated – especially where common yet influential rhetorical devices such as alliteration (which makes particularly salient for the reader the content it accompanies) and modality (which shapes reader belief and confidence in the information received) are concerned. Nevertheless, framing studies (see, for example, Baker 2006, 2007) and discourse analysis, both commonly applied in news translation research, indirectly justify this kind of focus. Reese defines frames as '*organizing principles* that are socially *shared* and *persistent* over time, that work *symbolically* to meaningfully *structure* the social world' (2001: 11; emphasis in the original). Baresch, Hsu and Reese (2012 [2010]: 641) cite the 'War on Terror' as an example. In addition, 'Reese's definition suggests that framing research not only examine the manifest or most salient content but also strive to catch the structure and pattern hidden in the media texts, and search for *what makes people take this latent structure and way of thinking for granted*' (Baresch et al., 2012 [2010]: 641; my emphasis). Discourse analysis draws upon stylistics (Schäffner, 2013: 48) but has yet to take proper account of combinations of stylistic elements in media texts.

Style can be defined as 'a choice of form ("manner") to express content ("matter")' (Wales 2001: 158). While we may not even notice stylistic elements when we read news texts, they nevertheless wield a lot of power. Baresch et al. evoke, for example, the potential role of 'allusion' or 'situational irony' in constructing underlying, organizing principles (2012 [2010]: 644–645). 'These devices will be difficult to spot, but the researcher must account for them' (645). Put otherwise, such devices are not obvious, they are under-researched, but they are a vital force in the way in which we interpret information. Therefore, '[a]t this early stage in new media scholarship', researchers 'must innovate methods for identifying, sampling, and analyzing data sets that will yield meaningful results' (645). Coming from a translation perspective, Boase-Beier, too, emphasizes the importance of 'stylistically-aware analysis' (2006: 111). Not only does it help 'the translator to describe and justify [...] stylistic decisions', but 'we can go further, and argue that knowledge of stylistics will allow the translator to consider how such aspects of meaning as attitude, implication, or cognitive state can be recreated in the target text' (2012 (Print, 2011)), Even when the aim is not translation in its narrower sense, that is from source text to target text, but news analysis and the way its discourse translates events, cultures or groups for an-other audience, looking at style 'will allow more detailed consideration of the interplay of universal stylistic features such as conceptual metaphor, culturally embedded imagery, and specific linguistic connotation' (Boase-Beier, 2012 (Print, 2011)). Working from a translation criticism perspective, Hewson (2011: 74–83) identifies alliteration and modality as two key foci for analyses seeking to describe stylistic effects. Alliteration/assonance and modality are explored in the following analysis.

Analysing *The Guardian* and *The Telegraph*

I chose to use articles from the *Guardian* and the *Telegraph* because they represent, respectively, more liberal-leaning and more conservative positions on the political spectrum. Given these political leanings and given the considerations above on terrorism reporting, crisis communication and style, I formulated the following hypotheses. In terms of general themes,

1) references to Britain/Britons, which journalists may use to make an article relevant for the domestic audience (Freedman, 2017: 215), would also be likely to heighten the sense of threat in both news sources, but the *Telegraph* would centre more on the home country and also portray it as superior;

2) representations of French society and of Muslims and/or Islam would be more negative in the *Telegraph*, given its alignment with conservative positions and policies, which are often anti-Muslim and also likely to find fault with the socialist government in place in 2016 in France.

The first hypothesis aligns with Cottle's assertion that '[w]hen reporting on distant disasters and humanitarian emergencies, [...] national news media often seek out stories populated by their own' citizens. 'This stock news cast of *dramatis personae* serves to "nationalize", personalize and "bring back home" the meanings of distant events and tragedies' (2012 [2011]: 482). Moreover, in relation to the second hypothesis, 'the global war on terror, inevitably, becomes reported through blood-flecked glasses tinted by national' and, I would add, political, 'interests' (483).

In terms of style specifically, I chose to focus on modality to flesh out my earlier findings; on alliteration because, to my knowledge, it has received no attention in news research. My hypotheses on these features were that

3) modal use would give suppositions a patina of factuality in both sets of news articles;

4) alliteration/assonance would predominantly accompany negative content and serve to emphasize and reinforce it, thereby giving it more weight, in both news sources. This in turn would be likely to fuel readers' sense of threat and 'of a state of emergency' (Federici).

Corpus and methodology

The corpus comprises thirteen online articles from the *Guardian* (including one technically from the *Observer*; 13,558 words) and 14 from the *Telegraph* (14,294 words) that were published from the morning following the attack, 15 July, through 18 July (see Table 9.1). Articles were included in the corpus if they addressed the Nice attack, were published during the defined time frame

Table 9.1 Synoptic table

Abbreviation	Source	Date	Short title	Author
TG1	*Guardian*	15.07.16	Why does France keep getting attacked?	Burke, J.
TG2		17.07.16	Police and academics search Nice attacker's history for a motive. Burke, J.	Burke, J.
TG3		16.07.16	As horror strikes again, all eyes are on how France reacts.	Nougayrède, N.
TG4		17.07.16	François Hollande pleads for unity amid anger over Nice attack.	Chrisafis, A.
TG9		15.07.16	From Charlie Hebdo to Bastille Day: France reels after new deadly attack.	Rawlinson, K., Chrisafis, A., & Dodd, V.
TG10		15.07.16	84 dead after truck rams Bastille Day crowd in Nice.	Chrisafis, A., & Dehghan, S. K.
TG11		15.07.16	'My daughters saw bodies. Lots of them': witnesses recall Nice truck attack.	Fischer, S.
TG12		15.07.16	France attack: use of truck in Nice demonstrates evolving nature of threat.	Burke, J.
TG13		15.07.16	France stunned after truck attacker kills 84 on Bastille Day in Nice.	Chrisafis, A., Fischer, S., & Rice-Oxley, M.

(continued)

Abbreviation	Source	Date	Short title	Author
TG14		15.07.16	Nice attack is a crisis for presidency of François Hollande.	Chrisafis, A.
TG15		16.07.16	Nice attack bewilders Mohamed Lahouaiej-Bouhlel's relatives.	Stephen, C.
TG16		16.07.16.	Nice truck attack: Islamic State claims responsibility.	Jones, S., Chrisafis, A., & Davies, C.
TGObs17	*Guardian/ Observer*	16.07.16	Tourism will not give in to terror, but the industry faces a rethink.	Doward, J.
DT5	*Telegraph*	15.07.16	Nice terror attack: Europe 'faces summer of copycat attacks'.	Farmer, B.
DT6		16.07.16	Nice attack: Truck driver who killed 84 named – the news as it unfolded on Friday, 15 July.	Boyle, D., Morgan, T., Chazan, D., Turner, C., Willgress, L., Allen, P., … Millward, D.
DT7		17.07.16	Bataclan brought us together – but this attack in Nice will drive a wedge into France.	Moutet, A.-E.
DT8		18.07.16	Mourners spit and throw rubbish on 'hate memorial' at spot Bastille Day terrorist was killed.	Morgan, T., Turner, C., Willgress, L., & Allen, P.
DT18		15.07.16	The Nice terror attack shows just how easy it is to commit an atrocity – and how hard it is to stop one.	Coughlin, C.
DT19		15.07.16	How the terror in Nice unfolded: Driver told police he was delivering ice creams – but instead delivered murder on a massive scale.	Mendick, R.
DT20		15.07.16	The crumb of comfort from the Nice attack is that even terrorists who plot alone can be stopped.	Blair, D.

(Continued)

Abbreviation	Source	Date	Short title	Author
DT21		15.07.16	Analysis: Nice truck attack shows France's acute vulnerability to terrorism.	Blair, D.
DT22		16.07.16	The best defence against terrorism is to show that it does not work as a way of changing government policy or public perception.	Barrett, R.
DT23		18.07.16	Who is the Nice terror attack suspect? Everything we know so far about Mohamed Lahouaiej Bouhlel.	Samuel, H., & Morgan, T.
DT24		18.07.16	French PM booed at Nice tribute for victims of terror attack.	Samuel, H., Chazan, D., Turner, C., & Willgress, L.
DT25		18.07.16	Nice terrorist attack on Bastille Day: everything we know so far on Monday.	Henderson, B., & Sabur, R.
DT26		15.07.16	How religion can drive someone to slaughter his fellow citizens – and believe they deserve it.	Meleagrou-Hitchens, A.
DT27		15.07.16	The Nice terror attack is why Donald Trump might win.	Stanley, T.

and came under the 'News' section of each website. This does not, however, mean that they all qualify as 'hard news', as is evident from the types of commentary a number of the articles contain.

I used the qualitative data analysis tool QDA Miner to explore themes (e.g. 'French Society' or 'Attitudes of/to Muslims') and stylistic elements in the corpus in an iterative process of category selection and definition, and then coded relevant textual segments within the established categories. I shall focus here on findings related to references to Britain/Britons, the portrayal of French society, alliteration and modality. Direct quotes were not included in the analysis, as my focus was the style of the text, not that of individuals who made statements or were consulted about events.

Instances of alliteration/assonance were tallied across the corpus and classified as negative, positive or neutral, depending upon the connotations of the content they accompanied. How is connotation understood here? It is true that various definitions of the term exist and take into account broader or narrower parameters. For instance, according to Osgood, Succi and Tannenbaum (1957), interlocutors react to words in terms of how positive or negative, strong or weak, active or passive the words are. Twenty years later, Chuquet and Paillard (1987), working from the perspective of a translator aiming to render a target text and the pitfalls she might encounter when dealing with connotation, restricted their concern to the positive vs. negative dimension. Don Bialostosky (2017) echoes common criticisms of such linguistic conceptions of connotation, which treat it as objectively classifiable and fail to take into account key factors in how a given word is interpreted, that is

> the kinds of situations and the kinds of utterances in which they are typically used, the kinds of speakers who use them, the kinds of hearers who hear them, and the kinds of emotional-evaluational tones with which they are used in those situations. We need to locate our individual associations in shared or at least shareable situations. (Bialostosky, 2017)

Nevertheless, I chose to use quite a narrow conception of connotation in this study, based on the positive/negative dichotomy. It is relevant to the topics being addressed and makes it possible to parse textual elements meaningfully, without being unwieldy. Moreover, I believe that the majority of readers of these news articles would make the same positive and negative associations. We share Anglo-Saxon culture; awareness of these news topics; knowledge of the news sources in question, their language, conventions and political leanings; and have chosen to read them. The assumption of shared associations could nevertheless be tested with further research.

Findings

Britain and Britons

In both sources, references to Britain and Britons work to 'bring the story home' (recall Cottle and Freedman) and appear to heighten the sense of crisis, although these effects seem even more pronounced in the *Telegraph* articles. Where the *Guardian* includes such references, France often still remains the central focus:

> TG9 France also suffered in August 2015 when a gunman opened fire on a high-speed train that was carrying more than 500 people, before he was overpowered by three Americans – two of whom were soldiers – and a British passenger.'

A *Telegraph* article stands in contrast:

> DT18 In Britain we suffered our own lone wolf attack when two Islamist extremists hacked to death Fusilier Lee Rigby on a south London street with machetes in 2013.

The relevance of the attack for Britons is nonetheless an important aspect of *Guardian* reporting:

> TG9 The UK Foreign Office called on all Britons in France to exercise caution and follow the instructions of local law enforcement officials.

> TG16 A number of Britons were also caught up in the attack.

(The heading of DT25, 'Britons caught up in *terror*' (my emphasis), while similar, is more dramatic.)

> TGObs17 The extension will see a visible security presence, both in Nice and across France, continued for another three months. This will entail more police and soldiers on the streets, a graphic reminder to Britons, who make 17 million visits to France each year, that the country, according to the Foreign Office, faces a 'high threat from terrorism'.

Particularly insidious is the *Telegraph*'s strategy of linking Lahouaiej-Bouhlel to an attack in Tunisia and to threats to Britons because the attack occurred near his home town:

> DT23 According to Tunisian security sources, he hailed from the Tunisian town of Msaken, which is close to the seaside city of Sousse, where 38 people, including 30 Britons, were gunned down by terrorists in June 2015.

Finally, the *Telegraph* even seems to suggest Britain is safer than France:

> DT21 Unlike Britain – which has always retained its frontier controls and has the natural advantage of being an island – France can do little to prevent the flow of suspected terrorists or weapons into its territory.

> DT20 Over the last decade, these vulnerabilities have been used to scupper one terrorist plot after another in Britain.

> DT20 Even if the plot avoids detection, the terrorists still face the problem of actually executing the attack. Here, everything depends on the quality of their training – and, in Britain at least, this has often been found wanting.

> DT22: In the United Kingdom, the Security Service (MI5) and the police have together disrupted seven terrorist attacks in the last 18 months.

French society

Multiple *Guardian* articles celebrate various aspects of Nice; not only its glamor, sun, sea (TG17) and 'festive [...] shoreline' (TG3), but its 'cosmopolitan' character, enhanced by the diverse mix of people who live and visit there (TG3), including '40,000 Tunisians' (TG15). In other words, 'France's proud cultural heritage' (TG3) is emphasized. The city's cultural standing is also underscored through a number of artistic and literary references, i.e. to Chekhov (TG3), F. Scott Fitzgerald (TG3 and 17), Picasso, or Oscar Wilde (TG17). This stands in contrast to the use of Camus in DT7 (Riggs 2018), which was both negative and unlikely to be accessible to a British readership. Yet the *Guardian* also recognizes that there is a darker side to 'the France of wine and charcuterie, chateaux and cheese' (TG1; note the alliteration). Indeed, the *Guardian* historicizes the 'impact of western colonialism' (TG2) in France, the enduring societal tensions that have resulted, and its consequences for '[d]isaffected youths in the region' (TG17).

The *Telegraph*, on the other hand, focuses on negative aspects of Nice. For instance, it emphasizes the terrorist threat that the city and the Côte d'Azur region represent: in DT25, the sentence 'Nice is considered a town under particular terrorist threat' appears twice. DT7 informs us that 'Nice has the dubious distinction [note the alliteration] of being the French city that sent the most volunteers to fight in Syria and Iraq'. What has happened there has ramifications for the entire Western world: 'Images of terrorism in Nice confirm Trump's narrative that the West has lost its way and new management is needed' (DT27).

In addition, The *Telegraph* rarely historicizes. One telling exception, though, is the assertion that 'in the Fifties and Sixties, Portuguese and Spanish immigrants moved into social housing and integrated into French society without complaint' (DT7), unlike those of Arab origin, who are clearly seen by the journalist as difficult, problematic, 'other'. In a similar vein, the *Telegraph* focuses on present results rather than past historical dynamics, in particular the 'failings' of integration (in segments coded for 'French society', such failings are emphatically referenced once in DT7 and twice in DT26, with security services and authorities also described as 'struggling' in DT18 or 'overwhelmed' in DT21). While the *Guardian* also refers to such shortcomings, they are objectively presented and/or contextualized. For instance, TG1 recognizes France's reliance, in intelligence and counterterrorism matters, on 'structures at a European level – which have been repeatedly found wanting'. The *Telegraph*, however, tends to blame the socialist government. A *Telegraph* excerpt cited above (DT21, 'Unlike

Britain [...]') also attributes France's problems with terrorism to open borders; the journalist believes that Britain is better off remaining outside the Schengen Area. Britain and the conservative policies in place there are portrayed as superior.

References to the Muslim countries that are major sources of immigration to France also play into the presence or absence of a historicizing perspective. Algeria is mentioned five times across the *Guardian* articles in relation to colonial history and immigrants. In contrast, it is mentioned just once in one *Telegraph* article, DT7. This article also attenuates the 'bitter' nature of the colonial legacy in favour of a discussion of radicalization, which is portrayed as being visited upon France from abroad. References to Tunisia appear in conjunction with either the perpetrator's profile, or contextualization. Tellingly, the country is mentioned in relation to the perpetrator eleven times in the *Guardian* and seventeen times in the *Telegraph* (recall the attack at Sousse). It is mentioned for purposes of contextualization four times in the *Guardian* but just once in the *Telegraph*.

Alliteration

The *Telegraph* articles include significantly more instances of alliteration than the *Guardian* articles. As Table 9.2 shows, by far the greatest number of occurrences is negative. In addition, there are 8 per cent more of these in the *Telegraph*, which also has 10 per cent fewer positive instances.

How does alliteration contribute to representing France, Muslims and the events in question? Both sources emphasize the trauma resulting from the Nice attack through use of alliteration, for instance 'try to come to terms with the terrible events' (TG11), 'stunned and sickened' (TG13), 'shell-shocked' (DT7), '[b]ut Bouhlel's rampage will take a devastating toll; the destruction will wreck families' lives forever' (DT19). However, the *Telegraph* uses it more frequently in conjunction with the violent aspects of the event itself ('ram raid', twice (DT5), 'killing and maiming the maximum number' (TG18), 'murder on a massive scale', 'smeared with dried blood while smashed children's buggies and

Table 9.2 Alliteration and connotation

Alliteration	Guardian	Telegraph
Negative	61%	69%
Positive	20%	10%
Neutral	19%	21%

other debris were strewn across the seaside promenade' (DT19), or 'method of murder', twice (DT20)).

Particularly telling are the findings on alliteration related to government or politics, on the one hand, and religion, on the other. Examples of these are presented in Tables 9.3 and 9.4.

TG1 acknowledges, and emphasizes through alliteration, not only the French authorities' 'failings' in response to terrorist attacks (also contextualized as part of a complex set of problems), but also improvements achieved thanks to measures introduced in 2014 but only now being demonstrated due to the 'time' needed to 'find and train' the requisite personnel. TG4, 13 and 14 highlight the difficulties President François Hollande is facing due to the attacks that have taken place on his watch. TG4 also reports criticism by the socialist prime minister Manuel Valls of the oppositions' proposals, and the journalist opts to include a critical reference by Valls to the right-wing Trump. Conversely, in DT27, devoted to Trump's chances in the upcoming election, while Trump is not portrayed as perfect (his 'proposed ban on Muslim immigration' is probably unconstitutional), he is seen as a viable response to the danger of terrorism (and the journalist claims that Hillary Clinton, Obama and the Democrats are worse than Trump). The first sentence from DT7 included in Table 9.3 highlights the tensions in France's political sphere; in addition, unlike the *Guardian* articles, DT7, 18, 19 and 26 alliteratively underline or question the authorities' weakness or ineffectiveness, with DT18 even including a jibe: that officials were surely 'quietly congratulating themselves' after France hosted the Euro 2016 football tournament without incident only to face this attack soon after. The political leanings of the sources come through in these examples, in part because they are reinforced via alliteration. While Richard Barrett (DT22) speaks out against 'a dramatic increase in the securitization of French society' and calls for inclusive dialogue between communities and officials, his unfortunately appears to be an anomalous position in the *Telegraph* articles analysed, despite the fact that he is the 'former director of global counter-terrorism operations for MI6'. Finally, while DT20 praises 'the success of the security forces', this refers to any forces facing the new 'lone-wolf' truck attack tactic, not French efforts specifically.

Let us now turn to the interplay between alliteration and the treatment of religion by the news sources. Table 9.4 presents the relevant textual segments.

I have discussed DT7 amply elsewhere (Riggs, 2018); among other issues was the question of journalist identity. The above results on alliteration show that

Table 9.3 Alliteration and government/politics

	Government/Politics
News source	**Textual segment with alliteration**
TG	
1	'failings of the fragmented bureaucratic and still under-resourced security services'
1	'time taken to find and then train'
3	'play out politically in France'
4	'president is under pressure'
4	'anger and accusations'
4	'pleading for the preservation'
4	'what he deemed divisive Donald Trump-style proposals'
13	'pressure to take more decisive action to defend France'
14	'constitutes a crisis for Hollande's premiership'
DT	
7	'France finds itself caught in a fatal loop of fear and recrimination, where each side's grievances fed [*sic*] from the existence of the other'
7	'mismanagement of security measures'
18	'suggests that the French security authorities are still struggling to come to terms with the sheer scale of the threat'
18	'their methods of monitoring'
18	'quietly congratulating themselves'
19	'unprepared and unable'
20	'success of the security forces. Suicide attacks have become so difficult that the terrorists have been forced to switch tactics.'
22	[no one is] 'complacent about continued success'
22	'government policy or public perception'
22	'development of a dialogue'
26	'state of security'
26	'increased police presence'
27	'the race to the Right'
27	'proposed ban on Muslim immigration contradicts that much misread document'
27	'responding to crises in a cool way' [criticism of Obama as only 'reactive'; Trump is different]

Table 9.4 Alliteration and religion

Religion	
News source	Textual segment with alliteration
TG	
1	'supposedly secular'
17	'accused of antagonizing Muslims'
DT	
7	'Money for mosques followed; then the imams to preach in them'
7	'Muslim men still disproportionately people'
7	'strive at school' [Muslim women–in part to 'escape' the 'domination' of Muslim men]
20	'contact with a charismatic preacher'
21	'Muslim minority'
26	'drive someone to slaughter his fellow citizens'
26	'a minority of French Muslims'
26	'the role of religion'
26	'the central role of religion'
26	'while it could be argued follows a flawed reading of the religion'
27	'stop Muslims from migrating to America'

while the kinds of positions taken in DT7 are more typical of *Telegraph* 'news analysis' articles, the case is not an isolated one. The results also confirm a more general trend: *The Telegraph* emphasizes religion much more than the *Guardian* does. TG1's reference to the 'supposedly secular' France is a criticism of the country's policy favouring assimilation over integration and multiculturalism, while TG17 observes that Nice's former mayor has been 'accused of antagonizing Muslims' and refers to an aggression against soldiers by 'a man', no religion indicated, 'outside a Jewish community center'. Thus examples of 'tensions in Nice' are provided without blaming a specific religious group.

The situation is quite different in the *Telegraph* 'news analysis' articles. As clearly seen in the examples of alliteration above, DT26 points the finger at Islam while for DT7, Muslims are a central 'problem'. Finally, whereas in DT27, reference to the Nice attack is mainly a pretext to talk about Trump and US politics, the link is clearly made between Muslims and terrorism, and credence given to an American public who, observing international events such as this attack, is likely, in the journalist's estimation, to elect the man who promises to 'stop Muslims from migrating to America'.

Interestingly, DT26's attention-grabbing headline about 'slaughtering fellow citizens' contradicts (a) assertions by both news sources that Lahouaiej-Bouhlel was not actually French after all and (b) the idea, dear to conservatives including the DT7 journalist, that terrorists are 'others' who 'flow' in from abroad.[2] It would be easy enough for UK readers to recall the London 7/7 attacks, in which all four perpetrators were UK citizens. In addition, the multiple attacks that have taken place in the UK *since* the Nice event, that *have* occurred despite border controls, also refute this position. The perpetrator in Nice was not a suspected terrorist and, while originally from Tunisia, had already lived in France for a number of years. It is true that the profile of terrorists in France has often been one of French sons of immigrant parents, as TG2 explicitly states: 'the classic profile of [the] French violent Islamic extremist' is that he was 'born in the country of immigrant parents'. Yet much debate surrounds the easy equating of such individuals' violence with being Muslim. The religion is nevertheless a central focus of news coverage generally and, in this corpus, strongly emphasized through alliteration in the *Telegraph* articles. Indeed, DT26, published on 15 July before much was known about the attack, centres on the debate between France's 'two most recognized experts on Islam in the West'. This kind of reporting choice immediately and unequivocally *makes it about Islam.*

Modality

As I have shown elsewhere, the use of modality in this corpus often serves to give suppositions a patina of factuality. Observing the instances of modality in more detail suggests that the two sources diverge in the way they address the claim by ISIS that Lahouaiej-Bouhlel acted on the terrorist organization's behalf. Both sources observe that the perpetrator had 'no known links' to ISIS or extremists (e.g. the exact phrase appeared in TG2 on 17 July; in both DT23 and DT24 on 18 July). Even more importantly, they do so *after* ISIS has claimed responsibility (16 July). However, through modal use in discussions of the claim, what is insinuated is that if the links are not (yet) known, they exist nonetheless. TG2, for instance, compares Lahouaiej-Bouhlel to other attackers proven to be terrorists. The argument turns around a 'lack of piety among militants' which the perpetrator also demonstrated. 'Lahouaiej-Bouhlel *certainly*[3] matches the classic profile of [the] French violent Islamic extremist in many ways', the journalist asserts, adding that the perpetrator's apparent disregard for religious precepts was *true* of the dozen or so French and Belgian young men involved in bombings and shootings earlier this year, and of Mohammed Merah, who committed the first major attack in France in 2012. (TG2)

By extension, it is insinuated, whereas the role of religion is debatable, Lahouaiej-Bouhlel is clearly an extremist. In addition, '*If true* [if Lahouaiej-Bouhlel is involved with Isis], this *would indicate* that Isis has continuing capacity for ambitious terrorist operations in Europe despite the pressure the group is under. And that *would be* a highly concerning prospect.' Note once again the move from supposition to fact (another instance of 'true'; the indicative 'has') which means that even though there is a shift back to supposition ('would be'), the idea that the information is factual – and now, extremely serious – is firmly in place.

What happens earlier on, before ISIS even claims responsibility? TG9 (15 July) evokes a '*possible* affiliation'. More interestingly, it maintains that there was more than one perpetrator (never proven), already suggesting a coordinated attack: '*it is difficult to conclude* that their assault *was not intended* to be directed at the heart of France's national identity'; '[i]nitial details *suggested* a tactic that jihadi propaganda has *suggested* for several years.' TG12 (also 15 July) makes a concession but gives credence to an authority figure's early conclusion that this was terrorism: 'even though there has been no *claim* of responsibility […] and no *confirmed* identification of the attacker', the French president has 'called' the event 'a terrorist act'. This is followed by yet another construction that moves from supposition towards fact: 'These *may* come shortly, and are *likely* to *confirm suspicions* of the involvement – direct or indirect – of either Islamic State or al-Qaida.'

Even though the tone changes the next day, paradoxically, in conjunction with the claim by ISIS (TG15 observes that '[i]t is still *unclear* whether he had any involvement in a terrorist organization', while TG16 refers to the '*claim*' seven times and uses the phrase 'no evidence' twice), the seed has been planted – this was a terrorist attack connected to an extremist group – and at a time when, in reality, there was still much uncertainty.

This 'patina of factuality' trend is also present in the *Telegraph* articles in the very early moments of reporting, and more insidious. Consider this sentence from DT18 (15 July):

> the *fact* that the key suspect in last night's attack was, *as far as we understand*, a French-Tunisian petty criminal known to the police *indicates* the French authorities *need to* improve their methods of monitoring *potential* Islamist terrorists.

'Fact', albeit tempered via a non-essential subordinate clause that introduces some doubt, carries the weight; furthermore, what is *also* presented as fact is the idea that (a) the perpetrator was an Islamist terrorist, (b) petty criminals are highly likely to become terrorists and (c) therefore, petty criminals should be put under surveillance. This reflects support for conservative policies of greater surveillance to enhance security. It also raises the thorny issue of who is to determine who constitutes a 'potential Islamist terrorist'. Similarly, the next day in DT6, the phrase 'no *known* links to terrorism'[4] is followed by '[t]he *fact* that the killer was known to the authorities *will be* of grave concern to those trying to prevent terrorist attacks in France'. The message: this was a terrorist attack. The journalist of DT22 (also 16 July), while far more measured, has clearly also assumed this was a terrorist attack.

Like the *Guardian*, the *Telegraph* texts refer to ISIS' claim often. However, whereas later in its cycle, the *Guardian* indicates multiple times that the 'claim' of responsibility by ISIS has not been substantiated, when the *Telegraph* indicates this, which is only once out of the eight times it refers to the claim (DT8, 18 July), it emphasizes the 'failure' of French authorities to establish the link, simultaneously discrediting them and giving credence to the claim: 'investigators have failed to establish links between the Bastille Day killer and Isil', 'despite the terror group *claiming* him as a "soldier of Islam"'. Furthermore, four news analysis articles, either emphatically (DT7, DT18, DT26) or subtly (DT27), blame Muslims, those assumed to be Muslim, or Islam.

Finally, in an interesting departure from the messages we have seen conveyed so far, DT25 gives credence to an alternative hypothesis, that the perpetrator was suicidal, rather than violently – and religiously – motivated. This is discussed further in the following section.

Conclusions

The period immediately following a terrorist attack, which is also the period during which these articles appeared, is characterized by feelings of fear, threat and doubts about certain societal groups. This is true not only for those who have had to experience the event, but also for those hearing about it via the news, albeit in a lesser measure. The following discussion sums up how the treatment of certain themes and the use of certain stylistic characteristics contributed to shaping crisis communication between the news sources analysed and their mainly British readership in the aftermath of the Nice attack.

In terms of themes addressed in the news articles, my initial hypothesis was that references to Britain/Britons would be frequent and likely to heighten the sense of threat in both news sources. I also expected that the *Telegraph* would centre more on the home country and portray it as superior, and that its reporting on French society and on Muslims and/or Islam would be more critical, given its alignment with conservative positions and policies.

Both sources did 'bring the story home' (Cottle, 2012 (2011)) to make it relevant for their readership; they did this in ways that seem likely to heighten the sense of crisis. These findings were more pronounced in the *Telegraph*, however. France remained the key context in the *Guardian* while the *Telegraph* steered the story back to the domestic context more frequently. In addition, Britain was presented as both safer and superior.

The *Guardian* portrayed France, including its multicultural society, in a more positive light than the *Telegraph* did. It also contextualized the country's problems and challenges much more. The *Telegraph* portrayed (Muslim) immigration as a threat, rarely historicized, criticized the French government and its policies more roundly, and one article even insinuated strongly that France is weakened by being part of the European Union.

In terms of style specifically, I thought instances of alliteration/assonance would predominantly accompany negative content and serve to emphasize and reinforce that content, thereby giving it more weight, in both news sources; and that this emphasis would be likely to fuel a sense of threat. I also believed modal use would give suppositions a patina of factuality in both sets of news articles. Alliteration did align with mainly negative content and also dramatize or even sensationalize that content, but these effects were more pronounced in the *Telegraph*. Thus alliteration contributed to emphasizing the negative tone of the *Telegraph* that we have seen in other parts of the analysis. When it was used in relation to the French government or politics, alliteration emphasized challenges in the *Guardian*, but criticism in the *Telegraph*. Politics was in fact an area where the political leanings of the news sources really showed through via the use of alliteration.

Alliteration did not frequently accompany content relating to religion in the *Guardian*; one article did subtly question the French emphasis on secularity and assimilation. In contrast, alliteration and commentary on religion co-occurred frequently in the *Telegraph*, which (a) was sometimes misleading about the source(s) of terrorism and the identities of its perpetrators, and (b) resolutely linked terror to Islam and Muslims. Thus, its texts are likely to heighten mistrust of Muslims and, in turn, contribute to polarizing communities.

Finally, further analysis of modality confirmed that both sources sometimes employ it to give suppositions a patina of factuality, in particular, and highly questionably, before the facts are really known. However, a *Telegraph* article used modality particularly insidiously, linking Islam, criminality and terrorism in order to argue for a far-reaching form of surveillance. This again correlates with its political alignment. Regarding the claim by ISIS that Lahouaiej-Bouhlel acted on its behalf, the *Guardian* emphasized that it was unsubstantiated while for the *Telegraph*, it provided another opportunity to criticize the French government.

During a recent lecture at the Reuters Institute for the Study of Journalism on the challenges and future of journalism, Marty Baron, the editor-in-chief of the *Washington Post*, said:

> The answer for us [journalists] is clear: Just do our job. Do it honestly, honorably, seriously, fairly, accurately, and also unflinchingly. 'To show, by our work', as David Shribman, editor of the Pittsburgh Post-Gazette put it, 'that the truth still matters'. (Baron, 2017)

This is laudable, but vague. Techniques of reporting that contribute to exacerbating tensions and heightening the sense of threat exist. They are highly questionable. But they sell news. This is one of many thorny questions currently facing journalism that do not have easy answers. In terms of religion and avoiding pre-emptively making terror 'about Islam', Seib (2017) has some sage advice: report on Islam regularly, not just when violence happens. If this were the case, 'perhaps news consumers would realise that there is far more to Islam than violence. And if antipathy toward Islam were to diminish, terrorists would lose a recruiting tool.' Indeed, the result 'of publishing texts which only narrate conflict-laden events which, in turn, are constantly linked to one community is that it constructs an image of Islam and terrorism as intrinsically connected'[5] (Piquer Martí, 2015: 143). Moreover, given that in the media, writing is always from the 'Us' perspective (Piquer Martí, 2015: 141), the Islamophobia present in society necessarily spills over into news articles. According to Piquer Martí, the way that the media portrays (Muslim) immigrants – through un-contextualized, isolated messages always bound up with violence and conflict – coupled with the public's relative ignorance of the Muslim world encourages negative stereotypes. Whether or not the alternative hypothesis presented in the *Telegraph* on 18 July (that the perpetrator was suicidal) marked a turning point in its reporting, that possibility was already unlikely to 'stick', given the messages, reinforced by stylistic choices, that preceded it. Journalists and other news actors need to turn 'a critical eye to their complicity in normalizing prejudice' (Allan, 2014 [2010]: 196); representational and stylistic choices, which play so subtle yet so central a role in shaping public opinion, are a good place to start.

Acknowledgement

This research is funded by the Swiss National Science Foundation, Grant number P2GEP1_171957.

Notes

1 This research is funded by the Swiss National Science Foundation [Grant number P2GEP1_171957].
2 In contrast, TG1 and TG3 refer to 'homegrown militants', part of the *Guardian*'s recognition that extremism in France has a complex background.
3 Modal elements are in italics.
4 It appears twice more, in DT23 and DT24 on 18 July.
5 Translations from Spanish are my own.

References

Allan, S. (2014 [2010]). 'Journalism and the Culture of Othering'. *Brazilian Journalism Research* 10(2): 188–203.

Baker, M. (2006). *Translation and Conflict: A Narrative Account*. London and New York: Routledge.

Baker, M. (2007). 'Reframing Conflict in Translation'. *Social Semiotics* 17(2): 151–169.

Baresch, B., Hsu, S.-H., and Reese, S. D. (2012 [2010]). 'Researching the Structure of Meaning in News'. In S. Allan (ed.), *The Routledge Companion to News and Journalism*. 2nd edition, 637–647. London and New York: Routledge.

Baron, M. (2017). *Reuters Institute for the Study of Journalism Memorial Lecture. When a President Wages War on a Press at Work*. Paper Presented on 16 February 2017. Oxford: Blavatnik School of Government.

Bialostosky, D. (2017). *How to Play a Poem*. Available online: https://books.google.ch (accessed 28 November 2018).

Boase-Beier, J. (2006). *Stylistic Approaches to Translation*. Manchester: St Jerome Publishing.

Boase-Beier, J. (2012 [Print, 2011]). 'Stylistics and Translation'. In K. Malmkjaer and K. Windle (eds), *The Oxford Handbook of Translation Studies*, 71–82. Oxford: Oxford University Press.

Canel, M.-J. (2012). 'Communicating Strategically in the Face of Terrorism: The Spanish Government's Response to the 2004 Madrid Bombing Attacks'. *Public Relations Review* 38(2): 214–222.

Canel, M.-J., and Sanders, K. (2010). 'Crisis Communication and Terrorist Attacks: Framing a Response to the 2004 Madrid Bombings and 2005 London Bombings'. In W. T. Coombs and S. J. Holladay (eds), *The Handbook of Crisis Communication*, 449–466. Oxford: Wiley-Blackwell.

Chuquet, H., and Paillard, M. (1987). *Approche linguistique des problèmes de traduction anglais-français* [A Linguistic Approach to Problems of English-French Translation]. Paris: Ophrys.

Cottle, S. (2012 [2011]). 'Global Crises and World News Ecology'. In S. Allan (ed.), *Routledge Companion to News and Journalism*, 473–484. London and New York: Routledge.

D'hulst, L., Gonne, M., Lobbes, T., Meylaerts, R., and Verschaffel, T. (2014). 'Towards a Multipolar Model of Cultural Mediators within Multicultural Spaces. Cultural Mediators in Belgium (1830–1945)'. *Belgisch Tijdschrift voor Filologie en Geschiedenis/Revue Belge de Philologie et d'Histoire* 92(4): 1255–1275.

Federici, F. M. (ed.) (2016). *Mediating Emergencies and Conflicts. Frontline Translating and Interpreting*. Basingstoke and New York: Palgrave Macmillan.

Freedman, D. (2017). 'Media Power and the Framing of the *Charlie Hebdo* Attacks'. In G. Titley, D. Freedman, G. Khiabany, and A. Mondon (eds), *After Charlie Hebdo: Terror, Racism and Free Speech*, 209–222. London: Zed Books Ltd.

Hewson, L. (2011). *An Approach to Translation Criticism: Emma and Madame Bovary in Translation*. Amsterdam and Philadelphia: John Benjamins.

Osgood, C. E., Succi, G. J., and Tannenbaum, P. H. (1957). *The Measurement of Meaning*. Urbana, IL: University of Illinois Press.

Piquer Martí, S. (2015). 'La islamophobia en la prensa escrita española: aproximación al discurso periodístico de *El País* y *La Razón* [Islamophobia in Spain's Written Press: A Study of Journalistic Discourse in *El País* and *La Razón*]'. *Dirāsāt Hispánicas. Revista Tunecina de Estudios Hispánicos [Tunisian Journal of Hispanic Studies]* 2: 137–156.

Reese, S. D. (2001). 'Prologue–Framing Public Life: A Bridging Model for Media Research'. In S. D. Reese, O. H. Gandy, and A. E. Grant (eds), *Framing Public Life: Perspectives on Media and Our Understanding of the Social World*, 7–31. Mahwah and New Jersey: Lawrence Erlbaum Associates.

Riggs, A. (2018). 'The Role of Stylistic Features in Constructing Representations of Muslims and France in English Online News about Terrorism in France'. *Perspectives* 1–19. doi: 10.1080/0907676X.2018.1478863.

Schäffner, C. (2013). 'Discourse Analysis'. In Y. Gambier and L. van Doorslaer (eds), *Handbook of Translation Studies, Vol 4*, 47–52. Amsterdam and Philadelphia, PA: John Benjamins.

Seib, P. (2017). 'Superficial, Speculative, Breathless: Outdated Terrorism Reporting Must Change'. *EJO - European Journalism Observatory*, 6 June. Available at https://en.ejo.ch/ethics-quality/superficial-speculative-hysterical-outdated-terror-reporting-must-change (accessed 28 November 2018).

van Doorslaer, Luc. (2012). 'Translating, Narrating and Constructing Images in Journalism with a Test Case on Representation in Flemish TV News'. *Meta: Translators' Journal* 57(4): 1046–1059.

Wales, K. (2001). *A Dictionary of Stylistics*. 2nd edition. London: Pearson.

Zelizer, B. (2015). 'Terms of Choice: Uncertainty, Journalism, and Crisis'. *Journal of Communication* 65(5): 888–908.

10

Re-Narrating Crisis: A Translation Perspective

Maria Sidiropoulou

As 'crisis communication becomes international in scope, it crosses national boundaries and becomes increasingly complex' (Frandsen and Johansen, 2010: 423). Although an important part of the literature refers to crises in business environments, the assumption in this chapter is that research on crisis communication will benefit from focusing on variability in a broad range of crisis types and management strategies across cultures. These strategies, or at least a significant amount of them, are put in place through forms of translation and interpreting, and, thus, investigating 'the complexity of emergency management' should include 'considerations of language barriers' (Federici, 2016: 3). It is also widely acknowledged that translated discourses reshape identities and worldviews in re-narrating stories to meet local expectations or construct intended ideological perspectives (Baker, 2006, 2007; Calzada-Pérez, 2014; Wodak and Forchtner, 2018). In intercultural transfer of crisis events, translated discourses published in the press often manifest systematic differences in the way in which crises are re-narrated in a target environment. This expected difference can shed light on the ways in which various cultures approach disasters (natural or man-made) to ensure local compatibility of crisis narration to activate local ethical sensibilities to suffering, thus enhancing the potential of risk reduction frameworks. If intercultural synergies are to be developed in setting up shared crisis management schemes, it is important for the crisis practitioners to be aware of variabilities in local conventions in crisis communication. Otherwise, the impact of crisis management discourses may be weak and intercultural synergies may not be effective. Besides, in the context of linguistic relativity, societies may wish to be aware of locally sanctioned interculturally variant approaches to crises.

If 'the critical component in crisis management is communication' (Coombs, 2010: 17), the study advances understanding of the communicators' role by analysing shifts in intercultural (ST English/TT Greek) communication on crisis events. It merges two research traditions within crisis communication research, the 'rhetorical text-oriented' and the 'strategic or context-oriented' tradition (Frandsen and Johansen, 2010: 427) taking into account all four parameters which 'mediate any kind of media communication (context, media, genre and text)' (Frandsen and Johansen, 2010: 432). It focuses on how traditional journalism [media] manages different types [genre] of crisis events [context], in news discourse [text] – as well as how affected institutions, bodies, corporations react and interact with the media that portray the crisis.

The chapter engages with concepts related to crisis management strategies, which may need to be renegotiated in as much the portrayal of crises is dependent on the effect of the intercultural transfer from the source culture in which the event took place, to the target culture in which the press represents the crisis from afar. The study focuses on traditional (printed) press data, which show that there are different conventions of emergency representation across cultures, and considers the contribution of visual material to the portrayal of crises. Results of this analysis confirm that genre represent a significant variable in crises communication (provided that 'context' and 'media' remain constant), not least across cultures, but also within the same culture. Findings in this study suggest that crisis management research should look into the translation perspective to do justice to significant aspects of intercultural crisis communication.

On crisis communication and translation

Crisis management literature confirms that threats to reputation 'can destroy, literally in hours or days' an image developed over decades (Regester and Larkin, 2005: 2) especially at a time when globalization and the internet are pushing us towards a world 'characterized by the intangible assets of reputation, knowledge [...] culture and loyalty' (Regester and Larkin, 2005). The view mostly refers to corporate crisis management, and it is referred to, here, because it manifests the power of public communication to reshape identities and affect the reputation of others. Assets seem to be negotiated through communication and renegotiated in cross-cultural contexts through mediated communication. Besides corporate and business assets, communication about and of crises also shapes the reception and reactions of audiences to them. It matters even more for crises happening abroad. Translation studies literature has also acknowledged the potential of translation to re-narrate knowledge and culture affecting reputation or loyalty connotations (Baker, 2007).

In the context of research on disaster response and recovery conducted by the Committee on Disaster research in the Social Sciences of the (US) National Academy, the 'Recommendation 4.6' suggests that '[m]ore cross-cultural research is needed on natural, technological and willfully caused hazards and disasters'. The analysis of translation practices and their products in the press is a route to cross-cultural research on hazards and disasters, as it is likely to bring out shifts in the perception of crisis events and vulnerability issues which have been registered in public discourse.

If notions such as 'insecurity' are social constructs (Monahan, 2010), the question arises as to what strategies construct concepts and ideas in societies, across cultures, which would facilitate the 'modalities of cooperation' in risk reduction frameworks as, for instance, the UN Sendai Framework for Disaster Risk Reduction 2015–2030, the ones which build resilience to disasters and develop policies, plans, programmes and budgets to eradicate poverty or protect vulnerable others. The five priorities of action suggested in the Sendai Framework are:

(a) To adopt a concise, focused, forward-looking and action-oriented post 2015 framework for disaster risk reduction.
(b) To complete the assessment and review of the implementation of the Hyogo Framework for Action 2005–2015: Building the Resilience of Nations and Communities to Disasters.
(c) To consider the experience gained through the regional and national strategies/institutions and plans for disaster risk reduction and their recommendations, as well as relevant regional agreements for the implementation of the Hyogo Framework for Action.
(d) To identify modalities of cooperation based on commitments to implement a post 2015 framework for disaster risk reduction.
(e) To determine modalities for the periodic review of the implementation of a post 2015 framework for disaster risk reduction. (2015: 9)

Risk reduction depends on communication; hence by extension, it is important to expect that printed and online journalism may play a significant role in sensitizing the public opinion to manage public response to crises. The assumption is that crisis communication is worth exploring especially where practice may reveal different culturally appropriate techniques of disaster reporting, which would facilitate intercultural communication and synergy during crises. For instance, the overwhelming inflow of migrants, asylum seekers and refugees into Europe of 2015 considerably affected Southern European counties, among which those with extensive coastlines, like Italy and Greece. Although the problem was shared, both countries were rather isolated in their attempt to cope with the increased influx and the emergency response it demanded (see also discussion in Chapter 11 in this volume). Focus on intercultural variation in the discourse of crisis reporting assumes a culture of emergency awareness, which is expected to facilitate synergies on crisis sites. Fairclough (1995) suggests that the literature on globalization lacks a discourse-level dimension. Studying the discourse of globalized crises like the refugee one (or even of local disasters triggered by natural hazards is a step towards highlighting the intricacies of local representations of global emergencies. This would enforce the discourse-level dimension of globalization, which Fairclough argues is missing.

Closely related to crisis management issues and the concept of entitlement (MKandawire and Aguda, 2009) is the concept of vulnerability, which has occasionally been understood as a state of susceptibility to harm from risk exposure. The study examines how vulnerability is constructed in crisis reporting in the press, with a view to unveiling cross-cultural variation in the way vulnerable others may be re-narrated in a target environment, in order for messages to be socio-culturally operative.

As '[d]isasters are more noteworthy than success' (Bignell, 2002: 85) in the press, newspapers are active in reporting disaster stories cross-culturally, which manifest cross-cultural pragmatics in operation, for instance, in reshaping construction of vulnerability and resilience, across versions of articles. Below I provide samples of data, which manifest different approaches to headline make-up across English-Greek traditional media on crisis events. The bottom-up approach of the study suggests that intercultural transfer of crisis events in communication is worth exploring for improving understanding of how vulnerability and resilience are constructed cross-culturally. The next section presents the theoretical underpinnings of the study and expands on its methodology.

The approach and methodological considerations

Ray suggests that '[a] crisis organization's primary vehicle for communication is the media' (1999: 53) and Tiernan (2007: 323) confirms that 'immediate delivery of corporate "messages"' in crisis communication response situations may be achieved through contact with journalists. The study analyses press discourse (Brown and Yule, 1983, Hussain and Munawar, 2017) to bring out varying tendencies in portraying crisis events across English and Greek news reports. As mentioned, it merges two research traditions within crisis communication research, the 'rhetorical text-oriented' and the 'strategic or context-oriented' tradition (Frandsen and Johansen, 2010: 427) considering all four parameters that 'mediate any kind of media communication (context, media, genre and text)' (ibid., 432). In crisis management situations, the crisis type is important (Holladay, 2010); '[t]he crisis type holds implications for reputation management strategies' (2010: 165) and – I would add – for assigning responsibility for the crisis. Blaming and assigning responsibility, in public discourses surrounding crises, is a speech act worth exploring in cross-cultural transfer, for its interdisciplinary nature – namely its overlap with the cross-cultural study of impoliteness (Culpeper, 1996) in linguistic pragmatics.

The study focuses on press headlines across English and Greek newspapers for the ideological potential they carry, with visuals occasionally complementing the ideological perspective carried verbally by the headline. Headlines are a central, short, compact and vibrant part of press articles, with their own conventions and, in combination with the visuals accompanying the article, are significant attention attractors. Headline transfer in the translated press is intriguing for translation scholars because it reveals shifting conventions in headline make-up cross-culturally. Allan (2004) confirms that the headline is crucial in highlighting how readers are to receive what follows. The headline, he suggests, is

> the principal topic or 'key fact' at stake in the account. To the extent that it is recognized as performing this function by the readers, it is likely to influence their interpretation of the account to follow. In this way, then it helps to set down the ideological criteria by which the reader is to 'make sense' of what follows. (2004: 83)

The data set comprises thirty headline pairs of 2017 English press articles on crisis events and their Greek translations retrieved from *I Kathemerini* (*Η Καθημερινή*) newspaper, a high-circulation broadsheet Greek newspaper. Although the actual bodies of the sample press articles are also enlightening as far as intercultural preference in discourse make-up is concerned, the study focuses on headlines and visuals only, because of their functionality and their potential to convey the gist of the producers' point of view. As generic conventions always matter in discourse, the search confirmed different conventions of headline make-up across English-Greek, namely, in articles on 'natural' disasters and 'man-made' ones. Different reporting conventions preferred locally in the press, for different crisis categories, are shown in this chapter. Photos, which accompany the headlines, may also vary systematically across English-Greek; this chapter also shows the potential of the visual material to contribute to messages conveyed verbally by the headlines.

Varied strategies of disaster reporting

In discussing disasters triggered by natural hazards as cultural discourse Bankoff (2003) points to Hewitt's (1983) view of vulnerability as a cultural construct.

> The Western discourse on disasters, whether it be about abnormal natural events or about vulnerable populations, still remains what Hewitt calls 'a socio-cultural construct reflecting a distinct, institution-centered and ethno-centric view of man and nature' (1983: 8). Health and disease, well being and danger are viewed as fundamentally dependent upon particular geographies. (2003: 14)

The data samples below show instances of different approaches into crises reporting, both within the target culture and across cultures, confirming the need identified by Recommendation 4.5 of the (US) National Academies that highlights the significance of cross-cultural future research on crisis events.

Disasters triggered by natural hazards

Examples 1–4 show different genre-specific patterns prevailing across versions in headline make-up, namely that (a) the earthquake magnitude is surfacing in the Greek version of headlines, together with (b) information on casualties and injured. These pieces of information on magnitude and number of casualties are emphasized in the Greek version of the headline (thematized in TT3 or simply added as in TT4). The English headline goes as far as to reporting a 'strong earthquake', a 'huge earthquake' (ST1, ST2, ST3). Furthermore, the magnitude aspect is often enforced visually in the Greek version, by pictures showing seismographic instruments. Greece is a country subject to repeating earthquakes and its population is used to magnitude measurements that immediately make sense for the general public.

ST1   "Strong earthquake rattles Tibet but only minor damage reported" *Reuters* 18 Nov. 2017

TT1   "Σεισμός **6,3 βαθμών** στο Θιβέτ" *Καθημερινή* 18 Nov. 2017 [+visual]
       BT.6.3 magnitude earthquake in Tibet

ST2   "Strong earthquake strikes east-northeast of Tadine, New Caledonia: USGS" *Reuters* 19 Nov. 2017

TT2   "Ισχυρός σεισμός **6,6 Ρίχτερ** στον Ειρηνικό Ωκεανό" *Καθημερινή* 19 Nov. 2017 [+visual]
       BT. Strong earthquake of 6.6 magnitude in the Pacific Ocean

ST3 "Mexico rushes aid to millions after huge quake; death toll at 96" *Reuters* 11 Sept. 2017

TT3 "Στους 96 οι νεκροί του σεισμού των **8,2 Ρίχτερ** στο Μεξικό" *Καθημερινή* 11 Sept. 2017

 BT. *The dead are up to 96 from the **8.2 magnitude** earthquake in Mexico.*

ST4 "Iran quake survivors complain of slow aid effort, battle freezing cold" *Reuters* 14 Nov. 2017

TT4 "Ιράν: Τερματίστηκαν οι επιχειρήσεις διάσωσης στις σεισμόπληκτες περιοχές - Περισσότεροι από **530 οι νεκροί**" *Καθημερινή* 14 Nov. 2017

 BT. *Iran: Rescuing in earthquake-stricken areas - More than 530 dead.*

Highlighting magnitude and casualties of earthquakes in Greek, when the (English) source is not as keen to do so, signifies a different approach to reporting on disasters triggered by natural hazards across English-Greek. The Greek version favours a more transactional approach to disaster headline make-up by highlighting the specifics of magnitude and casualties. The next section, on human-induced disasters, shows that the transactional approach is toned down in Greek, in favour of vagueness and expressiveness, which may facilitate (among other things) implications of responsibility.

Man-made disasters

In man-made disasters, the approach to headline make-up is different across English-Greek. The Greek version of headlines zooms out on the number of dead and injured, as examples 5 and 6 show, although the number of casualties does appear in the ST headlines. It is as if the intensity of the crisis event is more important than the number of casualties in Greek.

ST5 "Fire engulfs London tower block, **at least 12 dead**, dozens injured" *Reuters* 14 June 2017

TT5 "**Τραγωδία** σε φλεγόμενο ουρανοξύστη στο Λονδίνο" *Καθημερινή* 15 June 2017

 BT. ***Tragedy** in skyscraper on fire in London*

ST6 "Nigeria bombing: **50** killed in early-morning attack on mosque" *CNN* 21 Nov. 2017

TT6 "Νιγηρία: **Δεκάδες** νεκροί από επίθεση αυτοκτονίας σε τέμενος" *Καθημερινή* 21 Nov. 2017

 BT. *Nigeria: **Tens** of dead by suicide attack at a mosque.*

The data suggest that there are differences not least interculturally – but also within the same culture – in disaster reporting contexts, and that the type of crisis (genre) is of paramount importance as to how the crisis is to be re-narrated.

Another shifting convention seems to be that the national identity of the casualties may not survive, in the Greek version of headlines, evidently assuming human life is valuable, no matter the geographical origin of the victims. The Greek headline versions zoom out on nationality information. This is evident in TT7 where the Chinese identity does not make it in the Greek version. In the same vein, in another translated version of an article on the Malaysia Airlines accident, the Greek newspaper avoided the information that 'Most of the victims were Chinese.' The tendency of the Greek version to zoom out on nationalities allows the implication that humans – no matter where they come from – are vulnerable and exposed to hazards, which may have been someone's responsibility to prevent from happening. It also assumes awareness of and resistance to the view that 'health, disease, well being and danger are dependent upon particular geographies' (Bankoff 2003).

ST7   "Three **Chinese** students injured in car attack in **Toulouse**" *bbc.com* 11 Nov. 2017

TT7   "Αυτοκίνητο παρέσυρε [Ø] φοιτητές στη **Γαλλία** - Ψυχολογικά προβλήματα έχει ο δράστης" *Καθημερινή* 10 Nov. 2017
       BT. *A car has drifted [Ø] students away, in **France**. The agent has had psychological problems.*

Bankoff (2003: 17) argues that the 'geographies of risk' narrative is pervasive in disaster communication and disseminates a victimizing connotation:

> [T]ropicality, underdevelopment and vulnerability form part of the same essentializing and generalizing cultural discourse: one that designates large regions of the world as dangerous disease-ridden, poverty-stricken and disaster-prone; one that depicts the inhabitants of these regions as inferior, as untutored, incapable victims.

The assumption is that the Greek newspaper intends to resist geographies of risk, in favour of a more general risk-exposure assumption. In addition, the headlines in the Greek newspapers, reporting or introducing the same news items, seem to be keen on offering interpretation of situations, which allows implications of who is to blame and 'responsibility framing' (Olsson 2009). Social responsibility seems to be a value to be implicated, if not stated, in press news discourses. The responsibility implication may be facilitated through the added TT17 item *the agent has had psychological problems*, which seems to be an answer to a who-is-to-blame question. A similar approach appears in examples 8 and 9. The TT8 item *blocks* (*μπλοκάρει,* vs. ST8 item *wants exemption*), and TT9 item *indignation* (*αγανάκτηση*) are negatively charged and also allow the implication that 'someone is to blame' for the situation.

ST8   "Austria says **wants exemption** from EU migrant relocation system" *Reuters* 28 Mar. 2017

TT8   "Η Αυστρία '**μπλοκάρει**' πρόσφυγες" *Καθημερινή* 29 Mar. 2017
       *BT. Austria '**blocks**' refugees*

ST9   "Austria plays down spat with Italy over border controls" *Reuters* 5 Jul. 2017

TT9   "**Αγανάκτηση** Ιταλίας για τους πρόσφυγες" *Καθημερινή* 5 Jul. 2017
       *BT. Italy's **indignation**on the refugee issue*

An overall shift between the two versions may be described in terms of the two practices of democratic education in societies assumed in Ben-Porath (2006) who distinguishes between

- 'peace' practices favouring cosmopolitanism and liberal individualism, which attempts to construct society as a non-violent space, one 'which caters for the well-being of all citizens' (2006: 53) and assumes that peace is the norm and war an exception, and
- another practice which emerges as a response to perceived threats to security, namely, one which assumes that war is the norm and peace an exception, and intends to raise awareness of the latter perspective in citizens.

For instance, the former is a practice implemented in ST8 and ST9 headlines, the latter manifested in TT8 and TT9 headlines (through the TT items *blocks* and *indignation*, which cancel implications of the world being a peaceful space).

Likewise, in example 10, the family reunion issue is referred to in the Greek version to highlight refugee suffering.

ST10 "Refugees in Greece demand transfer to Germany, start hunger strike" *Reuters* 1 Nov. 2017

TT10 "Απεργία πείνας προσφύγων στο Σύνταγμα: «Θέλουμε να **ενωθούμε με τις οικογένειες** μας στη Γερμανία»" *huffingtonpost.gr* 2 Nov. 2017
       *BT. Refugee hunger strike at Syntagma (Square: "we want to **join our families** in Germany"*

Out of the three components of democratic citizenship identified in Ben-Porath (2006), namely 'civic participation', 'unity and solidarity' or 'public deliberation', the TT10 practice alludes to the 'unity and solidarity' component. These may be framing preferences, which need to be taken into account in intercultural communication on crises events.

In analysing disaster risk reduction in multilingual settings, Alexander (personal communication, Dec. 2017) refers to two approaches to planning responses to disasters caused by natural hazards. One approach is governed by a 'command' function principle, a proxy approach which is authority oriented, and a 'support' function principle which favours a more collaborative, participatory approach, where people take care of their own needs. The approach seems to tally with the distinction between high/low 'power distance' in Hofstede and Hofstede's (2005) interpersonal communication dimensions, which in this context is manifested interculturally (English-Greek) and intra-culturally (natural-hazards disasters vs. man-made in Greek). The distinction also pairs with the etic-emic one. The *etic* approach is manifested via reporting the specifics of magnitude and casualties in disaster situations (evidently provided by authorities), and the *emic* approach is manifested via a participatory, solidarity perspective which justifies the who-is-to-blame concern. The *etic* has a global resonance, as the specifics of magnitude and casualties are unambiguously transferable across the globe through technological communication means, and the *emic* approach is more clearly attuned to the local, its perspectives and interpretations. Table 10.1 summarizes the features of Greek disaster reporting conventions as manifested through English–Greek translation shifts.

The focus on earthquake magnitude and number of casualties (in disaster headlines) manifests a proxy, authoritative perspective, assessed on a global scale and technologically oriented (which may also be enforced through the added seismograph photos in the TT). The sample data provided above manifest implementation of the support function principle (with the expressiveness and interpretation tendencies made explicit in the TT), which are more culture-specific. The next section heightens awareness of the contribution of visuals that accompany the English–Greek versions.

Table 10.1 Greek conventions in natural and human-induced disaster reporting manifested through translation

	Natural	Human induced
Approach	etic	emic
Space resonance	global	local

Crisis management through press photos

As suggested, the verbal code seems to be highly eloquent in registering ideologically meaningful shifts across source and target versions (Coombs, 1995, 2010; Elmasry and Chaudhri, 2010). The visuals accompanying the source and target texts are also shifted in meaningful ways in intercultural transfer to contribute their own potential to the verbal message. They implicate intended perspectives, which complement the verbally conveyed messages. The visual shifts described below manifest the institutions' crisis management techniques, as their organizational DNA (Coombs, 2006). Refugees, for instance, are portrayed as less vulnerable, more resilient figures, in the Greek version of the TT11 photo (the solidarity, participatory perspective), conflicting with the perception foregrounded by the English visual which connotes vulnerability and helplessness, in relation to refugees (the 'geographies of risk', 'othering' perspective), and may activate painful memories of the 1923 population exchange between Greece and Turkey. In analysing international crisis management, Houben (2005: 7) suggests that 'an important place is given to certain socio-political phenomena such as dominant collective memories', which cannot be ignored, even though the nation-state may be declining nowadays.

ST11 "Ranks of world's refugees swell as asylum space shrinks: U.N." *Reuters* 2 Oct. 2017
https://www.reuters.com/article/us-un-refugees/ranks-of-worlds-refugees-swell-as-asylum-space-shrinks-u-n-idUSKCN1C718Q [accessed 18 Mar. 2018]
TT11 "ΟΗΕ: Τουλάχιστον δύο εκατομμύρια νέοι πρόσφυγες το 2017" *Καθημερινή* 3 Oct. 2017
http://www.kathimerini.gr/929092/article/epikairothta/kosmos/ohe-toylaxiston-dyo-ekatommyria-neoi-prosfyges-to-2017 [accessed 18 Mar. 2018]
BT.UNO: At least two million new refugees in 2017

The shift shapes more of an 'us' perspective (a resilient interpretation) in the Greek version, in relation to the refugees, vs. a 'them' perspective in the English version. Evidently, 'civic participation' (Weick and Sutcliffe, 2007; Schmidt et al., 2018) as a strategy of crisis management is pursued in different ways visually across cultures.

Children, as vulnerable age groups, may be portrayed in the Greek version through the visual, as the one accompanying target headline 12 on child labour exploitation, when no photo may appear in the English version, or when a different narrative (e.g. that of activism) may be foregrounded in the English version (ST12). Similarly, the photo pair accompanying example 13 registers a shift from portraying a female activist to children at work: the shift in the TT 'magnifies' the voice of the poor and marginalized (Chaney, 2017) to enforce the narrative of crisis exploitation (Boin et al., 2008) by the wealthy. The English visual heightens awareness of a participatory approach to the crisis, by showing a female activist fighting child labour exploitation.

ST12 "Syrian child refugees making British clothes in Turkey: BBC investigation" *Reuters* 24 Oct. 2016

https://www.reuters.com/article/us-europe-migrants-britain-retailers/syrian-child-refugees-making-british-clothes-in-turkey-bbc-investigation-idUSKCN12O0QK [accessed 18 Mar. 2018]

TT12 "BBC: Προσφυγόπουλα από τη Συρία εργάζονται σε εργοστάσια ρούχων στην Τουρκία" *Καθημερινή* 24 Oct. 2016

http://www.kathimerini.gr/880574/article/epikairothta/kosmos/bbc-prosfygopoyla-apo-th-syria-ergazontai-se-ergostasia-royxwn-sthn-toyrkia [accessed 18 Mar. 2018]

BT. BBC: Child refugees from Syria work at cloth factories in Turkey.

ST13 " Syrian refugee children found working in Next and H&M factories" *Independent* 1 Feb. 2016

http://www.independent.co.uk/news/world/middle-east/syrian-children-found-working-for-uk-clothing-suppliers-including-next-and-hm-a6845431.html [accessed 18 Mar. 2018]

TT13 " Σάλος στη Βρετανία με τα προσφυγόπουλα των H&M και NEXT" *AlfaVita Εκπαιδευτικό ενημερωτικό Δίκτυο* 1 Feb. 2016

http://www.alfavita.gr/arthron/prosfygopoyla-ergates-se-hm-kai-next-kai-ohi-mono-o-makrys-katalogos-tis-paidikis-ergasias [accessed 18 Mar. 2018]

BT. Agitation in Britain with the H&M and NEXT child refugees

The photos accompanying the next headline pair assume a resilient humankind, which will actually adapt to climate change. The scary power of nature, which connotes human race vulnerability, in the English visual is occasionally substituted by others, which connote some resilient human presence as in the visual accompanying TT14.

ST14 "Climate change made Lucifer heatwave far more likely, scientists find" *The Guardian* 27 Sept. 2017. https://www.theguardian.com/world/2017/sep/27/climate-change-made-lucifer-heatwave-far-more-likely-scientists-find [accessed 18 Mar. 2018]

TT14 "Οι απειλητικοί καύσωνες " *Καθημερινή* 28 Sept. 2017

http://www.kathimerini.gr/928481/article/epikairothta/perivallon/oi-apeilhtikoi-kayswnes [accessed 18 Mar. 2018]

BT. The threatening heatwaves.

Visual shifts in the Greek version strengthen the narrative of socio-ecological resilience by highlighting the potential for human adaptation to climate change (Coller et al., 2009).

Conclusions: Translation as a coping strategy

The illustrations discussed in this narrowly focused study are intended to zoom in on the cultural specificity of the headlines. Hence, this chapter focused on mediated headlines of crisis reporting in English, through translation into the Greek media, because the cultural specificity of crisis reporting strikingly manifests itself at the very outset of *introducing* a crisis to the Greek-speaking audiences. It showed that translation is perhaps another arena where mediated reality may be revisioned to narrate a different aspect of the story, which may de/mobilize audiences.

Translation practice seems to be highly important in crisis reporting situations. If '[i]nefficiencies in planning translate very easily into loss of life, injuries or damage that could have been avoided' (Alexander, 2012: 5), intercultural communication on crises is a worth exploring interdisciplinary area. Out of the four phases of a disaster cycle (mitigation, preparedness, response and recovery (ibid.)), the last two, namely

- response (the emergency actions taken during the impact and the short-term aftermath), and
- recovery (repairing the damage after the destruction has struck)

are the ones which translation studies seem to be able to significantly contribute to, as communication on crises can de/mobilize ethical responsibilities internationally. Coping strategies during a crisis 'involve a number of sequenced mechanisms for obtaining resources in times of adversity and disaster' (Wisner et al., 2004: 105). Translation is a strategy which may significantly contribute to the coping mechanisms, as, for instance, in avoiding or healing symptoms that may result from a crisis, a trauma or a critical incident (Thompson, 2004).

If the etic approach prevails in traditional journalism (Wisner at al., 2004, imposing the researchers' own perception and interpretation of vulnerability and crisis evoked by extreme natural events or social causation disasters), the translated version of this interpretation may not be an emic approach to crises (because it is similarly produced by another professional), but it could be assumed to convey an 'em-ish' perspective, in that it registers alternative culture-/institution-specific perceptions and interpretation of natural and man-made disasters. Analysing press data on crises, across press institutions, may reveal local aspects of hazard event reception in a target environment, which would make coping policies more socio-politically aware and flexible (Sawalha et al., 2017). In any case, there is a 'growing concern about the highly selective treatment of disasters by the Western media' (Wisner et al., 2004: 25) and this is another issue to be discussed through intercultural data.

Through its Higher Education Program, the US FEMA (Federal Emergency Management Agency) has developed standardized curricula on hazards and disasters and the courses developed have been social-science-related and have assumed awareness of social perception of crises. Such courses are 'Social Dimensions of Disasters', 'Sociology of Disaster', 'Social Vulnerability Approach to Disasters' and 'Public Administration and Emergency Management'. Translation practice would have enough findings to contribute to this social perception of crisis events and may need to be taken into account in the curricula. For instance, shifts in cross-cultural perception of social dimensions of disasters may be tangibly manifested in real-life translation contexts, through parallel versions of discourses (original and translated) which may register a target community's perception a disaster for the FEMA trainees. Monolingual researchers often doubt the power of professional translators' insight, which intercultural theorists and mediators highly appreciate.

In the same vein, the composition of the workforce in crisis situations usually reflects societal forces by taking into consideration features such as age, gender race and ethnicity. The analysis of the data in this study suggests that workforce development strategies should take into consideration the need for translators and intercultural theorists to participate in the workforce for ensuring greater socio-cultural sensitivity to vulnerability/resilience portrayal, and following intercultural conventions in both natural and human-induced disasters.

Acknowledgements

I am indebted to the Special Account Research Fund (ELKE) of the National and Kapodistrian University of Athens for funding this research, and to the editors for contributing invaluable suggestions.

References

Alexander, D. (2002/2012). *Principles of Emergency Planning and Management.* Edinburgh: Terra.

Allan, S. (1999/2004). *News Culture.* Berkshire: Open University Press.

Baker, M. (2006). *Translation and Conflict: A Narrative Account.* London: Routledge.

Baker, M. (2007). 'Reframing Conflict in Translation.' *Social Semiotics* 17(2): 152–169.

Bankoff, G. (2003). *Cultures of Disaster - Society and Natural Hazard in the Philippines.* London: Routledge-Curzon.

Ben-Porath, S. R. (2006). *Citizenship under Fire - Democratic Education in Times of Conflict.* Princeton, NJ: Princeton University Press.

Bignell, J. (1997/2002). *Media Semiotics.* Manchester: Manchester University Press.

Boin, A., Hart, P.'t, and McConnell, A. (2008). 'Conclusions: The Politics of Crisis Exploitation.' In A. Boin, A. McConnell, and P.'t Hart (eds), *Governing after Crisis–The Politics of Investigation, Accountability and Learning*, 285–316. Cambridge: Cambridge University Press.

Brown, G., and Yule, G. (1983). *Discourse Analysis.* Cambridge: Cambridge University Press.

Calzada-Pérez, M. (2014). *A propos of Ideology: Translation Studies on Ideology-Ideologies in Translation Studies.* London: Routledge.

Chaney, C. (2017). 'How Crisis Journalists Can Magnify the Voices of Poor, Marginalized Communities of Color.' *International Journal of Crisis Communication* 1: 2–8.

Collier W. M., Kasey, R. J., Saxena, A., Baker-Gallegos, J., Carroll, M., and Yohe., G. W. (2009). 'Strengthening Socio-Ecological Resilience through Disaster Risk Reduction and Climate Change Adaptation: Identifying Gaps in an Uncertain World.' *Environmental Hazards – Human and Policy Dimensions.* Special Issue: Climate Change as Environmental and Economic Hazard 8(3): 171–186.

Coombs, W. T. (1995). 'Choosing the Right Words – The Development of Guidelines for the Selection of the "Appropriate" Crisis-Response Strategies.' *Management Communication Quarterly* 8(4): 447–476.

Coombs, W. T. (2006). *Code Red in the Boardroom – Crisis Management as Organizational DNA.* Westport, CT: Praeger.

Coombs, W. T. (2010). 'Parameters for Crisis Communication.' In W. T. Coombs and S. J. Holladay (eds), *The Handbook of Crisis Communication*, 17–53. Chichester, UK: Wiley-Blackwell.

Culpeper, J. (1996). 'Towards an Anatomy of Impoliteness.' *Journal of Pragmatics* 25: 349–367.

Elmasry, M. H., and Chaudhri, V. (2010). 'The Press as Agent of Cultural Repair: A Textual Analysis of News Coverage of the Virginia Tech Shootings.' In W. T. Coombs and S. J. Holladay (eds), *The Handbook of Crisis Communication*, 141–158. Chichester, UK: Wiley-Blackwell.

Fairclough, N. (1995). *Media Discourse.* London: Arnold.

Federici, M. F. (2016). 'Introduction: A State of Emergency for Crisis Communication.' In F. M. Federici (ed.), *Mediating Emergencies and Conflicts – Frontline Translating and Interpreting*, 1–30. Basingstoke and New York, NY: Palgrave Macmillan.

Frandsen, F., and Johansen, W. (2010). 'Crisis Communication, Complexity, and the Cartoon Affair: A Case Study'. In W. T. Coombs and S. J. Holladay (eds), *The Handbook of Crisis Communication*, 511–526. Chichester, UK: Wiley-Blackwell.

Hewitt, K. (1983). 'The Idea of Calamity in a Technocratic Age'. In K. Hewitt (ed.) *Interpretation of Calamity from the Viewpoint of Human Ecology*. Boston, MA: Allen and Unwin.

Hofstede, G., and Hofstede, G. J. (2005). *Cultures and Organisations – Software of the Mind*. New York, NY: McGraw-Hill.

Holladay, S. J. (2010). 'Are They Practicing What We Are Preaching? An Investigation of Crisis Communication Strategies in the Media Coverage of Chemical Accidents.' In W. T. Coombs and S. J. Holladay (eds), *The Handbook of Crisis Communication*, 159–180. Chichester, UK: Wiley-Blackwell.

Houben, M. (2005). *International Crisis Management – The Approach of European States*. London and New York, NY: Routledge.

Hussain, S., and Munawar, A. (2017). 'Analysis of Pakistan Print Media Narrative on the War on Terror.' *International Journal of Crisis Communication* 1: 38–47.

Mkandawire, P., and Aguda, N. D. (2009). 'Characteristics and Determinants of Insecurity in Sub-Saharan Africa.' In I. N. Luginaah and E. K. Yanful (eds), *Environment and Health in Sub-Saharan Africa: Managing an Emerging Crisis*, 3–23. London and New York, NY: Springer.

Monahan, T. (2010). *Surveillance in the Time of Insecurity*. New Brunswick, NJ and London: Rutgers University Press.

Olsson, E.-K. (2009). 'Responsibility Framing in a 'Climate Change Induced' Compounded Crisis: Facing Tragic Choices in the Murray-Darling Basin.' *Environmental Hazards – Human and Policy Dimensions*. Special Issue: Climate Change as Environmental and Economic Hazard 8(3): 226–240.

Ray, S. J. (1999). *Strategic Communication in Crisis Management – Lessons from the Airline Industry*. Westport, CT: Quorum Books.

Regester, M., and J. Larkin. (1997/2002/2005). *Risk Issues and Crisis Management – A Casebook of Best Practice*. London and Sterling, VA: Chartered Institute of Public Relations.

Sawalha, I. H. S., Shamieh, J. M., and Fendi, U. A. (2017). 'Insights on the Influence of the Attributes of the Arab Culture on Crisis Communications.' *International Journal of Crisis Communication* 1: 21–28.

Schmidt A., Wolbers, J., Ferguson, J., and Boersma, K. (2018). 'Are You Ready2Help? Conceptualizing the Management of Online and Onsite Volunteer Convergence.' *Journal of Contingencies and Crisis Management*. Special Issue: The Citizen in Disasters: Organizing for Emergence? 26(3): 338–349.

Tiernan S., Igoe, J., Carroll, C., and O'Keefe, S. (2007). 'Crisis Communication Response Strategies: A Case Study of the Irish Tourist Board's Response to the 2001 European Foot and Mouth Scare.' In E. Laws, B. Prideaux, and K. Chon (eds), *Crisis Management in Tourism*, 310–325. Oxford: CAB International.

Thompson, R. (2004). *Crisis Intervention and Crisis Management – Strategies That Work in Schools and Communities*. New York, NY and Hove: Brunner-Routledge.

United Nations (2015). *Sendai Framework for Disaster Risk Reduction 2015–2030*. Geneva and New York, NY: UN. Available online: https://www.preventionweb.net/files/43291_sendaiframeworkfordrren.pdf (accessed 28 November 2018).

Weick, K. E., and Sutcliffe, K. M. (2007). *Managing the Unexpected – Resilient Performance in the Age of Uncertainty*. San Francisco, CA: John Wiley & Son, Jossey-Bass.

Wisner B., Blaickie, P., Cannon, T., and Davis, J. (2004). *At Risk – Natural Hazards, People's Vulnerability and Disasters*. 2nd edition. London and New York, NY: Routledge.

Wodak, R., and Forchtner, B. (2018). *The Routledge Handbook of Language and Politics*. London and New York, NY: Routledge.

11

Emergenza Migranti: From Metaphor to Policy

Federico M. Federici

In Italy, the concept of *emergenza migranti* – a sensationalist translation exaggerating and simplifying a humanitarian crisis that is considered here as a biased, conditioning and aggressive metaphor – altered not only the perception of the scope of arriving migrants in Italian harbours but also the linkage between the journalistic and political narrative, and the legislative actions justified by it. The bias became so extreme that the United Nations High Commissioner for Refugees (UNHCR) called journalists to develop an *ethical stance* in reporting about migration, so as to oppose the debasement of journalistic standards in favour of sensationalist figurative language. With its widespread adoption in the national press in Italy, the metaphor has become a political tool to justify incomplete policies of migration at national (and to some extent international) level.

Unparalleled numbers of people have become forced migrants in the last decade (over 70 million, according to UNHCR, 2018), a decade in which countries that were migrants' destinations were afflicted by the worst economic crisis in decades. This chapter argues that through metaphors such as *emergenza migranti* the deliberate choice of specific language is the manifestation of political agendas and it then becomes further concern for misplaced perceptions of migration flows in Italy. The powerful language affected the political debate in Italy culminating with the legislative changes introduced by the Decree of Law 113/2018, 5 October 2018 (the Salvini Act). The decree restricts applications for Italian citizenship (Art. 14) and applications for asylum (Art. 12), thus confirming the success of the hard-line right wing in power, which through its manifestation of a strong demagogic approach, contempt for cultural democracy and the belief in the regimentation of society along the lines of ethnic origins can be considered semi-fascist.

This chapter considers three dimensions of the skewed perceptions reinforced by the *emergenza migranti* metaphor: (1) the journalistic risk of endorsing a narrative frame over a long period of time; (2) the limitations of thirty years of Italian policies dealing with migratory flows as a contextual justification for embedding the discursive metaphor into legislative and political practices; (3) the shortcomings of letting the perceived migrants' emergency drive plans for intercultural communication, when it really deals with a crisis context. Subdivided into three sections, the chapter suggests provocative interpretations of the impact of the collocation *emergenza migranti*. Firstly, the phrase and its uses are discussed within the context of the movement for an ethical journalism, which upholds reporting values to protect the credibility of journalism. Secondly, the text argues that the discussion of news reliability has created a powerful and confusing form of oblique censorship, which makes extremist soundbites like *emergenza migranti* successful as useful shortcuts against complex debates, driving sloppy responses or arguably the complete lack of comprehensive responses called for by reality. Thirdly, it considers the social impact of these defective narrative shortcuts by reviewing Italian migration policies, which also focus on intercultural communication among a growing multilingual and multicultural society to support gradual integration of speakers of languages other than Italian. In the final remarks those three dimensions are brought together.

Code of conduct versus raging metaphors

This chapter is a thought contribution and is grounded on over ten years of observations and interpretations of the Italian news-making context discussed in master-level classes and at conferences. Although the imprint of those discussions and subsequent discussions is a priori academic, those debates occurred because they were triggered by the official and/or societal narrative that was questioned. The ensuing analyses were much less academic in nature and much more applying sound ethical grounds to the discourse in question. I have therefore focused on the ways in which Italian journalism has used *recognizable* national frames to introduce – via translated materials – information about 'the Other', more specifically *the foreigner*. In the 2010s, new migrant flows exacerbated the forms of national framing taking some extreme examples of vulgar, hatred-filled headlines (see Filmer, 2018: 166). These extreme reactions blossomed around such figures of speech as *invasion* and *emergency*.

Their power was so devious and the journalistic response to the phenomenon of displacement was such a negative framing that in 2013 the United Nations High Commissioner for Refugees (UNHCR) in 2013 felt compelled to be involved. As well, Italian associations of journalists began to call for adhesion to principles of the *Ethical Journalism Network* (EJN). Coinciding with the most profound investigation of journalistic practices of the British press, the Leveson Inquiry (2011–2012), the EJN is an international network that since 2011 draws on self-reflection and analysis of journalistic practices. At that time, following the initial social changes driven by a string of conflicts such as the Arab Spring, the wars in Iraq and Afghanistan, and the many forgotten wars in Africa, the EU and Mediterranean countries more in particular began experiencing increased migratory flows. The unprecedented numbers of displaced people in the early to mid-2010s, confused with the free movement of people across European member states, had fuelled an anti-migrant narrative. Journalists' reporting practices led to highly divisive civil societies in Europe until some journalists decided to take a step back and look at ongoing practices.

In Italy, the National Council of the Journalists' Association (CNOG) and the Italian National Press Federation (FNSI), sharing the UNHCR's concerns, saw the need to articulate a new charter of deontological behaviour for professional journalists: the *Charter of Rome* (2014). The Charter focuses entirely on reporting about the so-called migrant crisis and is a protocol in addition to the existing Italian Journalist's Charter of Duties, or code practice (*Carta dei doveri del giornalista*). The very fact that this document is an addition to the Charter of Duties indicates the seriousness of the association's concerns and the gravity of the ethics of reporting it was prompted by.

The Charter calls journalists to 'exercise the highest' care when they report on migration-related news items (2014: 1). They should do so by upholding four principles: (a) using appropriate terminology – as defined by the UN, 'asylum seekers, refugees, victims, of trafficking and migrants' (see also the relevant discussion in the Čemerin chapter in this volume); (b) avoiding 'spreading, inaccurate, simplified or distorted information as regards the latter groups'; (c) safeguarding their confidentiality in interviews; (d) consulting 'experts and organizations with a specific expertise on the subject so as to provide the public with information which is clear, comprehensive and also analyses the underlying roots of phenomena' (2014: 1).

However, the narrative framing of the arrivals of migrants in Italy as an 'emergency' had been long established by the time of the *Charter of Rome*. That framing obviously influenced the respective readerships and audiences but also political debates and legislation – not only in Italy, even though this chapter only focuses on the Italian contexts. Political debates and legislation were informed by the enduring, skewed perception. This influence led to confusing definitions of needs (between migrants, refugees and asylum seekers) and of support in establishing communication with the relevant Italian authorities – thus engendering a real crisis in terms of intercultural communication.

This chapter does not underestimate that the sheer number of arrivals was unprecedented during the 2014–2016 peak years of the refugee 'crisis' – following the EU definition of the phenomenon. Although the issue of scale was a legitimate concern that could have had an impact on the most robust and solid plans to deal with displaced people, behind the *emergency framing*, successive Italian governments had hidden the embedded behaviour of Italian politicians to ignore their own established policies and common theoretical planning, in favour of last-minute, ad hoc approach to highly predictable events. The Decree of Law 113/2018 represents only the last in line in this responsive legislation, which does not engage with the long-term but only the immediate political and electoral gain. Obviously, the way in which the press represented how human-made disasters and conflicts lead to large displacements of people, with their subsequent migration streams towards European countries in 2011–2016, goes beyond the Italian context. However, arguably, the Italian press chose very specific words that warranted a focus on the exceptionality of the phenomenon rather than an ethical representation of the many phenomena converging into the mass displacement of people.

In a strange sense of parallelism, the framing construed around the *emergenza* metaphor resembles press depictions of semi-predictable environmental disasters, for which Button (1999: 114) reminds us of 'how the media packages information and participates in the construction of reality and informs us of the ideological elements that work to maintain the status quo in the wake of a disaster'. By defining it an *emergenza*, nobody can mitigate its impact, as if the factors causing the displacement of people were not known. A further challenge emerged through the long-term humanitarian crises driven by conflicts and their cascading effects (Pescaroli and Alexander, 2015), because these effects showed up ineffectual solutions to the reception of migrants and the processing of applications for EU residence, via the Italian system. The frame of *emergenza* heightens the sense of unpredictability, which ultimately was not an element in the migration crisis of the second decade of the twenty-first century.

Ethics and journalistic frames of representation

The group of editors and journalists who funded and collaborated to the *Ethical Journalism Network* (EJN) – and still do – collected analyses of reporting on *migration* in the Mediterranean. In 2017, they conducted a large-scale study upon commission by the EUROMED Migration IV project (2016–2019),[1] in collaboration with the International Centre for Migration Policy Development (ICMPD, founded in 1993). Entitled *How Does the Media on Both Sides of the Mediterranean Report on Migration?* (2017), their study solicits serious reflections on reporting across Europe. Within this context, Masera (2017: 46–52) focused on Italy and provided evidence of the ways in which the tones used by the Italian press have changed over the last two decades. Their exacerbation and hyper-sensationalized undertones came under scrutiny when the 2013 tragedies in the Mediterranean brought about a revision of practices. The change of the tones used by most other Italian media, according to the study, was noticeable in 2016 and 2017. Outlets traditionally considered right wing or extreme right wing continued with their excessive and surcharged discourses. For instance, *Il Giornale* and *Il Fatto Quotidiano* famously used *invasione* – invasion – as the favourite term to discuss the arrival of migrants on Italian shores. The *emergenza migranti,* through the rhetoric of the right-wing, racist Lega Nord (Northern League) party[2] and its representative in the role of Ministry of Interior within the coalition government, perpetuates the metaphor through an aggressive (and for some illegal) anti-migration policy. The facts and figures tell a different story (see OECD, 2018) but because its pervasive nature – through media and politics – the narrative frame remains difficult to challenge. Undeniably, a ten-year-long plethora – if not outright bombardment – of repeated uses of figures of speech, firmly embedded in the political parlance by the right-wing coalition government led by Prime Minister Silvio Berlusconi from 2008, cannot be undone in lustre.

Daily newspapers: *La Repubblica, Il Corriere* and *La Stampa*

By researching the online and printed archives of three major daily newspapers *La Repubblica, Corriere della Sera* and *La Stampa,*[3] it is possible to track the spread of the *emergenza* expression via the newspapers with the largest (national) readership. Their usage of the expression arguably would reflect an established framing in televised news broadcasts. Its precursor, *emergenza clandestini* (emergency clandestine), used in the 1990s (see discussion below), functions as a reminder of the habitual use of the noun clause *emergenza*+noun in the journalistic variety of the Italian language. Such clause types represented a linguistic feature of the journalistic variety in the printed press, but seamlessly transferred into its online publications (Eco, 1971; Bonomi, 2002; Lorusso and Violi, 2015). Consulting on *corriere.it*, the subscription-only archives for the online and digitized printed versions of *Corriere della Sera*, the expression grows in significance and occurrences in the same years as it does for its competitors, but its usage seems to be less consistently present and tends to be limited to quotations. However, the *Corriere della Sera* archives also return a first-page heading 'Clandestini, emergenza in Sicilia' dated 3 August 1998; this was not necessarily the first occurrence for that expression, a predecessor of *emergenza migranti*, but it is a stern reminder of the long-term embeddedness of the syntagma, *emergenza*+noun, in the journalistic variety (of Italian).

Consulting the archives of *La Repubblica* – via its online (subscription-only) *repubblica.it* services providing access to paper and digitized printed versions – the expression *emergenza migranti* appears to be used for the first time from mid-May 2009 as if it were a regular collocation that is meaningful and accessible to the audience. In fact, it is not accompanied by any gloss, presuming therefore that the readers recognize this collocation. There is no evidence of any occurrence in the archived materials of *Repubblica*, which date back to 1 January 1984. Since its first recorded occurrence until December 2018, there are, however, over 830 occurrences in the intervening years.

The online archives of *La Stampa* support the perception that this newspaper became more attentive to avoiding the expression from early on. Anna Masera, the copyeditor of its main online pages, being a regular collaborator of the EJN, steered this newspaper towards a more considerate use of negative frames on the migrant crisis.

These cursory observations and findings based on rudimentary frequency scores of *emergenza emigranti* – already very telling – intend to capture the undertones in its usages. However, I would not expect these minimalistic insights on the linguistic facts to necessarily persuade readers that this approach would be enough to justify this interpretation of the linguistic phenomenon. As a phenomenon of usage in written press and, most certainly, in broadcast (see Figure 11.1), the study of this expression would require a more profound stand-alone systematic scrutiny.

The purpose here is to contextualize how an expression repeated consistently almost every two days across two of the major national newspapers came to undermine political policies to deal with migration. Until the time, in 2011,

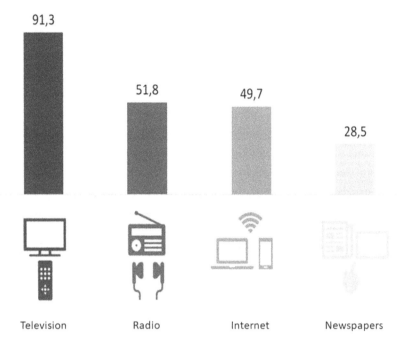

91,3

51,8

49,7

28,5

Television   Radio   Internet   Newspapers

Figure 11.1 Access to information in Italy.

Source: Autorità per le Garanzie nelle Comunicazioni (AGCOM), Rapporto sul consumo di informazioni (AGCOM, 2018).

when the expression itself gave way to a political use of special finances to fund the *n*th ad hoc solution to engage with the migratory flows in the Mediterranean, when the expression was used to justify the declaration of a state of emergency (see Filmer and Federici, 2018). The next section shows how the political force of this framing gradually led to a legislative, rather than a political, use of the expression.

Framing is neither new, nor surprising

Nobody ever expects narratives from news organizations to attempt uncensored and unbiased presentation of events (Zelizer and Allan, 2010; Zelizer, 2015). However, the exacerbation shown in 2016 and 2017 of politically driven concepts of *mistrusts* in traditional journalism with the US executive giving enormous exposure to the misleading concepts of 'fake news' and 'alternative facts' boosted the growth of a new form of journalistic ethical censorship. The focus for this chapter lies with the representative force of figurative language

(Montgomery, 2008) in relation to the *emergenza migranti* collocation and it does not intend to be a blind attack of the press. Quite the contrary, the chapter aims to support freedom of the press as in the duty to report on reality in truthful manners and as such aims to combat the situation in which freedom of the press is under attack, like in Italy but also in other G20 countries.

Since 2016, right-wing, populist, identitarian (often discriminating or racist) politicians, or supremacist ones even, in Italy (e.g. Salvini), the UK (e.g. Farage) and the United States (e.g. Trump) more extensively than elsewhere have been conducting attacks to esteemed members of the press. They do so when journalists ask questions that such politicians perceive to be difficult or irrelevant to their worldview and to be disjoint from the opinion of the countries they represent (composed of those who voted for them or for other candidates). Emerging from populist contexts, and fuelled by conspiracy theories online, these voices until recently were considered marginal, extremist and reactionary political positions, which laid secretly at the background of G8 countries that considered themselves as democratic. Suddenly, the darkest manifestations of these populist, isolationist and outright reactionary positions have become a worldwide phenomenon (see as well Slavtcheva-Petkova, 2016). Even more recently, they have been shown to pertain to the Italian context quite poignantly by investigative reports such as the one by the *New York Times* (Horowitz, 2017) and *BuzzFeed* (Nardelli and Silverman, 2017).

Damocles' sword is ever-pending over the Italian contexts. On the one hand, the phenomenon of a 'journalism under attack' is particularly worrying – if not dangerous in the long term in relation to the very existence of democracy – as it has been subject of over thirty years of interference of its news system by media tycoon Silvio Berlusconi and recently has been overtaken by an even louder and more censoring interference by self-proclaimed beholders of all truths, the right-wing coalition of the *Movimento 5 stelle* (5-Star Movement, 5SM) and the Northern League. On the other hand, journalists themselves have been responsible for enforcing and showcasing ever more inappropriate and unacceptable terms and narratives as if they are the ultimate entitlement of freedom of speech. The excesses in narratives going well beyond the threshold of denoting reality as per the Italian coalition government formed in June 2018 – three months after a general election – led Mr Matteo Salvini, at the time of writing the incumbent Minister of the Interior of Italy, to deny NGO boats as well as migrant boats in trouble in Italian waters access to Italian ports. The reactive action was transformed towards the end of 2018 into the Decree of Law 113/2018 that sanctioned restrictions to the conditions for asylum applications (Art. 1 and Art. 2) whilst simultaneously simplifying procedures for deportation, re-entry and repatriation (Art. 4, 5, and 6). To reach this extreme political action, the government benefitted from the previous ten years of framing of the isolation of Italy when dealing with migratory flows, and its uniqueness in having to deal at the same time with the effects of substantial displacement movements (due to conflicts and socio-political causes) and migration streams (due to economic and personal reasons) that landed onto its shores, whilst being the 'backdoor' to Europe (Filmer and Federici, 2018).

Reflections on international journalism and its needs for credibility are becoming ever more necessary at the time of news processing by artificial intelligence (Clerwall, 2014). International journalists have discussed yet another crisis of journalism (Zelizer, 2015) from first decade of the twenty-first century in which citizen journalism has seen a sudden growth (Allan, 2006). The last decade and the last lustre have seen the problem emerge as a scourge of current democracies: new forms of cyber-propaganda via news tweets have appeared together with open channels that reject notions of evidence, proofs and any concept of *reliable, credible* and *fact-checked* sources. In this mixture, the use of coloured and negatively biased collocations such as *emergenza migranti* as a way of offering a transparent access to other worldviews risks being ever more skewed towards forms of oblique censorship (Federici, 2011). It could be argued that strong collocation 'migrant crisis', which is the preferred label used by the EU institutions to refer to the increased displacement of people after the Arab spring, the war in Syria, the prolonged conflict in Afghanistan since 2012, might have led to alternative perception of the phenomenon, as one in need of concerted, rationalized and pondered solutions for the long-term, rather than a short-term, unexpected emergency.

Emergenza migranti can be plotted as a different translation solution of the different conceptualization of the phenomenon as a crisis. The EU-preferred collocation entails that the current events are due to affect people for a long time, whilst the Italian *emergenza* is an emergency requiring immediate and strong action with resources and response (on the differences between crisis and emergency, see Alexander and Pescaroli, 2016). Filmer and Federici (2018: 230) emphasize: 'On 7 April 2011, the then Prime Minister Silvio Berlusconi declared a "state of national emergency" due to increased migratory flows following the Arab Spring, which *de facto* endorsed the media discourse on "migrant emergency" by activating special governmental powers'. By interlocking people's displacement with notions of emergency that legally frame the deployment of financial resources in the case of disasters triggered by natural hazards in Italy, the *emergenza migranti* collocation became a powerful political tool.

The next section further emphasizes the political and social significance of this linguistic choice by considering it as a form of oblique censorship. *Emergenza migranti* becomes as metaphor that stifles political and social debates on migration routes, with the purpose of simplifying the evolution of societies in a globalized twenty-first century world. Any other analysis of the migration phenomenon became secondary and attributed to *buonismo* (a negative connotation to describe those who keep an open mind on social issues, rather than compartmentalize and group people; normally attributed by right-wing politicians to moderate and left-wing intellectuals and politicians). It is therefore useful to consider this concept in the next section.

Conceptualization of oblique censorship

Bunn's (2015) revisits established notions of censorship in New Censorship Theory and puts forward a very powerful argument that we should rethink censorship as relativistic forms of freedom of thought. Such conceptualization will be applied in the specific of this chapter to a relativistic form of freedom of press. For Bunn (2015: 43): 'It may ultimately turn out that effective authoritative censorship is not simply external, but insinuates itself into the circuits of communication, not simply coercive but also mobilises powerful social currents, not simply repressive but also generates new forms of speech and thought.' The conceptualization of censorship as part of a continuum within channels of communication and actors alike may appear ethically disturbing at first, yet it is a powerful instrument to investigate mass phenomena that discredit experts, science and evidence-based (fallible but tested) notions in favour of unfounded, memetic rumours that have their main power in numbers – and hence in their easily dissemination open to easy manipulation. The linguistic roots of this political power is well explained in a long Western tradition of rhetoric from the sophists, Aristotle, to Gramsci, before Bourdieu discussed it in sociological terms. To understand the actors in the linguistic process of censorship, many areas should be investigated. For Bunn (2015: 44), '[s]uch an investigation entails examining the actual practice of censors, not as external actors within a system of communicative control, but as the surprisingly undertheorised and unappreciated cogs within communication networks in which powerful forces like the state invariably operate.' Arguably, page editors choosing headlines and sub-headlines with easy collocations censored other perspectives on the migration phenomenon.

Definitions of censorship abound; it is useful to juxtapose here the definition of Billiani to that of Bunn. She proposed it and used it specifically to conduct research into the relationship between translation and censorship, 'Censorship itself must be understood as one of the discourses, and often the dominant one, produced by a given society at a given time and expressed through repressive cultural, aesthetic and linguistic measures or through economic means' (2007/2014: 2). This definition can extend into a notion of 'oblique censorship' of alternative views – for instance, seeing migratory phenomena in the context of global, socio-economical changes that lead to a long *crisis* until a solution is found. The rhetoric behind emergency as a choice, which diminished after the *Charter of Rome*, presents an example of this exclusion of ideas by omission, an oblique censorship.

The open manipulation of credibility, in smear campaigns targeted to vulnerable groups or individuals, but also in consolidated propaganda, is an equally well-known historical phenomenon (see for instance Neander and Marlin, 2010) and one with new permutations that is growing in significance worldwide, with increasing levels of unchallenged populistic views. However, in Italy, the demagogic forms of populism have taken specific aim to discredit both investigative journalism and the role of expertise and scientific competences. For instance, an extensive, commercially funded and scientifically unfounded no-vaccination (termed as 'no-vax') campaign – driven by the unruly and uncritical dissemination of the theory presented in the now-retracted article by Wakefield et al. (1998) led the Italian government to put forward a Decree of Law (no. 73, 7 June 2017) to avoid epidemics in young children. The growth of the inconsiderate and erroneous belief that vaccinations carry higher levels of risk for individual than benefits for the public health of the population illustrates a significant issue in trusting alternative sources of journalism (Horowitz, 2017; Nardelli and Silverman, 2017), because shortcuts taken by traditional journalism had already undermined their credibility.

The need for the *Charter of Rome* in 2014 proved that this fear came to be acknowledged by journalists in relation to reporting the migrant crisis. However much the trend is global and determined by circulation of rumours on social media, the Italian manifestations are particularly relevant because the current government coalition includes a party whose ideas are too often based on generic internet sources, with no fact-checking, and no scientific or rigorous backing (the 5SM). Their resulting rhetoric is an incarnation of the Orwellian nightmare where serious situations that need solutions are made banal to be dismissed with extraordinary measures, rather than with institutional plans. The *emergenza migranti* encapsulates, metaphorically, the preference for ephemeral, untested, inefficient and ineffective patchwork solutions over accepting the complexity of twenty-first century and working to mould a political strategy that works towards accommodating its challenges, rather than around them. The *emergenza migranti* enforces a sense of intercultural emergency without an emergency plan.

A substantial number of social media accounts, ranging from blogs, Twitter, and Facebook to Instagram, support circulation of misinformation in attempts to discredit any traditional source of information in Italy. The Italian anomaly is that the largest party with the relative majority after the 2018 election seems to be reliant on entirely web-based sources. The 5SM *was at its core* a social media movement, grown into a party by a new typology of media tycoon, the webplatform owner Gianroberto Casaleggio. Born in the name of a web democracy, this party creates proselytes online by means of ill-informed news pieces controlled by a small number of individuals (not unlikely from 'traditional' or 'old' media in the hands of an invasive tycoon, who completely hide behind their internet platforms). Through control of misinformation and use of social media, they discredit science, scientists and discoveries by opposing their forms of web-based 'revealed' truths to the scientific method (to which we can still impute many limitations, but not strive to revise, review and reconsider theories on the ground of evidence). This political movement has created a shift in journalism happening as it did alongside the exponential growth of social media; traditional press, however, had been caught in this self-defeating spiral once it established its preference for loud refrains, such as *emergenza migranti*, as continuous simplifications of very complex situations. Over time with the financial crisis of 2007, still affecting the Italian economy, the perceived *stato d'emergenza* has been ingrained in the population.

In this context, a polarization between 'old' and 'new' media has emerged in Italy stronger than seen elsewhere, also as a result of intimidating, violent and repeated attacks on the Italian press, as Natale reminds us (2016: 594), 'in the rhetoric of the [Italian] 5-Star Movement, the country is seen as divided into two contrasting blocks, "one which finds information in the Web, the other which finds disinformation in newspapers and television" ' (Grillo, 2008). Most Italians access news via TV broadcasts (91.3 per cent; see Figure 11.1) and newspapers are the fourth source of information, but, of course, their relevance combining web-based and printed access remains significant. Nevertheless, collocations usable in oral broadcasts become standard coinage in the printed and digital press; hence *emergenza migranti* achieved its spread because of political and televised use but was embedded in the narrative by the continued use in Italian newspapers for over ten years. The next section expands on earlier critical reflections on the sematic of the misused noun *emergenza* (Federici, 2016) in relation their significance within policy making.

New approaches are documenting how difficult it is for audiences to discern information provided by credible and reliable scientific sources (McKnight and Coronel, 2017), when alternative sources are used to corroborate discussions on polarizing topics. Adaptations of news items such as the *migrant crisis* more ruthlessly as *an emergency* become means of purporting views in an instrumental way: the EU crisis becomes a catalyst point only in Italy; it becomes such a breaking point that, similarly to the onset of a disaster, foregrounds the need for immediate and urgent action, rather than a systematic approach.

Although their content is public and visible, social media groups (on numerous platforms with diverse audiences but similar purposes, Instagram, Facebook, Twitter, and many country-specific others) do not represent an open dialogue. Conversations tend to be compartmentalized into closed bubbles, cyclically dialoguing within closed, exclusive communities. Social media–based exchanges are even more closed in-group conversations than traditional media in as much as they use polarized forms of dialogue. Soundbites like *emergenza migranti* amass in the faceless cauldron of rage that is Twitter. And even when the real peak of 'going viral' for the bitesize phrase and sentence phenomenon is over (see Reynolds, 2018), the compromised expression lingers on (and is available online to be stumbled across by people who are unaware or outright ignorant). There was no major advantage in conducting an extensive analysis of social media regarding its use of the *emergenza migranti* metaphor, as recent research has shown that social media in Italy create such a closed and polarized dynamics that debunking false information online, truly 'fake news', is *de facto* unfeasible (Zollo et al., 2017), in the polarized and 'tribalised' audiences (Orengo, 2005).

Emergency discourse: The language issue

There is no novelty in saying that powerful language shapes the ways in which we think. Lakoff and Johnson (1985) showed the cognitive footprint of metaphors. There are situations though, such as the metaphor of *emergenza migranti*, that can and do operate as catalyst points to understand the cascading effects of yielding the power of language. Its destructive consequences allow us to identify the explicit connections between political narratives, their journalistic echo-chambers and the correlation with policies or laws. There is no intention of accusing journalism for its tones and rhetoric, as this is not a polemical pamphlet. There is, however, the need for reflections on the power that figures of speech have not as stylistic tools but as political tools. The increased usage of *emergenza migranti* corresponds to the introduction of new measures on regulating in equal manner integration or expulsion of non-European residents from Italy in response to migrant flows. According to the extensive DEMIG (2015b) project on migration policies (2011–2014), Italy has seen between 150 and 200 changes to migration policies since 1918 (DEMIG, 2015a). Studying these policies recently for a case-study analysis of their application (Filmer and Federici, 2018), extensive connections became evident between the emergency narrative of the *emergenza migranti* and the changes in legislation on *politiche di accoglienza* (immigration policies).

The most recent legislative processes have been studied in other disciplines (for informative introductions, see Marchetti, 2011; 2014), but it is worth focusing on those of the last two decades and especially those of the last decade as they correlate with the spread of the *emergency* narrative. Over the century-long engagement with migration policies, only nine of the 200 or so mentioned in DEMIG, were made between 1990 and 2011, which are the years in which politicians saw in the movement of people a growing social concern related to recent historical changes (dissolution of Yugoslavia, 1990s recession, wars in Bosnia-Herzegovina and Kosovo, Iraq, Afghanistan, Sierra Leone, etc.), the most restrictive one coming once the measures of the previous governments (themselves guilty of using emergency solutions) had reduced the number of migrant arrivals in Italy by creating sub-humane conditions in detention centres in Libya.

Fragmented regulatory framework and emergency

Italy signed the International Covenant on Economic, Social and Cultural Rights promulgated by the United Nations General Assembly UN (1966) in 1967. However, it ratified it only in 1978. However, the first full national law on immigration, which refers to refugees' resettlement, is Act 39 of 28 February 1990 (or the 'Martelli law'). This legislative phase occurred at the beginning of the largest arrivals of migrants into Italy through the Adriatic Sea, especially from Albania and former Yugoslavia. This phase saw the recurrent use in journalistic Italian of the synecdoche *barconi* (fluvial barges) to indicate large groups of migrants crossing to Italy on makeshifts boats to escape poverty and insecurity. The expression lingered in the journalistic variety and continues to be used to depict the instability and danger of sea crossing in unsuitable vessels.

From its inception, the Martelli Law on migration created legislative confusion. Its categories included all typologies of migrants alongside the international category of refugees (Marchetti, 2011; 2014: 53–54). Further clarity arrived following the implementation of European Council's Directives (e.g. 2001/55/EC; ED 2004/83/CE).[1] In 2001, the *Programma nazionale asilo* (PNA, National Asylum Plan) led Italian city councils to underwrite a plan with the Office of the United Nations High Commissioner for Refugees (UNHCR) pertaining to the status of asylum seekers and refugees in Italy. This plan was redrafted into Act 189 of 20 July 2002 (the 'Bossi-Fini Law') to become the *Sistema di protezione per richiedenti di asilo e rifugiati* (SPRAR, System for the protection of asylum seekers and refugees), which still underpins the resourcing and management of the Italian reception centres, including support for intercultural communication and mediation. To this legislative amendment corresponded the introduction of the term *clandestino* (clandestine, illegal immigrant) which entered the journalistic variety as a category to identify groups of peoples much broader than those who could be legally defined as illegal immigrants.

Table 11.1, however, shows the most direct relationship between very recent policy changes and the surrounding political debates. The incremental distribution of *emergenza migranti* maps on the overall frame to discuss migration trends and to restrict access to migrants.

From the DEMIG classification and coding of the migration policies, two features are particularly relevant to this discussion: the policy area and the target group (for a detailed explanation of the coding, see De Haas, Natter, and Vezzoli, 2015). Policy area refers to 'what' is the core focus of the policy, whilst the target group refers to 'who', i.e. the groups who are affected by the policy. The magnitude of the policy is an indication of the degree of legislative change applied by the policy to the existing legal framework; in this perspective, the case of the 2009 changes, the security (anti-migrant) revision is a minor change and revision for graduates is the second most important category of change in the DEMIG approach. These details are important because they show how the legislative changes map on the aggressive political debate of 2009–2011 and resurface as soon as these subterranean debates in the fringes of right-wing movements became the flagship policies of the right-wing coalition government in power since 2018.

Table 11.1 Adapted excerpt from the DEMIG POLICY database

Year	Policy change	Policy area	Policy tool	Target Group	Target Origin	Restrictiveness	Magnitude
2009	2009 Law 94 or Part II of the 'Pacchetto Sicurezza' ('Security Package') made it possible to keep illegal immigrants up to 180 days (previously 60 days) in so called Identification and Expulsion Centres	Border and land control	Detention	Irregular migrants	All foreign nationalities	More restrictive	Minor change
2009	2009 Law 94 or Part II of the 'Pacchetto Sicurezza' ('Security Package') made conditions easier for foreigners graduating from an Italian university, who now have 12 months to find a job	Integration	Work VISA/ permit	International students	All foreign nationalities	Less restrictive	Mid-level change
2011	Decree 181/2011 converted into law 129/2011 – authorizes the expulsion from Italy of EU citizens who do not meet the requirements of the European Directive on free movement (targeting Roma community in Italy).	Exit	Expulsion	Specific categories	EU citizens	More restrictive	Mid-level change
2011	Decree 181/2011 converted into law 129/2011 – extended the maximum duration of detention of undocumented foreigners awaiting deportation from 6 months to 18 months	Border and land control	Detention	Irregular migrants	All foreign nationalities	More restrictive	Minor change

Year	Description	Policy area	Sub-area				
2011	Implementation of 2009 law – Introduces Language test (A2 CEFRL) required to obtain the long-term residence permit.	Integration	Access to permanent residency	All migrants	All foreign nationalities	More restrictive	Major change
2012	Presidential Decree 179 of 10 March 2012 – stipulated that non-EU foreigners intending to stay longer than one year must sign a point-based Integration Agreement with the Italian State (implementation of 2009 law) – (A2 Italian language, civic principles, within 24 months)	Integration	Language, housing and cultural integration programmes	All migrants	All foreign nationalities	More restrictive	Major change
2018	Decree 113 of 5 October 2018 restricts the definition of asylum seekers and imposed reductions on times for assessment of application, as well as closing the CARAs (Reception centres for asylum seekers).	Border and land control	Detention, deportation, and repatriation	All migrants	All foreign nationalities	More restrictive	Major change

Source: The table adapts (DEMIG, 2015a) examples relevant to Italy from the DEMIG database integrating data on the most recent policy revisions.

The system 'works because it's an emergency'

These legislative and policy actions regulate the management of the *Centri di Accoglienza per Richiedenti di Asilo* (CARA, Reception centres for asylum seekers) and pertain to SPRAR's ordinary management, whereas the *Centri di Accoglienza Straordinari* (CAS, Extraordinary Refuge Centres) were set up in 2014, thus marking the need for additional, hence 'extraordinary', centres operated by local authorities to deal with the increased migrant flows. Marchetti (2014: 68) discusses the mindset behind this duplicate system of reception centres with the introduction of the CAS, whose creation was also driven to prove that the Italian government was working without support, as the EU had organized only uncoordinated efforts to support those member states, like Italy, who had seen an enormous increase in migrant arrivals. For the purpose of this chapter, the very name of the centres, which are *straordinari*, shows the continued perception of the state of emergency, aligned with the figurative language of the *emergenza migranti*.

The discourse has affected also provision of language services to migrants. The perception of people displacement as an emergency is reflected in the ways in which established academic centres of excellence in pedagogy and training in public service interpreting (Trieste, Bologna-Forlì, Pisa) and their training systems were excluded by a major attempt to devise a policy to establish a national threshold for the professionalization of intercultural mediators. Curricula, pedagogists, educationalists and coordinators of the interpreter programmes of these institutions were not consulted by the special commission of the Italian Ministry of the Interior. The ministerial commission, funded by the EU, with the purpose of organizing and enhancing provision of services for language and culture mediation did not involve these institutions extensively (at all?). The very limited (if any) involvement is surprising considering that these institutions have had interpreting and translation at the core of their research, training offer and teaching activities for decades and are recognized against international standards as centres of excellence. In theory, the legislative push for defining the professional status of *mediatori linguistici* or *mediatori culturali* (language or culture mediators) dates from 2009, but a further push came from the perceived *emergenza*. For speakers who need interpreting and translation from languages that are not converted in formal, academic education in translation and interpreting, there is often an issue of recruitment (besides obvious issues of quality). Hence reflections on intercultural mediators, coming from practices of integration in the schooling systems (mediatori culturali) rather than from public services interpreting approaches and research, seemed to prevail.

The prevalence of the approach towards 'integration' rather than language service provision can be discussed in positive terms (e.g. gradual integration by limiting language barriers for the migrants) as much as in negative terms (e.g. there is no money available for the necessary provision of suitable support to intercultural communication, or, even worse: immigrants are left to their own devices).[4] These debates are beyond the scope of this chapter, but they are not to be underestimated. Concerning the prevalent sense of urgency determined by the *emergenza* narrative, the institutional approach seemed to move to the application of the language policies set out by the Presidential Decree (DPR) 179 of 14 September 2011. Entitled 'Regolamento concernente la disciplina dell'accordo di integrazione tra lo straniero e lo Stato' (*Regulation regarding the integration agreement between a foreign person and the State*), the DPR was enacted in 2012 and it lays out the legal principles that regulate language use in relation to migration. According to the DPR 179/2011, the Italian State and non-EU foreign residents willing to integrate into the Republic (be they economic migrants, asylum seekers or refugees) enter into a contract, termed the Integration Agreement (Di Muzio, 2012: 8). The DPR creates a point-based system to obtain the permit and a pathway to integration; it foresees the potential allocation (art.2, par.2) of 'credits' for the applicants' competence in the Italian language, culture and knowledge of the institutions of the Republic of Italy in compliance with art. 5 of Act 286 of 25 July 1998, regulating the status of immigrants in Italy. The DPR therefore presupposes a phased emancipation from the reliance on translators, interpreters and cultural, or linguistic, mediations; *it henceforth anticipates them* as being needed upon arrival in Italy.

The provision of translation and interpreting services is perceived as part of the initial phase of interactions between migrants and Italian institutions. Gradual acquisition of the language is intended in the legal framework as intertwined with socio-cultural integration, thus incorporating provision for issues such as education, employment and health in the point-based pathway to integration. In terms of language policy, its long-term focus is as well its strength and fatal flaw: the Integration Agreement leads non-EU migrants to EU citizenship through a direct route of the Italian visa, which can be perceived in the EU as a backdoor pathway and a problem of securitization (Guild, 2014a; 2014b). Furthermore, with its focus on long-term, permanent migrants, it could be reasonably argued that the policy is potentially irrelevant when it comes to addressing the sudden increase of 'humanitarian immigrants' (using OECD terminology) experienced in the six years following its 2012 ratification.

If social and language needs connected to the Integration Agreement stayed more or less the same over the first two years after its ratification, Italy then indeed saw a 'sharp rise in humanitarian immigration', however, that 'coincided with a wider picture of overall immigration reduction (21% in total)' (OECD, 2017: 16; 2018). The change to humanitarian integration was conflated in the political framing underlying the *emergenza migranti* narrative. In turn, the legislative flexibility on community-specific contexts becomes a lack of clarity and support. When the number of humanitarian migrants increased suddenly, it generated pressure on the reception system as a whole. The increase in numbers of people arriving and the growing needs and demands raised barriers for humanitarian migrants to communicate with the Italian institutions and vice versa (for a case study, see Filmer and Federici, 2018). Language needs for non-permanent migrants in the already-overstretched system in place for asylum seekers and VISA applicants increased following the regulatory changes. These unveil the overall lacunae of the Italian, as well as European, immigration policies in the response to the linguistic emergencies, whereby the system according to intercultural mediators involved works *only* 'because it's an emergency' (see Filmer and Federici, 2018: 234).

Fragmented intercultural communication policies

In 2009, those involved in intercultural communication with migrants became formally called and recognized as *intercultural mediators*. Their role was to support changes in social expectations recorded in the previous decade. Morniroli et al. (2007: 5) considered migrant flows towards Italy as no longer embedded in notions of emergency but as already 'organised and structured' phenomena belonging to the socio-economic composition of Italian society. From this perspective, the increased demand for such services as intercultural mediation, interpreting and translation across the Italian peninsula are due to the country's socio-cultural transformations. The Italian definition of intercultural mediators draws from research in the early 2000s in relation to language support in the classroom and the legal term became the most common after the DPR179/2011 was ratified. The statutory mechanisms of DPR179/2001 for language provision are disseminated in the dedicated portal entitled *Integrazione Migranti Vivere e lavorare in Italia* (Migrant Integration: Working and living in Italy). The portal summarizes how the legal framework organizes the professional role of *intercultural mediators*. These figures cover a variety of communicative needs that range from first response to asylum seekers, refugees and visa applicants' support. Although it is true that training in intercultural mediation ought to engage with the latest societal needs (Kelly, 2017), the sudden obligation for autochthonous (often economically deprived) communities to integrate newcomers in uncontrolled and disorganized processes is a consequence of the political narrative filtering into institutional practices, and in turn cementing the public's concerns and fears around a phenomenon that is not a state of emergency from the perspective of the accommodating host society and its duty of care but a dramatic state of displaced people and a complicated intercultural and transnational crisis.

A 2014 report offers the most recent figures collected and shows how there is demand and intent to establish a training pathway to prepare intercultural mediators to deal with the changing needs of migrants in their pathways to integration (Melandri et al., 2014). Within the legislative framework established by the *emergenza*, the twenty regions of Italy could define professional intercultural mediators in as many as twenty different ways. The pervasive rhetoric of emergency seems to influence the ways in which the most significant voices of translation and interpreting training programmes in Italy were excluded from the public consultation towards defining the profiles of *intercultural mediators*. Urgency once again seems to prevail over planning. Associated by the law to reflect community-specific needs at local level, such flexibility impedes local authorities from deploying established and efficient practices developed elsewhere so as to maximize resources. Arguably, such application of the law to training policies for intercultural mediators attests to embedded political disregard towards the wider societal training needs as much as existing literature was virtually ignored in the plans to support formal training of intercultural mediators (including the works by Angelelli, 2004; Corsellis, 2008; Hale, 2007, 2011). The metaphor of *emergenza migranti* achieved exactly this result and, with the Decree of Law 113/2018, it achieved its greatest victory as Italy has created a policy of closure in favour of adopting migration policies from all the countries who signed up the agreements on asylum applications. It also means that the focus has shifted to only one category of migrants, the humanitarian migrant seeking asylum only within those under 'international protection' (art.12, par. 4).

Concluding remarks

In Italy, the metaphor of *emergenza migranti* has taken a life of its own, accentuating political discontent and unrest. In an interview given in September 2017 to BBC, former Minister of the Interior for the previous government, Mr Marco Minniti, who organized in 2017 the controversial agreement with Libya to control dangerous crossing towards Southern Italian harbours, analysed the reasons for the electoral victory of populist parties over the centre-left groups to which he belongs. His analysis of the election results, clearly from the side of the losers, engages with the issue of migration and attributes the loss to the delay of his party to address that issue, which caused a sense of fear and anger. Minniti explains: 'We lost the election for two reasons [...]. We did not respond to two feelings that were very strong: anger and fear. We lost contact with a big part of public opinion' (Reynolds, 2018). Audiences had been listening for almost a decade of framing of the *emergenza migranti*, which in fact comes in the interview with Minniti:

> Mr Salvini [right-wing, Northern League, current Minister of the Interior] has won headlines by turning away foreign-flagged rescue boats –and by asserting that he's the politician who's finally got a grip on migration. But in terms of reducing migrant numbers, it's Marco Minniti who's had by far the most impact –not Matteo Salvini.
>
> 'The point is this. Italy managed to show Europe and the world that you can manage migration, keeping two principles in mind: humanity and security. Now we're in another phase. There is no migrant emergency in Italy,' [Minniti] replies.

In this interview, Minniti's words underline his bitterness in having to *prove* what Italy could do about the migrant flows in isolation, unaided by the EU institutions – a common refrain accepted by all Italian parties without being challenged or proven otherwise by the EU institutions themselves. The United Nations Support Mission in Libya released the full grim details of the Libyan detention centres, in its report entitled *Desperate and Dangerous* (2018).

By looking at a figure of speech that has influenced political and social debates, through its frequency in the journalistic variety of Italian, there are indications that this powerful metaphor entrenched the perception of the global phenomena of migration into a reductive notion of emergency – which does not cover the causes of the displacement or the needs in terms of reception and accommodation but only relies on imagery in which the migrant and the refugee are a burden. This notion then so coloured the political debate in Italy to be reflected in flimsy and confused legislative approaches oscillating between punishment and integration. In this context, the notion of emergency came to overshadow a problem that needs to be discussed as a social crisis. As such, the crisis needs to be addressed with long-term plans and articulated, not punitive, solutions: it needs long-term determination, motivations and ingenuity so as to imagine and develop alternative ways to deal with migrations. For its geography, Italy has a role to play whilst protecting all of its residents and receiving asylum seekers, temporary refugees, as well as social and economic migrants. It also has demands from the European Union and a role to play to steer immigration and integration policies. In other words, Italy ought to have looked at ways to unshackle itself from the *emergenza migranti*. The need for reception centres and revised policies to deal with *transmigrants* (see discussion in Chapter 2), people who arrive in Italy to reach their intended countries of destination, was not an emergency; the situation was handled so that it managed to hide a complex crisis and partial legislative restrictions replaced socio-political solutions for the long term.

Notes

1   The overall objective of the project is to support EU Member States and ENI Southern Partner Countries in establishing a comprehensive, constructive and operational framework, with a particular focus on developing evidence-based and coherent migration policies and activities (ICMPD online, https://www.icmpd.org/our-work/migration-dialogues/euromed-migration-iv/).

2   Already in 2009 a debate in the European Parliament was held over the 'clearly racist and xenophobic' posters used by the Northern League (EU Parliament, Parliamentary Questions, online http://www.europarl.europa.eu/sides/getDoc.do?pubRef=-//EP//TEXT+WQ+E-2009–3471+0+DOC+XML+V0//EN&language=EN).

3   Based on data about national distribution retrieved from AUDIPRESS 2018.

4   This is not exclusively the terrain of Italian right-wing politics. In Belgium, in Flanders more in particular, the requests for community interpreting – a right for every person who does not master the Dutch language – has risen by 24 per cent since 2015. In March 2019, the Flemish Minister for Integration Liesbeth Homans communicated her plans to have users of this service – which allows non-speakers of Dutch to visit a GP for instance – pay for it themselves. Dressed as a practical concern and aiming at saving taxpayers' money in Flanders, Belgium, the core of the intended policy was one of stigmatizing those who do not master Dutch and as such aligning a narrative of *us vs them* with tax revenue on the one hand and 'foreigners' on the other.

References

AGCOM (2018). *Rapporto sul consumo di informazione*. Rome and Naples: AGCOM. Available online: https://www.agcom.it/documents/10179/9629936/Studio-Ricerca+19-02-2018/72cf58fc-77fc-44ae-b0a6-1d174ac2054f?version=1.0 (accessed 21 March 2019).

Allan, S. (2006). *Online News: Journalism and the Internet*. Maidenhead, UK: McGraw-Hill Education.

Angelelli, C. V. (2004). *Medical Interpreting and Cross-Cultural Communication*. Cambridge: Cambridge University Press.

Billiani, F. (2007/2014). 'Assessing Boundaries – Censorship and Translation'. In F. Billiani (ed.), *Modes of Censorship: National Contexts and Diverse Media*, 1–25. London and New York, NY: Routledge.

Bonomi, I. (2002). *L'italiano giornalistico. Dall'inizio del '900 ai quotidiani on line*. Florence: Franco Cesati Editore.

Button, G. V. (1999). "The Negation of Disaster: The Media Response to Oil Spills in Great Britain." In A. Oliver-Smith and S. M. Hoffman (eds), *The Angry Earth*, 113–132. New York, NY and London: Routledge.

Bunn, M. (2015). 'Reimagining Repression: New Censorship Theory and After'. *History and Theory* 54: 25–44.

Clerwall, C. (2014). 'Enter the Robot Journalist: Users' Perceptions of Automated Content'. *Journalism Practice* 8(5): 519–531.

Corsellis, A. (2008). *Public Service Interpreting: The First Steps*. Basingstoke and New York, NY: Palgrave Macmillan.

De Haas, H., Natter, K., and Vezzoli, S. J. C. M. S. (2015). 'Conceptualizing and Measuring Migration Policy Change'. *Comparative Migration Studies* 3(1): 15.

DEMIG (2015a). demig-policy-database_italy_version-1-3. In *DEMIG POLICY, version 1.3, Online Edition*. Oxford: International Migration Institute, University of Oxford. Available online: http://www.migrationdeterminants.eu/ (accessed 21 March 2019).

DEMIG (2015b). *DEMIG POLICY, version 1.3, Online Edition*. Oxford: International Migration Institute, University of Oxford. Available online: https://www.imi.ox.ac.uk/data/demig-data/demig-policy-1/download-the-data/demig-policy-data-downloads (accessed 21 March 2019).

Di Muzio, G. (2012). 'Italy'. *Focus Migration Country Profile 23*. Available online: http://www.bpb.de/gesellschaft/migration/laenderprofile/145671/migrationspolitik (accessed 21 March 2019).

Eco, U. (1971). 'Guida all'interpretazione del linguaggio giornalistico'. In V. Capecchi and M. Livolsi (eds), *La stampa quotidiana in Italia*, 335–377. Milan: Bompiani.

Federici, F. M. (2011). 'Silenced Images: The Case of *Viva Zapatero!*' In R. Wilson and B. Maher (eds), *Words, Sounds, Images*, 139–157. London: Continuum.

Federici, F. M. (2016). 'Introduction: A State of Emergency for Crisis Communication'. In F. M. Federici (ed.), *Mediating Emergencies and Conflicts. Frontline Translating and Interpreting*, 1–29. New York, NY: Palgrave Macmillan.

Filmer, D. (2018). 'War of the Words: Dialectics and Discourse on the "Migrant Crisis" and "Islamic Terrorists" in British and Italian Newspapers'. *InVerbis* 1: 165–186.

Filmer, D., and Federici, F. M. (2018). 'Mediating Migration Crises: Sicily and the Languages of the Despair'. *European Journal of Language Policy* 10(2): 229–253.

FNSI (2014). *Charter of Rome*. Rome: FNSI. Available online: https://mediacompolicy. univie.ac.at/wp-content/uploads/2016/06/CODE-AND-GLOSSARY-ENGLISH.pdf (accessed 21 March 2019).

Grillo, B. (2008). *Le due Italie*. Blog entry. http://www.beppegrillo.it/2008/10/le_due_ italie.html (accessed 22 March 2019).

Guild, E. (2014a). 'Conflicting Identities and Securitisation in Refugee Law: Lessons from the EU'. In S. Kneebone, D. Stevens, and L. Baldassar (eds), *Refugee Protection the Role of Law: Conflicting Identities*, 151–173. London and New York, NY: Routledge.

Guild, E. (2014b). 'Migration, Security and European Citizenship'. In E. F. Isin and P. Nyers (eds), *Routledge Handbook of Global Citizenship Studies*, 418–426. London and New York, NY: Routledge.

Hale, S. (2007). *Community Interpreting*. Houndmills, Basingstoke and New York, NY: Palgrave Macmillan.

Hale, S. B. (2011). 'Public Service Interpreting'. In K. Malmkjær and K. Windle (eds), *The Oxford Handbook of Translation Studies*, 343–356. London and New York, NY: Routledge.

Horowitz, J. (2017). 'Italy, Bracing for Electoral Season of Fake News, Demands Facebook's Help'. *The New York Times, International Edition*. 25 November 2017. Available online: https://search.proquest.com/docview/1968183526?account id=14511 (accessed 21 March 2019).

Kelly, D. (2017). Education for Community Translation: Thirteen Key Ideas. In M. Taibi (ed.), *Translating for the Community*, 26–41. Bristol: Multilingual Matters.

Lakoff, G., and Johnson, M. (1985). *Metaphors We Live By*. London and Chicago, IL: University of Chicago Press.

Lorusso, A. M., and Violi, P. (2015). *Semiotica del testo giornalistico*. 2nd edition. Rome and Bari: Laterza.

Marchetti, C. (2011). 'Assistiti o segregati? I grandi centri per richiedenti asilo in Italia'. *La società degli individui* 41(14): 57–70.

Marchetti, C. (2014). 'Rifugiati e migranti forzati in Italia. Il pendolo tra "emergenza" e "sistema"'. *REMHU-Revista Interdisciplinar da Mobilidade Humana* 22(43): 53–70.

Masera, A. (2017). 'The Temperature Is Down, but Media Coverage Still Fails to Tell the Full Migration Story'. In *How Does the Media on Both Sides of the Mediterranean Report on Migration?*, 47–51. Brussels: European Union. https:// ethicaljournalismnetwork.org/resources/publications/media-mediterranean- migration/italy (accessed 22 March 2019).

McKnight, J., and Coronel, J. C. (2017). 'Evaluating Scientists as Sources of Science Information: Evidence from Eye Movements'. *Journal of Communication* 67(4): 565–585.

Melandri, E., Carbonari, L., and Ricci, A. (2014). *La qualifica del mediatore interculturale. Contributi per il suo inserimento nel futuro sistema nazione di certificazione delle competenze*. Rome: Gruppo di Lavoro Istituzionale (GLI) sulla mediazione interculturale. http://www.integrazionemigranti.gov.it/Documenti-e-ricerche/ DOSSIER%20DI%20SINTESI%20QUALIFICA%20MEDIATORI_28_07.pdf.

Montgomery, M. (2008). *An Introduction to Language and Society*. London and New York, NY: Routledge.

Morniroli, A., Cipolla, A., and Fortino, T. (2007). *Dialoghi: metodologie e strumenti di mediazione linguistica culturale*. Naples: Dedalus.

Nardelli, A., and Silverman, C. (2017). 'One of the Biggest Alternative Media Networks in Italy Is Spreading Anti-Immigrant News and Misinformation on Facebook'. *BuzzFeed News*. 2 November 2017. Available online: https://www.buzzfeed.com/ albertonardelli/one-of-the-biggest-alternative-media-networks-in-italy-is?utm_ term=.qqXDPqQgoL#.nlogYlwb91 (accessed 21 March 2019).

Natale, S. (2016). 'There Are No Old Media'. *Journal of Communication* 66(4): 585–603.

Neander, J. and Marlin, R. (2010). 'Media and Propaganda'. *Global Media Journal* 3(2): 67–82. Available online: https://core.ac.uk/download/pdf/26945870.pdf (accessed 21 March 2019).

OECD (2017). *International Migration Outlook 2017*. Paris: OECD.

OECD (2018). *International Migration Outlook 2018*. Paris: OECD.

Orengo, A. (2005). 'Localising News: Translation and the "Global-National" Dichotomy'. *Language and Intercultural Communication* 5(2): 168–187.

Pescaroli, G., and Alexander, D. E. (2015). 'A Definition of Cascading Disasters and Cascading Effects: Going beyond the "Toppling Dominos" Metaphor'. *Planet@Risk* 3(1): doi: https://planet-risk.org/index.php/pr/article/view/208.

Reynolds, J. (2018). 'Marco Minniti: The Man Who Cut the Migrant Flow to Italy'. *BBC News*. Available online: https://www.bbc.co.uk/news/world-europe-45575763 (accessed 21 March 2019).

Slavtcheva-Petkova, V. (2016). 'Are Newspapers' Online Discussion Boards Democratic Tools or Conspiracy Theories' Engines? A Case Study on an Eastern European "Media War"'. *Journalism & Mass Communication Quarterly* 93(4): 1115–1134.

UNHCR (2018). *Mid-Year Trends 2018*. Geneva: United Nations High Commissioner for Refugees. Available online: https://www.unhcr.org/statistics/ unhcrstats/5c52ea084/mid-year-trends-2018.html (accessed 22 March 2019).

UNHCR (2019). *Desperate and Dangerous: Report on the Human Rights Situation of Migrants and Refugees in Libya*. Geneva: United Nations High Commissioner for Refugees. Available online: https://www.ohchr.org/Documents/Countries/LY/ LibyaMigrationReport.pdf (accessed 21 March 2019).

Wakefield, A. J., Murch, S. H., Anthony, A., Linnell, J., Casson, D., Malik, M., and Harvey, P. (1998). RETRACTED: 'Ileal-Lymphoid-Nodular Hyperplasia, Non-Specific Colitis, and Pervasive Developmental Disorder in Children'. *The Lancet* 351(9103): 637–641.

Zelizer, B. (2015). 'Terms of Choice: Uncertainty, Journalism, and Crisis'. *Journal of Communication* 65(5): 888–908.

Zelizer, B., and Allan, S. (2010). *Keywords in News and Journalism Studies*. Maidenhead, UK: Open University Press.

Zollo, F., Bessi, A., Del Vicario, M., Scala, A., Caldarelli, G., Shekhtman, L., and Quattrociocchi, W. (2017). 'Debunking in a World of Tribes'. *PLOS One* 12(7): e0181821. doi: https://doi.org/10.1371/journal.pone.0181821.

Index

ACAPS 5
accredited social health activists (ASHAs) 117
activism 28, 30–1, 153, 155, 157, 159, 161, 163, 165, 167, 225
  prosocial 156
activist artists 21
activist community 24, 77, 155
activist mediators 30–1
Acute Stress Reaction 108
Adriatic Sea 246
advocacy 10–11, 116, 149, 153, 155
Afghanistan 6, 70, 158, 165, 180, 235, 241, 246
Afghans 41, 69, 73
AFP 87, 97
  resided 91
Africa 39, 235
African countries 5, 28–9, 59
AGCOM (Autorità per le Garanzie nelle Comunicazioni) 239
Agerholm 179
Aguda 218
AIIC 68
Ajdaraga, Adelina 160, 167–8
Akhoyan 91
Alavi, Simona 163, 167
Albania 246
Albanian (language) 54–5, 58, 158–9
Albanian refugees 162
AlfaVita *Εκπαιδευτικό* 226
Algeria 203
ALNAP 5, 15
American Red Cross 118
Amharic (language) 45, 47, 58
Android 117
Anganwadi workers 117
ANMs (auxiliary nurse midwives) 117
anti-migrant 235, 247
anti-Muslim 196
Arabic 29, 46–8, 50, 52–5, 58, 71–5, 82, 84, 89, 92, 96, 159, 163–4, 180

Arabic varieties and dialects 48, 53, 75, 84, 96, 165
Arab origin 202
Arab Spring 39, 235, 241
Are You Syrious community 43
Aristotelian rhetoric 121
Aristotle 242
ASHAs (accredited social health activists) 117
Ashkali populations 158
Asia 39
assimilation 206, 210
asylum 8, 11–12, 21, 32, 34, 41, 45, 48, 68, 105, 158, 249, 253–4
Asylum Act (Croatia) 45
asylum applications 2, 21, 27, 28, 32, 45, 180, 217, 247
asylum seekers 3, 21–3, 31–3, 41, 45, 48, 116, 153, 158, 175, 180, 217, 235–6, 247, 249–52
  formal 53
  political 32
  procedures 32, 34
  process 45, 51
  standard 34, 45
Atlas Servicios Empresariales 71
AUDIPRESS 255
Australia 58, 127, 149, 181
Austria 56, 223

Bacillus anthracis 119
Bādīnān (language) 58
Balkan Peninsula 39, 40, 57
Balkans migration route 39, 43, 54–5, 57
Bámbara (language) 73
Bapska 49
Basque (language) 64
Bastille Day 193, 197, 199, 209
Bataclan 193, 198
BBC (British Broadcasting Corporation) 174, 226, 253, 258
Beirut 72

Belgium 255
Belize 33
Bengali (language) 58
bias 12, 233
    dangerous 160
    personal 142
    unconscious 82
biased lenses 12
Bisnode Ltd 56
Blace 158, 160–2
BMA (British Medical Association) 174–6,
    186
    Library 186
    News 186
    Refugee Doctors Initiative 175, 186
BMP 179, 183
BMP project 181
Bosnia 17, 40–1, 78, 158, 246
Bosnian (language) 54–5
Bosnian Muslims 41
Bosnian War 158
Bossi-Fini Law 247
Bourdieu 31, 242
Bregana 44, 49
Brexit vote 193
Brijuni 59
British Broadcasting Corporation. *See* BBC
British Medical Association. *See* BMA
British Medical Journal 113, 175
Brucella species 119
Budapest 166
Building Bridges 175, 179, 186
Bulgaria 40, 56
Burkholderia mallei 119
Burkholderia pseudomallei 119
Burmese (language) 58
BuzzFeed 240

Cairo 72
Canadian Convention 33
Casa Árabe 74
Catania 32
censorship 242–3, 256
    effective authoritative 242
    ethical 239
    oblique 13, 234, 241–3
Cervantes Institute 72
Charlie Hebdo Attacks 193, 213
Charter of Duties, *See* Charter of Rome
Charter of Rome (*Carta dei doveri*) 235,
    243

child 4, 26
child labour exploitation 225
    female activist fighting 226
child mortality 118
children
    of refugee families 99
    separated 107
    young 162, 243
Chinese (language) 71, 75
choral music 120–1
Christchurch 6
Cilicia 88
citizenship 22, 24–6, 34, 48, 81, 251
clandestine 238, 247
Clinton, Hillary 204
CNI (National Intelligence Agency, Spain)
    64, 69
CNOG (National Council of the
    Journalists' Association Italy,
    *Comitato Nazionale dell'ordine dei
    giornalisti*) 235
CNP (National, Police Force, Spain) 64,
    69, 74
code-mixing 52
codes
    ethical 122
    professional 156
    verbal 225
Cold War 59
Common European Framework of
    Reference for Languages 40
communication 1–5, 14–15, 21, 53, 65–6,
    111–14, 116–20, 122–3, 129, 136–8,
    140–1, 167–8, 177–9, 214–18
    clinical 113, 182
    crisis relief 7
    disaster 222
    emergency 65
    flow of 139–41, 145–6
    health-related 66
    inter-community 88
    inter-group 90
    interlingual 58
    international 21, 24
    mediated 9, 157, 216
    medical 114, 156, 177
    multilingual 1, 3, 14, 111
    non-verbal 58, 143–4
    public 216
    verbal 88, 96
communication skills, clinical 176

communities 1–2, 5–6, 24, 27, 121, 130,
        134, 149, 156–7, 164, 248, 253, 255
    affected 65
    immigrant 73
    polarizing 210
community engagement 13
concepts 9–10, 12, 18, 25, 84, 101, 117,
        140, 147, 154, 216–18, 233, 239,
        241–2
    cultural 131, 143
    flexible 68
    intangible 8
    medical 128
conduits 10, 122, 156
    invisible 136
conflicts 9, 14, 39, 41, 60–1, 66–8, 76,
        157–8, 163, 211–13, 235–6, 241
Corriere della Sera 237–8
    archives 238
Costa Rica 141
Côte d'Azur 202
Coventry 180
Creative Commons 54
Croatia 39–41, 43, 45, 47–50, 53–7, 158
Croatian (language) 9, 46, 47–8, 52, 54–6,
        58
CSID (Military Intelligence, Spain) 64,
        69
Cultural Competence 132
cultural competency 139, 146–8, 184
Culturally and linguistically diverse
        (CALD) communities 1, 10
cultural mediators 8, 21, 23–7, 29, 31–3,
        35, 48, 68, 120, 194

Damascus 72
Dari (language) 45, 58, 72–4
DEMIG 246, 247, 248, 249
Democratic Republic of Congo (DRC) 4–5
DHC. *See* Disaster Healthcare
Dikran 91
Directive 2010/64/EU 71, 74
Disaster Healthcare 108
Disaster Medicine 106, 108
DM. *See* Disaster Medicine
Doctors Without Borders 10, 106, 111,
        113, 117, 118, 120, 122
DRC (Democratic Republic of Congo) 4–5
Dutch (language) 255
DWB. *See* Doctors Without Borders

Eastern Armenian 89–91
Ebola 4–5, 15–16, 66, 107, 112
Egypt 59
EJN. *See* Ethical Journalism Network
ELF 21–4, 28–9, 35
empathy 1, 3, 5–7, 9, 11, 13, 15, 31, 51, 83,
        108, 154–8, 163, 166
    affective 154
    automatic 166
    cognitive 154, 156
    conflict transformation studies 155
    Einfühlung 154
    essence 155
    teach 167
empathy and activism 153, 155, 157,
        159, 161, 163, 165, 167
English (language) 180, 181, 184, 185, 186
ETA 64
Ethical Journalism Network (EJN) 235,
        237–8
ethics 16, 110, 132, 169–70, 235, 237
ethnic groups 4, 51, 82, 84, 95, 228
    foreign 73
    homeland, perceived 82, 85–6, 95–6
    individual 51
EUROMED Migration IV Project 237
Europe 23, 39–40, 57, 64, 76, 107, 193,
        198, 208, 217, 235, 237, 241
European Council's Directives 247
European migrant crisis 40, 158–9, 164

Farsi (language) 45–6, 48, 50, 52–5, 58,
        72–5, 159, 166
Fatto Quotidiano, Il 237
FEMA trainees 228
fidelity 74
    linguistic 30
Finnish military interpreters 66
First World War 85
5-Star Movement 240, 244
FNSI (Italian National Press Federation,
        *Federazione Nazionale Stampa
        Italiana*) 235
Foreign Office UK 201
France 12, 34, 193, 195–205, 207
freedom 174, 240, 242

Gaza 34–5
gender-binaries 84
    gender 228

gender-representative support 3
General Medical Council UK (GMC)
 173–7, 184–6
genre 13, 112–13, 122, 216, 219, 222
Germany 56, 64, 98, 158, 223
Gevgelija 158, 163, 165
Ghana 26
Giornale, Il 237
Global Compact 2, 3, 7, 15
Globalization 25, 216, 218
GMC. *See* General Medical Council
Google Translate 46–7, 53
Gramsci, Antonio 242
Grand Bargain 2
Greece 57, 60, 158–9, 164, 218, 220, 223,
 225
Greek (language) 12, 54, 55, 165, 220–5
Greek camps 50
Greek-Cypriot Community 100
Greek-Macedonian border 158
Guardia Civil (Spain) 64, 69
Guardian, The 32, 196–7, 200–3, 206,
 209–12, 226
Guinea 4

Hausa (language) 28
hazards 46, 76, 217, 222, 228
 natural 12, 65
headlines 12, 219–20, 222, 227, 242, 254
health 43, 81, 105, 107, 117, 119–22, 138,
 178, 181, 220, 222, 251
 mobile 117
healthcare 4, 105–6, 109–11, 113–14, 127,
 129, 131–3, 135, 137, 139, 141, 143,
 145, 147, 149, 183
 intercultural healthcare
  communication 132, 147
 interpreters 10, 127–9, 133, 140, 145, 147
 patient-centred 149
 personnel 66, 71
 practitioners 178
 professionals 3, 73, 107, 108–9, 111–12,
  120, 175, 186
 providers 127, 133–4, 137–8, 140, 178
Herzegovina 41, 158
Hindi (language) 58, 74, 117
HIV 120–1
Hofstede, Geert 224
Hollande, François 197–8
 difficulties President 204

humanitarian crises 43, 106, 115–17, 233
 long-term 236
human rights 2, 31, 158
Hungarian (language) 54, 56
Hungary 40, 43, 56
Hyogo Framework 217

identities 8, 21–3, 26, 31, 34, 82–3, 156,
 194, 210
ideological 85, 120, 219
 elements 236
 ranking 22
Idomeni 164
IELTS. *See* International English Language
 Testing System
IFRC. *See* Red Cross and Crescent
 Societies
immigrants 60, 63–4, 82–4, 96, 115, 193,
 203, 211, 251
 detainees 116
information 5, 7, 14, 50–1, 53–5, 70–1,
 106–8, 112–19, 121–2, 129–31, 161,
 194–5, 220, 234–5, 244
 critical 119
 crucial 3
 management 65
Instagram 244–5
institutions 8, 29, 42, 71, 73, 86, 109, 122,
 132, 137, 161, 241, 250–1,
 254
intercultural mediation 3, 14, 48, 127–8,
 130, 132, 135, 138, 145, 147, 149,
 151, 252
intercultural mediators 8, 12, 14, 23, 51,
 131, 250, 252–3
International English Language Testing
 System (IELTS) 175, 181, 183–6
interpreters 9–11, 23, 30, 45–8, 50, 63–9,
 71, 73–7, 115–16, 127–9, 132–3,
 135–49, 153–4, 156–60, 162–70
 community 23, 156
 conflict 76, 164
 local 75, 163
 non-professional 33, 166, 168
 untrained 168
interpreting 2, 10–11, 58, 138–9, 149–50,
 153–4, 156–7, 159–61, 163–7, 250
 for refugees 153, 155, 157, 159, 161,
  163, 165, 167
InZone 2, 68

IRA 64
Iran 48, 221
Iraq 48, 57, 66, 165, 180, 202, 235, 246
Iraqi (people) 41, 53, 89, 96
ISIS 76, 194, 207–9, 211
Islam 194, 196, 206–7, 209–11
    Islamophobia 12, 211
Israel 72, 127
Istanbul 72
Italian (language) 238, 249, 251
Italy 8, 13, 23, 27–8, 33, 158, 218, 223, 233,
    235–7, 239–45, 252

Japan 66, 127
Jesuit Refugee Service 42–3, 48, 51, 53
Ježevo 49
Jordan 66, 74
journalists 12, 194, 196, 202–4, 207, 209,
    211, 218, 233, 235, 237, 240, 243

Kanuri (language) 28
Kató platform 46
Kenya 66
Khmer 58
Kivu 4
knowledge 14, 21, 28, 74–5, 84, 91, 143,
    147, 163, 168, 173, 176, 195–6, 200,
    216
    cultural 74, 108
knowledge management 63–4
Kosovo 79, 158–60, 162–3, 246
Kurdish (language) 45, 48, 50, 52, 58
Kurmanji (language) 45–6, 58
Kuwait 72

Lahouaiej-Bouhlel, Mohamed 193, 207–8,
    211
language barriers 2, 46, 76–7, 89, 137, 177,
    215
    limiting 251
language brokers 163, 168
language mediation 8, 14, 40, 50–1, 53,
    57–8, 66
language mediators 9, 37, 40, 42, 47–8, 51,
    56, 61
Language Policy 70, 76, 251, 256
legislation 28, 71, 74, 174, 236, 246
Levantine Arabic (language) 45, 74
LGBT population 165
Liberia 4, 15

Libya 48, 246, 254
lingua franca 8, 21, 28, 75
    translational 23

Macedonia 56, 158–60, 162–5
machine translation (MT) 46, 58, 67, 78–9
Maghreb 53
Malawi 6
Malaysia Airlines 222
Martelli Law on migration 246, 247
Masera, Anna 238
Médecins Sans Frontières. See Doctors
    Without Borders
mediators 5, 8, 23, 26–31, 42, 47–54, 63,
    111, 147, 155, 157, 228
    gender 52
medical interpreters 127–30, 133–7,
    140–1, 143–9
    licensed 109
    professional 127, 148
Mediterranean 24, 39, 61, 158, 237, 239
Merah, Mohammed 208
metaphor 13, 194, 233, 235, 237, 239,
    241–3, 245, 247, 251, 253–5
    conceptual 196
MFH Project Group 148
mHealth 117, 118
MI5 201
MI6 204
Middle East 48, 72, 82, 93
migrant crisis 39, 41, 43, 45, 47, 49, 51, 53,
    55, 57, 241, 243, 245
migrants 2–3, 8, 21–5, 27–35, 39–41, 43,
    46, 53, 85, 233, 235–6, 246–7, 250–4
    forced 13, 84, 86, 95–6, 233
migration, forced 81, 83–4, 89, 92, 97, 157
Military Intelligence 64, 69
Mineo Reception Centre (CARA) 32,
    249–50
Minniti, Marco 253–4
minority 9, 85, 94, 157
    communities 163
    cultures 148
    ethnic 149
    groups 86
    linguistic 2, 3, 27, 147
Movimento 5 stelle. See 5-Star Movement
Mozambique 6
Msaken 201
MSF. *See* Doctors Without Borders

MT. *See* machine translation
multilingualism 28, 71
Muslim 193, 196, 203, 206–7, 209–11

narratives 8–9, 12, 67–8, 75, 106, 111, 167, 239–40
National Health Service UK (NHS) 11, 173–4, 176, 179, 181, 184, 186
   NES (NHS Education for Scotland) 186
   NHS Scotland 186
nationalities 41, 157, 222, 248
Netherlands, The 6
newspapers 218–19, 237–8, 244
news sources 196–7, 200, 204, 207, 209–10
New Zealand 6, 127
NGOs (non-governmental organizations) 2, 8, 40, 42–4, 69, 71, 73, 88–9, 91–4, 106, 109, 111, 116, 118, 120, 122
NHS. *See* National Health Service
Nice attack 193, 197–8, 203, 206, 209
Nigeria 26, 28, 221
Nigerian English (language) 28–9
non-governmental organizations. *See* NGOs
Northern Ireland 64, 174
Northern League, *Lega Nord* 237, 240, 254–5
NPOs (non-profit organizations) 57

Obama, Barak 204–5
Observer, The 197–8
OECD terminology 251
OET (Occupational English Test) 175, 184–5
Office for the Coordination of Humanitarian Affairs (OCHA) 118
Ofilingua 71
organizations 5, 7, 14, 44, 48–50, 53–4, 57, 65, 70, 137, 139, 168, 174–5, 179, 186
OSCE mission 162
Ottoman Empire 85

Pakistan 41, 158, 180
Palestine 34, 74
Pashto (language) 45, 58
Pashtun 72, 74–5
Patient-centered care 113, 130, 181
Patient Centred Translation (PCT) 114

patients 26, 107, 109, 111–12, 114–15, 128–49, 156, 169, 176–8, 181, 185
   patient care 138–9, 148, 173
perception 12–13, 18, 44, 64, 83–4, 87, 96, 217, 225, 227, 233, 238, 241, 250, 254
phases 1–2, 109–10, 227, 246, 254
Picasso 202
Pidgin English 28–9
Pisa 250
PLAB. *See* Professional and Linguistic Assessments Board
PNA 247
policies 81, 210, 217, 233, 235, 237, 239, 241, 243, 245–7, 250–1, 253, 255
population
   affected 4–5, 50, 65, 106–7, 112
   crisis-affected 1, 7, 14
   disaster-affected 12
   local 90, 96, 120
   vulnerable 79, 106, 220
post-traumatic stress disorder (PTSD) 108, 118–19
power 6, 22, 194–5, 216, 228, 233, 235, 245–7
   power asymmetries 109
   power imbalances 21, 155
practice
   best 5, 26, 58, 230
   clinical 113, 175, 177
   medical humanitarian 121
   predominant 31
preparedness 109–10, 113, 119, 227
   medical 112
press 194, 215–19, 236, 238, 240, 242
   institutions 228
   national 233
   press data 13, 216, 228
   traditional 244
   translated 219
Prishtina 162
Professional and Linguistic Assessments Board UK (PLAB) 175, 181, 183, 186
   tests 175–6, 181, 186
protection
   civil 15, 43
   civilian 64
   legal 168
protection services 39
PTSD. *See* post-traumatic stress disorder

race 83, 85, 157
  close 85
RAF 64
Ramon y Cajal Hospital 73
Reception Centres for Asylum seekers and
    Refugees (SPRAR, Italy) 27, 30,
    217, 247, 249–50
Red Cross and Crescent Societies (IFRC)
    2, 48–51, 163
  Asylum and Migration Department
    and Search Service 49
  Red Cross Emergency 118
Refugee Doctors Initiative (RDI) 175,
    186
refugees 6, 8–9, 11, 39–41, 43, 45–51,
    53–7, 153–5, 157, 173–6, 185, 225,
    235–6, 246–7
  camps 11, 41, 66, 112, 119, 153, 158–9,
    164
  crisis 40–2, 47, 57, 153, 159
  groups 55, 157, 160–1, 164, 166, 186
  refugee health professionals 175–6,
    179–81, 184–6
  Refugee Phrasebook 42–3, 54
  Refugees Doctors Programme 186
  status 168–9
  women 162, 164
ReliefWeb 118
Repubblica, La 237–8
Republic of Armenia 81, 83, 87, 93, 95
resources 4, 23, 70, 108–9, 116, 121, 159,
    180, 182, 186, 241
  wasted 175
respondents 42, 44, 47, 50–3, 73, 75, 133,
    183
responders 44, 106–7, 112, 116, 120,
    122–3
response 65, 69, 109, 117, 119, 127–8, 134,
    139, 166, 168, 174, 178, 204, 223,
    227
Reuters 220–1, 223, 225–6
right wing
  coalition 237, 240, 247
  extreme 237
  hard-line 233
  politicians 242
  Trump 204
Roma (people) 58, 158, 163, 248
Romanian (language) 73
Rome (Italy) 36, 235, 243, 255

Russia 87, 96
  Russian news 87
  Russian TV 87
  Russian (language) 71, 74–5, 82, 84, 86–7,
    91, 96

Salvini, Matteo 240, 254
Salvini Act 233
Sanskrit (language) 58
Schengen Area 39, 203
schools 86–9, 96–7, 231, 250
Scotland 175, 186
  Scottish Government 186
security 43, 64, 74, 84, 162, 193, 201, 209,
    223, 247–8, 254
security forces 204–5
Sendai Framework for Disaster Risk
    Reduction 217
Seprotec 71
Serbia 40, 49, 56, 159, 162–3
  Serbian camps 40
Serbian (language) 54–5, 158–9
services 8, 14, 47–8, 54, 58, 91–2, 127,
    131, 136–7, 148, 156, 159, 250, 252,
    255
  linguistic 138
  medical 46, 138
Sicily 31–2, 124, 238, 256
Sierra Leone 4, 246
Skopje 162
Skype 159
Slovenia 43, 49
social media 16, 39, 117, 125, 244–5
soldiers 68, 74, 200–1, 206
solidarity 9, 24, 225
Somalia 6, 48, 66, 158
  Somali 52
  Somali communities 133–4
  Somali migrants 52
Sorani (language) 45–6, 58
Sousse 201, 203
Soviet Union (USSR) 82, 85, 87
  policy-makers 86
  values 86
Spain 63–4, 69, 71, 74–5
Spanish (language) 64, 70, 72–5, 111, 118
Spanish immigrants 202
Spanish institutions 9, 70–5
  grants support 72
spontaneous volunteers 44, 54, 58

SPRAR. *See* Reception centres for Asylum
    Seekers and Refugees
Stampa, La 237
    support 238
standards 11, 136
    international 250
    medical interpreting 135
    professional 177
stereotypes 12, 141
    negative 48, 211
Storie Migranti 22, 33
Sub-Saharan Africa 4, 230
Sudan 6, 48
support 2, 5, 68–9, 89, 116, 118, 163,
    165–6, 179–80, 183–4, 186, 234,
    236, 250–3, 255
    institutional 159
    medical 108, 161
    psychosocial 49
    specialist 75
support asylum claims 116
Syria 9, 48, 57, 66, 70, 74, 88–90, 93–4, 96,
    158, 163, 165, 178, 180, 184
Syrian Armenians 81–2, 84–5, 88–96
Syrian Civil War 39, 88
Syrian (people) 41, 85, 93, 163
    Syrian refugee children 226

Tabanovce 159
Tadine 220
Tamil 58
Tel Aviv 72
Telegraph, The 196–7, 201–3, 206, 209–11
terminology 37, 89, 121, 235
terrorist organization ETA 64
Tibet 220
Tigre (language) 58
Tigrinya (language) 45, 58
Tovarnik 49
TOXNET 119
training 30–2, 48, 72, 75, 142, 146, 154, 157,
    159, 165–6, 179, 183, 186, 250, 252
    crisis situation 108
    cultural 131
    informal interpreting 168
    medical 11, 188
translators 30–1, 33, 46, 54–7, 64,
    66–9, 73–5, 77, 106, 108–9, 115–16,
    120–3, 169–70
    care 107

medical 105, 108, 112–14, 119
    non-professional 122
    professional 47–8, 63, 67, 69, 111, 228
    volunteer 54, 57
translators and interpreters 9, 30, 45, 63–4,
    66–7, 69, 74–5, 116, 122
Translators Without Borders (TWB) 46,
    50, 79, 106–7, 114
Trnovec 49
Trump, Donald 132, 193, 199, 202, 204–5,
    240
    Trumpist America 4, 204, 206
trust 5, 29, 68, 83, 120, 130–1, 134, 141–2,
    156–7, 160, 162–3, 166, 168, 243
    established 160
    relationships of 155, 157, 167–8
Tunisia 201, 203, 207
Turkey 41, 57, 66, 72, 78, 81, 225–6
TWB. *See* Translators Without Borders
Twitter 117, 244–5

Ubani Case 176
UHC. *See* universal health coverage
UK. *See* United Kingdom
UNHCR (United Nations High
    Commissioner for Refugees) 25, 37,
    81–2, 89, 105, 124, 157–9, 161–6,
    168, 233, 235, 247
    Blace border team 159, 161
    Emergency Handbook 39
    interpreters 162, 164
    Prishtina team 162
UNICEF 166
UNISDR 65
United Kingdom (UK) 56, 63, 69, 74, 116,
    173–87, 193, 201, 207, 240
United Nations 16, 80, 168, 231
United Nations General Assembly 246
United Nations High Commissioner for
    Refugees. *See* UNHCR
United States 63, 70–1, 73–4, 76, 127, 131,
    149–50, 193, 240
    US Border Patrol 27
    US FEMA 228
    US National Library 119
universal health coverage (UHC) 116–17,
    125
UPWEB project 15
Urdu 45, 47, 58, 73, 74, 159, 166
USSR. *See* Soviet Union

values 46, 68, 82, 85–7, 93, 95, 114, 120, 122, 138, 143, 146, 155–6, 222
  cultural 11, 115–16, 143
Victorian 14
vocabulary 55, 84
  feminizing 84
  gendered 84
Voice of Croatia 57
volunteering 52
  digital 57
volunteers 10, 14, 40, 42–4, 47, 51–7, 110, 202
  uncoordinated 44
vulnerability 164, 201, 218, 220, 227
  vulnerable groups 10, 75, 153–4, 157, 160, 165–6, 168, 243
  vulnerable migrant groups 61

Wales 174–5, 195
Wales Deanery Website 176

war 70, 73, 105, 163, 173, 175, 180, 185, 223, 235, 241, 246
Warsaw Pact 59
Washington Post 211
West Africa 4–5, 15–16, 74
WHO. *See* World Health Organization
WISER 119
World Health Organization (WHO) 4, 80, 112, 117–18, 125

Yazidis 165
Yemen 5
Yerevan 89–96
Yersinia pestis 119
Yoruba (language) 28
YouTube 116
Yugoslavia 16, 41, 48, 246

Zagreb 49
Zimbabwe 6, 120

Lightning Source UK Ltd.
Milton Keynes UK
UKHW020700210521
384111UK00003B/74